SWEET LAND
OF
LIBERTY

SWEET LAND OF LIBERTY

A HISTORY OF AMERICA IN 11 PIES

ROSSI ANASTOPOULO

ABRAMS PRESS, NEW YORK

Chapter Six has been adapted from the author's article "The 'Pie Engineer'
Who Designed a Dessert for the Jazz Age," first published by *Atlas Obscura*
on March 24, 2020.

Chapter Nine has been adapted from the author's article "The Radical Pie That
Fueled a Nation," first published by *TASTE* on November 13, 2018.

Chapter Twelve has been adapted from the author's article "Why Apple Pie Isn't
So American After All," first published by Food52 on October 8, 2021.

Recipe for Karo Pecan Pie on page 119 courtesy of ACH Food Companies, Inc.

Recipe for Tofu Cream Pie on page 242 reprinted with permission from *Pie Any
Means Necessary: The Biotic Baking Brigade Cookbook* (Oakland, CA: AK Press,
2004), 108.

Library of Congress Control Number: 2022933714

ISBN: 978-1-4197-5487-6
eISBN: 978-1-64700-305-0

Printed and bound in the United States
10 9 8 7 6 5 4 3 2 1

Abrams books are available at special discounts when purchased in quantity
for premiums and promotions as well as fundraising or educational use.
Special editions can also be created to specification. For details, contact
specialsales@abramsbooks.com or the address below.

Abrams Press® is a registered trademark of Harry N. Abrams, Inc.

ABRAMS The Art of Books
195 Broadway, New York, NY 10007
abramsbooks.com

For my yiayias.
To my Yiayia Harriet, whose pies started this all.
And my Yiayia Rosie, who taught me to
meet everything with a laugh.

LAND ACKNOWLEDGMENT

The majority of this book was written on the ancestral homelands of the Tongva people, who were enslaved, assimilated, and forcibly removed through colonization. I honor their right to this land and pay my respects to generations past, present, and future.

CONTENTS

INTRODUCTION

ON FEBRUARY 1, 1960, Ezell Blair Jr. entered the F. W. Woolworth's lunch counter in Greensboro, North Carolina, along with several of his friends, took a seat at the counter, and ordered coffee and a slice of cherry pie.

Woolworth's was a popular lunch destination in Greensboro, a place where you could go for a quick burger or sandwich, maybe a cup of coffee with a slice of pie on the side. The interior was basic but comfortable—a row of metal-backed stools lined a long counter littered with sugar canisters and salt and pepper shakers, behind which servers in paper hats took orders and refilled coffee cups.

It was the sort of democratic spot that served a large cross-section of the town's population, from local lawyers in suits to thrifty college students from nearby UNC Greensboro.

There was one exception to this clientele, however. Woolworth's did not serve Black customers.

Ezell Blair and his three friends, all of whom were Black, knew this when they entered Woolworth's that winter day. As freshmen at the local North Carolina Agricultural and Technical State University, they were accustomed to the strict racial codes that governed Greensboro, dictating where they could eat and shop and live.

Therefore, unlike all other patrons, their trip to the Woolworth's lunch counter that day was meticulously planned.

Inspired by nonviolent protest, including a television program he had previously watched about Mahatma Gandhi, Blair had joined his friends in organizing a deliberate civil rights protest by staging a sit-in at the all-white Woolworth's lunch counter. The tactic—which had already been employed several times in lunch counters throughout the South—was decided after the group dared each other to do it during a campus bull session. Determined to be organized and disciplined, the students planned their approach deliberately, plotting their route to ensure success.

First, the group stopped at a nearby store owned by white businessman Ralph Johns, a social activist who supported the NAACP and was sympathetic to their cause. Next, the four young men visited the Woolworth's five-and-dime store, where they purchased several items and carefully saved their receipts. Finally, they took their seats at the Woolworth's lunch counter and politely placed their orders, with Ezell Blair Jr. requesting coffee and cherry pie.

It seems no coincidence that Blair ordered pie during this historic moment. The dish was a staple of Southern diners and lunch counters, part of the distinctly American cuisine such establishments served, and it could be found in similar lunch spots across the region. Pie was a familiar order. It was also deeply and traditionally American—a direct product of the United States. It seemed that if a Black American could eat pie—this symbol of American innovation and identity—at a lunch counter in North Carolina or anywhere else in the South, he or she might be considered just as equal an American citizen as anyone else.

Seated calmly at the lunch counter, the four men were immediately denied service. Unfazed, they remained, refusing to be denied. Blair waited for his slice of pie.

Unlike white Woolworth's patrons, he didn't receive it.

And thus, with one order, Ezell Blair Jr., Franklin McCain, Joseph McNeil, and David Richmond sparked a wave of social protest that ignited throughout the region. The next day, more students from North Carolina A&T arrived at Woolworth's to protest alongside the four men. Two days later, Black protesters were seated in sixty-three of the restaurant's sixty-six seats, with employees occupying the remaining three. The protest rippled out beyond Greensboro to Charlotte, Winston-Salem, and Durham, and eventually as far away as Jackson, Mississippi.

While pie was ordered by civil rights activists in sit-ins throughout the '60s, it played a different role in these protests for white people intent on opposing the fight for desegregation. For Black customers and protestors at lunch counters, being served pie was a symbol of equality, but segregationists instead turned the dish into a weapon of division. In many instances, the white reaction to Black protesters became violent, and when this happened, they often pelted activists with food and smeared them with pie.

Ann Moody, a participant in a sit-in at a Jackson, Mississippi, Woolworth's in which angry white high school students began violently attacking the protesters, recalled: "We bowed our heads [to pray], and all hell broke loose. . . . The mob started smearing us with ketchup, mustard, sugar, pies, and everything on the counter." In these instances, pie became politicized and racially charged. Now, transformed into an object used for intimidation and power, it was a weapon for those aiming to preserve the status quo.

In these lunch counter settings—battlegrounds over which some of the fiercest wars of the Civil Rights Movement were waged—control over pie became a metaphor for racial victory. For Black Americans, being served pie represented a win for equality and justice; meanwhile, white Americans sought to reclaim the dish by using it as a tool in physical assaults. Underlying this struggle is the fact that—like much of the food prepared at these Southern lunch counters—the pie being served was a descendant of both Black and white culinary influences.

The segregationists' violent efforts were to no avail. Six months after the original Greensboro Four calmly took a seat at the all-white lunch counter, Woolworth's officially desegregated.

And when, over a decade after he had first placed his fateful order at the Greensboro Woolworth's lunch counter, Ezell Blair (by then known as Jibreel Khazan after he joined the Islamic Center of New England and changed his name in 1968) returned to the same Woolworth's for a reunion with the three other men alongside whom he had shaped history, the *Greensboro Daily News* proclaimed, "First Sit-In Participant Finally Gets Cherry Pie."

And with one slice, victory had finally been achieved.*

PIE IS, NEEDLESS to say, not the most natural medium through which to navigate American history. I've received more than enough curious looks when explaining the premise of this book to confirm this (although I relish the opportunity to be an obsessed pie lady, as many people now seem to view me).

The idea that food can be a lens through which to examine issues of race, class, and gender in our society is not a new one, or even a particularly radical one. I am far from the first person to step into such deep and rich waters, and it thrills me that I will not even come close to being the last.

* Joseph McNeil had returned to the Woolworth's to order pie the autumn following the sit-in. According to him, "The pie wasn't very good."

But though food as a medium for social history is not a novel concept, using pie to do so certainly is.* Served everywhere from greasy-spoon diners to holiday tables to hipster bakeries, it's a dish so common that it's easy to overlook its power. Though it may seem mundane, pie's broad exposure means that, in a way, this humble dish is a touchstone for almost all of us.

Many of us can recall fond childhood memories in which pie makes an appearance—a comfortable, familiar presence on the table. Maybe it was your aunt's sweet potato pie at every Thanksgiving dinner, generously spiced with black pepper and always served first to Grandpa before anyone else could even think about taking a bite. Perhaps it's the slice of chocolate cream pie waiting in the cooler at the diner where your dad would take you after Saturday T-ball games, resplendent under fluorescent lights. Pecan pie might remind you of the chocolate version served at the church potluck on Sundays; tomato pie might conjure the dish your mom made every year during the height of summer, when the small patch of tomatoes she dutifully tended in the backyard ripened in abundance.

You might be the kind of person who's terrified at the thought of making pie crust and won't come within ten feet of a rolling pin, so when your best friend brings over a cherry pie after your new baby is born, it tastes all the sweeter. Or maybe you're a baker, and you dream about endless filling combinations and artful lattice designs.

For me, thinking about pie always conjures the apple pie I make for my father's birthday every year. Never a fan of cake, he's requested apple pie to celebrate for as long as I can remember. (As

---

* Not to say others haven't written about pie history. Food historian Janet Clarkson's *Pie: A Global History* is a wonderful book and invaluable resource.

he is a very Greek man, it's a little funny to me that he wants such a stereotypically American dish.) It's the first pie I ever made, and still the only one I can make without a recipe. At some point, inspired by the headnote from the original recipe we used, my mother suggested we cut my dad's name into the crust, and now his apple pie isn't complete without a craggy, lopsided "Akim" carved into the golden-brown canvas.

My dad's apple pie technically doesn't *mean* anything—the recipe itself came from the first cookbook we decided to look in decades ago, and when we eat it every year, the main takeaway is mostly, "Delicious." (And "Dad is old," but we don't say that one out loud. At least, not to his face.)

But every year, as the smell of cinnamon and nutmeg and butter wafts from the oven, a simple apple pie becomes the center point around which the various far-flung pieces of my family are gathered. Sloppy, warm slices become harbingers of nostalgia and memory and identity. The simple act of making this pie is an expression of love, and the act of eating it one of community.

And I know I'm not the only one with a pie memory like this.

Pie is baked and eaten all over our country every day, and it has been for centuries, since the very beginning of the United States. Nearly every person in the US has some memory or association with pie, and so too have endless generations that came before us, from the Black Muslim on the streets of Brooklyn to the Midwest housewife struggling through the Great Depression to the activist fighting against globalization in San Francisco. Pie, in a way, is a common thread woven through the fabric of American history, one that has evolved and mutated throughout the years right alongside our country.

Pie is more than just a widespread, commonly known dish. There are three reasons in particular why pie is such a unique vehicle for this type of social study. Firstly, it is one of the few quintessentially American dishes we have. Though "American pie" (shout out Don McLean . . . and Jason Biggs) is directly descended from pie in other countries like England and the Netherlands, not to mention the dish itself originated thousands of years ago, pie as we know and eat it in the United States doesn't really exist anywhere else. There are savory bisteeyas in Morocco and sweet galettes in France and flaky empanadas in Spain. But for us, pie is (for the most part!) a sweet dish with at least one crust, often two, molded in a pie plate and filled with any number of things. These include, but are certainly not limited to, almost any type of fruit, various spins on cream, chocolate, Jell-O, beans, crackers, and so much more.

Here is probably the best place to point out that this arbitrary definition of American pie is limited, porous, and by no means strict. In fact, at least one pie in this book breaks the very rules I've just set out. When it comes to defining pie, it might be best to adopt the attitude of a certain Supreme Court justice about a certain type of adult film: *I know it when I see it.*

Which leads to the second characteristic that makes pie such a good barometer for American society—it is endlessly adaptable. The fact that pie is so malleable and hard to define is the very reason it is so revealing. Because of its flexibility, pie is frequently molded to the situation that it's in, shaped by such varying factors as the ingredients available, the amount of time or energy the baker has to make it, the kitchen in which it's made and the tools on hand, the eating habits or dietary restrictions of the people eating it, and even the weather outside or time of day. (Is it any coincidence that the pie originating at our country's southernmost point—the key lime pie—is made with a graham cracker crust that calls for melted butter rather than the ice-cold butter needed for traditional flaky pastry? Maybe . . . but also maybe not.) As such, pie is somewhat of a blank canvas whose many quirks and intricacies become revealing insights into the place and time in which it is made.

Finally, pie is so powerful because, frankly, it's pretty unnecessary. Unlike, you know, *dinner*, we only make and eat dessert because we want to. In times of hardship or stress—everything from war to revolution to poverty—there's really no point in making dessert. So when someone does make a pie in these circumstances, it begets one very big and very obvious question: Why? The answer to that question, as you'll find in many of these chapters, can be quite illuminating.

I might add one fourth and irrelevant reason why pie makes an excellent foundation for a book like this—pie is delicious, and delicious things, I've found, have a tendency to capture the imagination (mine, at the very least).

But while we can say that these are the pies that tell the story of America, this country's history cannot always be collapsed into scrumptiously comforting desserts. As exceptional as it is, pie does not actually correlate to every ebb and flow of our country's trajectory. Not to say I didn't try to will this into fact. Abandoned chapter ideas, which fell to the wayside as soon as I realized their symbolism existed mostly in my own head and not really anywhere else, include: key lime pie and Cuban relations, shoofly pie and nineteenth-century European immigration, campfire pie and westward expansion, and some pie—any pie!—and the Cold War. (I wanted a Cold War pie *so badly*.) There was also a tremendously salty suffragette recipe that begged to be included, but try as I might, I ultimately couldn't make it support a full chapter. Nevertheless, gaze upon the "Pie for a Doubting Husband," which appeared in 1915's *The Suffrage Cook Book* and calls for:

1 qt. Milk of Human Kindness
8 reasons:
War
White Slavery
Child Labor
8,000,000 Working Women
Bad Roads
Poisonous Water
Impure Food

Mix the crust with tact and velvet gloves, using no sarcasm, especially with the upper crust. Upper crusts must be handled with extreme care for they quickly sour if manipulated roughly.

THOUGH, IN THE end, not every nuance of American history is represented by a circular dessert in a crust, you'd be surprised by just how much of our past can be told through pie.

Pumpkin pie, for instance, captures stories about the very beginnings of the United States—the Indigenous people who lived here before European colonizers arrived, what these two populations ate separately and then together, and how that history eventually played out. Pumpkin pie didn't exist at the first Thanksgiving (or, at least, an approximation of what we typically like to think of as the first Thanksgiving), yet by the mid-1800s it was popping up in Thanksgiving-themed poetry, and today we eat it every year on the fourth Thursday of November while our cousins yell at the Cowboys and at least one uncle is napping from too much ~~beer~~ turkey. Why? And how?

Molasses pie, meanwhile, captures some of the worst crimes of the United States and the legacies of racial trauma and oppression passed down from our country's history of slavery. Sweet potato pie, on the other hand, emerged from a complicated origin amidst enslavement to be reclaimed by the Black population originally forced to bake the dish and barred from eating it. The dish proved so powerful that it even helped fund the historically Black college that would go on to become Bethune-Cookman University, as the university's founder Dr. Mary McLeod Bethune sold sweet potato pies to earn capital and keep the school open when it still had just five students. And many decades later, a bean-based pie emerged once again as a weapon in the fight for racial equality to become a radical symbol of Black power. (Not to mention, the alleged cause of Muhammad Ali's most famous boxing loss.)

A quirky pie like the mock apple pie (made with crushed crackers and literally no fruit) pops up during two of the most severe economic crises our country has faced, and its endearing filling embodies the creativity and ingenuity employed by housewives trying to preserve an air of normalcy amidst drastic upheaval and uncertainty.

Of course, pie has also been entwined in gender relations on both sides of the divide. In the twentieth century, food corporations marketed pie recipes using their products to capitalize on the domestic pressures of modern housewives tasked with providing traditional meals for their families. Later, in reaction to Second-Wave Feminism, men seized upon a very specific type of pie as a barometer to define arbitrary rules of masculinity and gender roles. They also deeply misunderstood satire in the process, because *classic*.

And at one point, political activists in the late twentieth century became so fed up with the dire state of global affairs that they took a cue from the Three Stooges and began literally hurling pie in people's faces. The movement led to fabulous puns like the hand-book *Pie Any Means Necessary*, not to mention the rise of such noto-rious individuals as Aron "Pieman" Kay, an anonymous thrower known only as Agent Apple, and the infamous "Cherry Pie Three." Truly terrifying stuff.

These are just some examples of the stories you'll find between these pages. They range in scope and subject, touching upon such hefty topics as war, nationalism, race, industrialization, poverty, environmental degradation, gender, and even Hollywood. Narra-tives range from ongoing, multi-decade epics to brief flashes in the pan (or, erm, stints in the oven). There are heartbreaking histories and amusing anecdotes, and one character quite literally dubbed "The Pie King." From the marshy lowlands of the South to the crowded streets of New York to the suburbs of the Midwest to the bright lights of California, pie stretches across the broad expanse to touch nearly every corner of our country.

Ultimately, the story of pie in the United States is a story of America itself, following the narrative of our country and its evolu-tion across centuries of innovation and change.

It's time to dig in.

ALL-BUTTER PIE CRUST

MAKES 1 CRUST FOR A 9-INCH (23-CM) PIE

Crust is pretty much the unifying factor when it comes to pie. This fluid, flexible, feisty dish morphs into countless shapes and styles, but you can count on the final result having some sort of crust. It won't get too much attention in the following chapters—with a notable exception here and there—as most pies are distinguished by their filling. But don't let that fool you. The crust is our trusty friend, a guide into the wide and wonderful world of pie. It will be the common thread woven through the rest of this book, even if it often goes unacknowledged.

So let's lay the foundation here with a go-to recipe. Everyone has their favorite pie crust recipe, and this just happens to be mine. Everyone also says their crust is the very best—the flakiest, the most flavorful, the most shrink-resistant. I will make no such claims of this recipe, because I don't think the "perfect pie crust" actually exists. Experiment with adding vinegar or vodka, shortening or lard, and feel free to use the pie crust recipe that best suits you. I've used this one for years and love the fact that (1) it's all butter so you only have to worry about keeping one kind of fat in your kitchen and (2) it doesn't require any odd ingredients or complicated methods. It's simple and straightforward, and for a dish as humble and quotidian as pie (and for a baker who can be both lazy and time-constrained), it suits just fine.

One final note on this recipe—I usually don't measure the salt or sugar. Just a big scoop of each. I also never measure the water, as the amount of water you'll need to bring the crust together depends on many factors, and the exact measurement will differ each time you bake. Once you've made enough crusts, you'll be able to go by feel instead of measurement; until then, use the amounts below as a guide and trust your gut. Happy baking!

> 1¼ cups (155 g) all-purpose flour
> ½ teaspoon salt
> 1 teaspoon granulated sugar
> 8 tablespoons (1 stick/115 g) unsalted butter, cold, cut into
>   ½-inch (12-mm) chunks
> 3 to 6 tablespoons ice water

In a large mixing bowl, combine the flour, salt, and sugar. Add the butter to the flour mixture and lightly toss until all the butter is coated in flour, then use your fingers to work the butter into the flour, smashing the butter into flat pieces as you do so.* Do this until you have a crumbly mixture that's still full of large, visible butter chunks, about the size of dimes or lima beans.

Drizzle in the ice water 1 tablespoon at a time, lightly stirring the mixture until you have a shaggy, mostly cohesive dough. It's okay if there are still dry patches—in fact, that's ideal. Gently form the dough into a disc, then wrap tightly in plastic or a reusable alternative and chill in the refrigerator for at least 30 minutes before using. You can store the chilled crust in the fridge for a few days before using and for a few months in the freezer.

To prepare for a standard 9-inch (23-cm) pie, roll out a disc on a lightly floured work surface until about 12 inches (30.5 cm) in diameter. It's now ready to line a pie plate or top a double-crusted pie.

---

* Working the butter in with your fingers can be physically difficult for some people, so you can easily do this part with a pastry cutter or food processor, or even in the bowl of your stand mixer.

CHAPTER ONE

APPLE PIE

IT SEEMS INEVITABLE, doesn't it, that this book would begin with apple pie. Easily the single most famous pie, if not dish, in the United States, it harkens all the way back to the country's beginning, and even well before. It's no surprise, then, that apple pie parallels America's birth. Originating on foreign shores, the dish arrived in the New World with British colonists before evolving with the early United States, culminating with the first truly American apple pie recipe arriving at nearly the same time as our Constitution.

Ultimately, the story of American apple pie's creation is that of America's itself. And telling that story means going back to the very beginning.

American cuisine is a vast, deeply multicultural landscape with influences from a remarkable number of cultures that have relocated here. To say that it is exclusively Western, European, or British would clearly be misguided. Yet in a general sense, there still exists a certain through line of British and Western European influence that speaks to this country's start as a collection of not-very-well treated colonies—coincidentally (or not) the first time apple pie was consumed on North American shores.

Obviously, it would be not only naive but also dumb to pretend that Western Europeans were the first people to call this verdant landmass home. And indeed, the next chapter of this book dives deeply into the influence of Indigenous people on the United States of America and on our collective pie consumption habits. But in tracing the thread that eventually became both apple pie and the republican democracy that we know of as the USA, we typically begin with the first of the British colonies.

Of course, that's not really where it all began, either. Rather, we might go even further beyond that, back across the pond and into England. Because here, amidst a monarchy and a lot of ale and some very dirty streets, is where our country really originated, with some royal charters authorizing the colonization of North America. It's where our beloved apple pie got its start, as well.

And if we want to get the full lay of the land and go very deeply down the rabbit hole, we could go all the way back to ancient civilizations in the Mediterranean, where both modern Western government and pie originated. Unsurprisingly, both looked a little different way back then. Pie, for instance, had an oil-based crust that was pretty nasty tasting and basically inedible. It was also mostly savory at that point, built on the basic concept of enclosing meat in a pastry made from ground wheat and oil. Government, meanwhile, was mostly democratic in nature and occupied almost exclusively by white men who all hated each other.

So actually, maybe only one of them has evolved in the last few thousand years.

To continue the long story of pie and the United States, we can jump into one of those warp-speed flashes through history, like the opening of *The Big Bang Theory*, through the evolution of Europe into a loose collection of feuding states and territories and families. This brings us to England in the Jacobean Era, on the brink of establishing another colony in a faraway land upon which it should seemingly have no jurisdiction. In this instance it was the New World, an untapped wonderland that was definitely full of gold and definitely not full of people already living there.

Colonial expansion was fueled by a number of social, political, and economic factors in England at the dawn of the seventeenth century. Rapid population growth had put a strain on resources, prompting an economic recession that left many struggling to support themselves. Poor crop yields only made things worse. In addition, industrial development had created a thriving textile industry that demanded wool, and as a result, landholders transformed farms into land for sheep grazing, leaving many farmers without work. Add to this a huge swath of second and third sons who, being left out of the inheritance reserved only for firstborns, sought other opportunities to make their name and fortune. In all, England at the time was home to quite a number of people with nothing to lose and everything to gain, a situation that, in addition to motivating gamblers throughout the course of history, also turned out to be quite good for breeding colonists.

The establishment of joint-stock companies was the final push to the exodus launched across the Atlantic Ocean, providing financial backing that funded colonial expansion as a commercial venture. With joint-stock companies, multiple investors pooled their resources to fund journeys west, sharing the financial risk and potential profits that might result. Incidentally, such companies were also the precursor to modern-day corporations, which have impacted the trajectory of American history as much as any social or political force.

And so, with financial investment and a royal charter burning a hole in their pockets, British settlers embarked by the boatload, lugging with them their clothes and customs and cooking, the latter of which contained one distinctly British dish that had evolved to become a culinary staple in the last few hundred years.

I'm speaking, of course, of apple pie.

Apple pie emerged from a pie culture that evolved from those early crude pies in the ancient Mediterranean. The dish had become deeply entrenched in the British Isles since the Middle Ages, when societies in Northern Europe began using butter and lard in their pastry instead of oil to create a dough that could more easily be rolled and shaped. The Middle Ages were also when the crust began to be eaten along with the filling, whereas it had previously only been used as a receptacle for the meat within. These crucial changes eventually birthed what we would consider the "modern pie." The dish, however, still looked rather different than the pie we know and love today—pies were freestanding and portable, and they were also known as "pastry coffins"* because the crust was hard, dense, and several inches thick (to withstand long baking times).

With the Renaissance and its onslaught of cherubic painted babies, irascible geniuses, and ornate architecture came a new artistic evolution for pie that nudged it toward a dish more familiar to modern bakers. Pastry cooks began developing lighter, easier-to-handle doughs, particularly in France, though the trend soon expanded north. By the time 1685 rolled around, English cook Robert May published *The Accomplisht Cook*, with fourteen different recipes for paste ("paste" being the word used for crust or pastry at the time).

The Renaissance also saw the crucial transition from savory to sweet pies, paving the way for apple pie and a legacy of mostly dessert pies that would eventually become a distinctly American culinary tradition. In England, bakers began creating sweet,

---

* Incidentally, a pastry coffin is also what I would like to be buried in. Relatives, please take note.

fruit-based pies. One of the first recipes for apple pie appeared during the beginning of this era, found in *The Forme of Cury* by Samuel Pegge in 1390. A compilation of recipes by the master cooks of King Richard II, this cookbook included a recipe "For to make Tartys in Applis" (warning: confusing Middle English ahead):

> Tak gode Applys and gode Spyeis and Figys and reysons and Perys and wan they are wel ybrayed co-lourd wyth Saffron wel and do yt in a cofyn and do yt forth to bake well.

By the mid-sixteenth century, sweet fruit pies, and particularly apple pie, had gained a stronger foothold in British cuisine and daily life. One mid-sixteenth-century cookbook, *A Proper Newe Booke of Cokerye*, featured instructions "To make pyes of grene apples," which included directions to add cinnamon, sugar, and ginger to season the apples, resulting in a pie very much resembling the dish we enjoy today. The recipe went as follows:

> Take your apples and pare them cleane and core them as ye wyll a Quince, then make youre coffyn after this maner, take a lyttle fayre water and half a dyche of butter and a little Saffron, and sette all this upon a chafyngdyshe tyll it be hoate then temper your flower with this sayd licuor, and the whyte of two egges and also make your coffyn and ceason your apples with Sinemone, Gynger and Suger ynoughe. Then putte them into your coffin and laye halfe a dyshe of butter above them and so close your coffin, and so bake them.

Meanwhile, apple pie was also becoming ingrained in everyday British culture. The sixteenth-century English dramatist and poet Robert Greene once praised a lovely lady by writing that "Thy breath is like the steame of apple-pyes." Really, I could think of no higher compliment. Swoon. And later, in 1713, an English poem summed up just how beloved apple pie had become to the British in a poem titled "Apple Pye," declaring:

> Of all the Delicates which Brittons try
> To please the Palate, and delight the Eye,
> Of all the several Kinds of sumptuous Fare,
> There's none that can with Apple-pye compare
> For costly Flavour, or substantial Paste,
> For outward Beauty, or for inward Taste.

And none other than Jane Austen herself weighed in, writing to her sister Cassandra in a letter, "Good apple pies are a considerable part of our domestic happiness."

It's worth noting that England was not the only country baking and eating apple pie at this time. The Netherlands, in particular, was known for apple pie, with one recipe book as far back as 1514 including a recipe for Appeltaerten made with pastry, sliced apples, warming spices like cinnamon, cardamom, and nutmeg, and some very creative cooking methods that included baking the filling, removing the crust to mash it up, then serving. Versions of Dutch apple pie have endured, served as a distinct style in America today—typically covered with a crumb topping and with cream added to the filling. This iteration is not, however, what we think of when we proclaim something as "American as apple pie," and that is because the dish that has cemented its legacy as our national symbol remains firmly rooted in double-crusted British tradition, just like our nation's founding.

This brings us back to the fledgling United States and the intrepid colonists making their home in the New World, who would go on to (quite literally) plant the seeds of our apple pie tradition. Following the lost colony of Roanoke in 1585 (the original cold case), the British established their first colonies in Jamestown in 1607 and later Plymouth Rock in 1620. Life at the time was, to put it mildly, hard. Colonists struggled to feed themselves, because, as it turns out, not everything you're used to growing and eating on an island on the other side of the ocean is possible to cultivate on a completely different continent. Not to mention, many settlers had little experience in farming or hunting, more accustomed instead to purchasing their food. Just how the British solved the rather large problem of feeding themselves is detailed further in the following chapter, but one very crucial and very familiar food source is worth discussing here: apples.

Because when they arrived, these boats full of weary travelers found that one particularly beloved and useful fruit was not available in their new home. That's right—the foundational ingredient of our country's most cherished and iconic dish didn't even grow here four hundred years ago.

What did grow here were crab apples—small, shrunken little fruits that were sour and bitter. They could barely be eaten, let alone transformed into pie, and colonists gradually learned these would not fill the apple-size hole in their diets (and hearts).

Though it somewhat pains me to admit it, apples weren't only valued for their ability to make excellent pie. They were also a tremendously useful dietary staple, as they were hearty, grew easily and with little maintenance, and, perhaps most importantly, could be dried and stored throughout the winter. Plus, they were great for making cider, and alcohol can go a long way when you're moored on a hostile coast thousands of miles away from your friends and family (and, sure, need a safe drinking source too). As a result, colonists sought to introduce apples to North American soil, thus making their mark on the future of America's agriculture and diets.

Originally, settlers attempted to bring grafted apple saplings from England, but the harsh sea voyage and subsequent New England winters proved precarious for the young trees. So instead the colonists pivoted, relying on apple seeds. Though this strategy worked better than the grafted saplings, the crop still struggled. As a result, settlers likely began cross-breeding these newly grown apples with the continent's native crab apples to produce varieties more suited to the climate, mostly notably with the creation of the Hewe's Crab Apple. A cider apple, it was an extremely popular fruit variety grown in 1700s Virginia, including at Thomas Jefferson's Monticello. In so doing, they created a distinctly American crop, one literally created from both English and native origins.

And that crop took to the North American landscape like a duck to water; by 1850, the country boasted thousands of different types of apples, which was largely possible due to the plant's ability to cross-pollinate.

Though it seems small in the grand scheme of things, and even in the food scheme of things (apples, after all, were far from the only crops the British and Europeans introduced to the New World, and not as influential as others like sugar, wheat, and rice), this was a crucial development that introduced a newly created variety of apples to America and enabled centuries of national mythmaking for one dessert. It enabled the eventual creation of *American* apple pie, a key distinction that came to mean so much more than its British predecessor.

Had the British not begun planting apples in North America, who knows what our national dish would be? Another type of pie? A cake? Something savory? (The baker in me shudders at the thought.)

In a way, the colonists' introduction of apples was yet another way for them to plant their flag on this new continent, reshaping the land to suit their dietary needs. It was a form of cultural dominance, designed to introduce traditions and customs to solidify British ownership of a land to which they technically had no right. And the roots of this ideology went far deeper than those of these settlements' new apple trees.

In North America, the British were creating an entirely new *society*, built from scratch and on the back of English culture. And eventually, as we all know, they would go on to do more, establishing an entirely new country complete with a new government, social hierarchy, and economic system. But in the meantime, they also wanted to transplant their familiar way of life from their homes in England to their new outposts on foreign soil in the process.

One of the primary ways the British went about re-creating their accustomed lifestyle was through their food, a practice that indirectly led to apple pie's introduction to the New World. In addition to the usual continent-conquering goods like weapons, the colonists also brought along domestic guides to provide advice on farming, homemaking, and cooking.

One such book was Thomas Tusser's *Five Hundred Pointes of Good Husbandrie* (including one section on "Huswiferie"), originally published in 1573 and brought to the New World at some point in the seventeenth century. Another, likely much more helpful, example was Gervase Markham's seventeenth-century book *The English Huswife, Containing the Inward and Outward Virtues Which Ought to Be in a Complete Woman*. Aside from a somewhat bombastic title, this book contained advice for nearly everything a housewife might be faced with, including the plague, a headache, and a hungry husband. Replete with recipes and domestic advice, the book offered a blueprint for re-creating an English home on foreign shores. And somewhere amidst all of that sage advice, the book also contained a recipe for apple pie, making it one of the earliest recorded recipes for apple pie used in America.

In fact, the book technically provided two recipes for apple pie, demonstrating the dish's popularity. Using the term "pippin," which referred to apples, the book shared recipes for A Pippin Pie and A Pippin Tart. Ironically, the tart is much more similar to what we would think of as pie than the actual pie recipe. Markham's Pippin Pie, for instance, calls for whole cored apples and bears a resemblance to a kind of dumpling. The Pippin Tart, on the other hand, instructs the baker to take apples and "pare them, and then divide them just in the halves, and take out the cores clean." The apples are then spiced and placed in a pastry-lined dish, and finally covered with yet another layer of pastry, making a dish that very much resembles the type of pie we're familiar with today.

As the colonies continued to grow and develop over the course of the seventeenth and eighteenth centuries, more British cookbooks like *The English Huswife* and their accompanying recipes for apple pie proliferated. Susannah Carter, for example, included a recipe for apple pie (well, technically "apple or pear pie") in her book *The Frugal Housewife, or Complete Woman Cook*, which was originally published in England and later reprinted in the colonies in the 1770s.* Her apple pie recipe was also notable for another reason: It was lifted nearly verbatim from an earlier cookbook, *The Art of Cookery Made Plain and Easy* by Hannah Glasse, which was

* Fun fact: The plates used to illustrate the American edition of her book were made by the one and only Paul Revere.

published decades prior, in 1747. Apparently such blatant plagiarism really wasn't that uncommon back then, but still!

Regardless of who actually developed it, this apple pie recipe was likely popular in early America due to the success of *The Frugal Housewife*. Though not an exact reproduction of modern apple pie, it called for techniques and ingredients that we would be familiar with—pared and cored apples, sugar, lemon, cloves—as well as a bottom and top crust of flaky puff pastry, a style that was on its way to becoming standard. It goes:

> Make a good puff paste crust, lay some round the sides of the dish, pare and quarter your apples, and take out the cores; lay a row of apples thick, throw in half the sugar you intend for your pie; mince a little lemonpeel fine, throw a few cloves, here and there one, then the rest of your apples, and the rest of your sugar. You must sweeten to your palate, and squeeze in a little lemon juice. Boil the peeling of the apples and the cores in fair water, with a blade of mace till it is very good; strain it, and boil the syrup with sugar till it is rich; pour it into your pie, put on your upper crust, and bake it. You may put in a little quince* or marmalade, if you please.

These published recipes—originally written for English cooks—circulated among women in early America, who tweaked or modified as needed to serve their families. They reflected the eating habits of colonists, many of whom turned to apple pie at all

---

* Pie maven Kate McDermott, author of a book named *Art of the Pie*, also cites quince as a secret weapon in her apple pie fillings. These ladies were on to something!

hours of the day to eat for breakfast, lunch, and/or dinner. "Aple" pie, for instance, made an appearance in a 1769 entry in the diary of a minister named John Page, listed alongside mince pies in an extensive list of dishes that included a "roasting pig."

While writing home to Sweden in 1759 about a settlement in Delaware, the Swedish parson Dr. Israel Acrelius shared: "Apple pie is used throughout the whole year, and when fresh Apples are no longer to be had, dried ones are used. It is the evening meal of children. House pie, in country places, is made of Apples neither peeled nor freed from their cores, and its crust is not broken if a wagon wheel goes over it." His community's pies, evidently, were still made in the rustic style that emulated Medieval British "coffins," with a hard, unbreakable crust (not even a wagon wheel could shatter it!) and whole, uncored apples. Acrelius also referenced dried apples, which turned apples into pantry staples for the lean years of winter. By drying the fruit, North American settlers made it possible to prepare apple pie at any time of year, even when fresh apples were no longer accessible.

Overall, as demonstrated from the number of variations and iterations of apple pie that proliferated, from dumpling-style pies with whole uncored apples to Dr. Acrelius's unbreakable coffins to more familiar double-crusted pastries, the dish was evolving with the colonies, beginning its slow transformation from purely British invention to American staple.

AS VERSIONS OF British apple pie adapted to a new American environment, local government in the colonies also evolved from a foundation built on existing English systems. In the Massachusetts Bay Colony, for example, the population developed a system of local governance that mirrored England's Parliament. The General

Court, as it was known, was divided into two houses that mimicked the House of Lords and the House of Commons; in Massachusetts, they were known as the House of Assistants and the House of Deputies, respectively. Rooted in the church, this original system emulated the values and structures that governed England. But soon, evolving philosophies and belief systems challenged this status quo, leading to new, distinctly American forms of government.

In Rhode Island, for example, Roger Williams established a new settlement with a government that emphasized more democratic ideals. Williams had been banned from the Massachusetts Bay Colony for having the gall to advocate for such outlandish ideas as separation of church and state (absolutely bonkers). Arriving in Rhode Island in 1636, he set up a new settlement, one with a government based on the consent of the people, religious tolerance, and the separation of church and state. Sound familiar?

And he wasn't the only one—in Hartford, a settlement founded in 1636 along the Connecticut River by Reverend Thomas Hooker, the people were governed by a system rooted in democratic control by all citizens that did not limit voting rights to members of the Puritan church; it was also shaped by the Fundamental Orders of Connecticut, which influenced elements of the eventual United States Constitution. As colonies continued to develop throughout the next few decades, particularly in the middle and northern territories, many reflected these new liberal and democratic ideals, including William Penn's Pennsylvania.

And as government began to develop, so too did social ideology. Isolated in the New World, the colonies underwent their own periods of moral, social, and religious revolution that separated them from their English origins. During the Great Awakening of the 1730s and '40s, which was anchored by Jonathan Edwards's sermon "Sinners in the Hands of an Angry God" and George

Whitefield's travels to preach throughout the thirteen colonies, America experienced a wave of religious revivalism that impacted American culture for years to come. It established a religious climate that emphasized individualism and nationalism and began to plant the idea that colonists were American rather than just British expatriates.

Meanwhile, the Enlightenment—whose American poster boy was history's most famous kite enthusiast, Benjamin Franklin—was also going on in Europe, and its influence spread across the sea to the colonies. Also known as the Age of Reason, the Enlightenment emphasized logic, education, and science, ushering in a new era of modern thought. It also promoted ideals like balance and order, which laid the groundwork for an eventual American governance structure built on a system of balance of power.

We know, of course, how this whole story ends. Colonists eventually embraced their American identity wholeheartedly, breaking from the British and their ties to England. With the Revolutionary War and powerfully symbolic touchstones like the Declaration of Independence and the Liberty Bell, Americans created a new code of nationalism and patriotism, one isolated to the societies of North America and the newly created United States.

Not coincidentally, it was also right around this time that apple pie fully broke from its British roots, and the first truly American apple pie entered the picture.

It came in the 1796 cookbook *American Cookery* (whose full title was *clears throat*: *American Cookery, or the art of dressing viands, fish, poultry, and vegetables, and the best modes of making pastes, puffs, pies, tarts, puddings, custards, and preserves, and all kinds of cakes, from the imperial plum to plain cake: Adapted to this country, and all grades of life*), believed to be the first cookbook published in the United States, arriving less than a decade after the official ratification of the Constitution in 1787 and only a few years after George Washington's election as the country's first president.

As we have seen, the recipe books American housewives had previously used were English creations born from a purely English lifestyle. Amelia Simmons, the author of *American Cookery*, set out to change the game. Instead, she wrote a distinctly American cookbook that embraced the spirit of the newborn country, employing ingredients that could be found in the States and formalizing American recipes that had developed over the previous two centuries. She even made this mission clear in the title, if you happened to have the patience to read all the way to the end.

Unfortunately, we don't know much about Amelia Simmons herself, despite her unbelievably significant role in the course of apple pie history. As culinary historian Karen Hess explained in a modern printing of Simmons's book, she was an orphan (she's literally listed on the book's cover as "Amelia Simmons: American Orphan") and came from a modest background; likely because of these origins, her book demonstrates a keen understanding of social hierarchies and the difficulties many women from less prosperous backgrounds might face, with a particular affinity for other orphans like herself. As such, *American Cookery* is somewhat of a democratic text that sought to help women by fortifying them with essential domestic knowledge.

That egalitarian framework is just one of the ways Simmons's book embodied the new American spirit. Even more importantly, Simmons's recipes focused on using ingredients found in North America, an area in which English cookbooks' knowledge was severely lacking, having been written for English pantries and all. Indeed, as Hess wrote in the introduction of that modern *American Cookery*: "So, again, what makes *American Cookery* so very American? It is precisely the bringing together of certain native American products and English culinary traditions." For instance, Simmons included many recipes using cornmeal, one of the foundations of the American diet and a substitute for English oats; such recipes included dishes like Hoe Cake and Indian Slapjacks.

Catering to a definitively American kitchen, *American Cookery* was extremely popular, so much so that it was kept in reprints for thirty-five years after its initial publication in Hartford. Needless to say, food and cuisine play a tremendously important role in developing a common national identity, and Simmons's *American Cookery* proved particularly influential in this regard, due to its spirit, ingredients, and groundbreaking status as the first such book published in America. By explicitly recording the way people ate and cooked in the young United States of America, Simmons created a guideline of domestic American life and culture that was inextricably linked to food. As culinary historian Mary Tolford Wilson has written, "Amelia Simmons's work was, in its minor sphere, another declaration of American independence."

American Cookery knowingly leaned into this role, too—the book's second edition included recipes for Independence Cake and Election Cake. And even though it didn't have such an extravagant name, the inclusion of apple pie was no less patriotic.

Up to this point, apple pie had long been a culinary staple for colonists, as we well know, and it had emerged more than perhaps any other variety as the definitive pie of America. Simmons herself called out apples in a section titled Fruit, in which she wrote:

> Apples, are still more various, yet rigidly retain their own
> species, and are highly useful in families, and ought to
> be more universally cultivated, excepting in the most
> compactest cities . . . If the boy who thus planted a tree,
> and guarded and protected it in a useless corner, and

carefully engrafted different fruits, was to be indulged free access into orchards, whilst the neglectful boy was prohibited—how many millions of fruit trees would spring into growth—and what a saving to the union. The net saving would in time extinguish the public debt, and enrich our cookery.

Amelia Simmons proposed that apples could literally save the country, defeating the two-headed monster that brings down all empires: crippling national debt and bad cooking.

Therefore, it's no surprise that Simmons included not one but two recipes for apple pie in her book, as well as a recipe for apple tart. The two pies are fairly similar, but the second recipe, Buttered Apple Pie, might be considered a bit more standard to our twenty-first-century eyes, mainly because it explicitly calls for pared, quartered apples and a top crust. Observe:

A Buttered Apple Pie: Pare, quarter and core tart apples, lay in paste No. 3, cover with the same; bake half an hour, when drawn, gently raise the top crust, add sugar, butter, cinnamon, mace, wine or rose-water.

Really, this recipe isn't all that different from some of the previous versions produced during America's early decades. In particular, it harkens back to the more refined English styles of British cookbooks like *The Frugal Housewife* and *The Art of Cookery* (a connection that's more than just implicit—turns out our girl Amelia also allegedly indulged in a little creative shoplifting throughout *American Cookery*).

But what made this pie recipe so groundbreaking was the fact that by recording it, Simmons ultimately established a definitive version of American apple pie. This exact recipe hasn't endured, of course, but certain hallmarks have become standard, including cut apples, warming spices like cinnamon and mace (or nutmeg), and of course, the signature top crust, designed to be edible and tender, rather than a hard pastry like early British coffins and Dr. Acrelius's indestructible shell. Though Simmons's recipe for Buttered Apple Pie calls for the apples to be baked in the sealed crust and the spices, sugar, butter, wine, and rosewater to be added afterward by lifting the top crust, a practice we would never engage in today (can you imagine the stress of handling that top crust?!), the distinction of sealing a spiced and sweetened apple filling between two layers of pastry remains.

By setting forth this version of apple pie in the first cookbook of the United States, Simmons (perhaps unwittingly) established the outline of a national symbol that would endure as much as any other piece of patriotic propaganda from the era.

And, like much of the broader foundation of the new United States, her book established how the apple pie emerged from English origins to create something new and distinct. Indeed, Harriet Beecher Stowe just about summed it all up in 1869 when she wrote, "The pie is an English institution, which, planted on American soil, forthwith ran rampant and burst forth into an untold variety of genera and species."

This moment comes at the very beginning of our nation's birth, in its infant stages. The narrative, as we know, is just beginning. Apple pie, like the United States, has a long way to go to become the dominant force that we know it as today. But already, before the catchy sayings and the near-mythological status, it was there at the very beginning of the United States, solid and comforting, a harbinger of all that our country had already undergone.

A BUTTERED APPLE PIE

Adapted from *American Cookery* by Amelia Simmons

MAKES ONE 9-INCH (23-CM) PIE

Unlike Amelia, we will not be lifting the top crust after baking to add all the ingredients, though feel free to experiment with that technique if you so desire. I like this pie made with white wine (and tend to have that available in my kitchen more frequently), though you can also take Amelia's other suggestion and use a splash of rosewater instead.

2 All-Butter Pie Crusts (pages 12–13)

4 to 5 medium-to-large apples, peeled, cored, and cut into ¼-inch (6-mm) slices

½ cup (100 g) granulated sugar

¼ cup (30 g) all-purpose flour

½ teaspoon mace or nutmeg

2 teaspoons ground cinnamon

2 tablespoons white wine or rosewater

½ teaspoon salt

2 tablespoons unsalted butter, cold, cut into ¼-inch (6-mm) chunks

1 large egg, lightly beaten, for brushing the crust

Preheat the oven to 425°F (220°C). Line a 9-inch (23-cm) pie pan with one of the prepared crusts. Place in the refrigerator while you make the filling.

In a large bowl, toss the apples with the sugar, flour, mace, cinnamon, white wine, and salt. Arrange the apples in the prepared crust, then dot with the chunks of butter. Top the filling with the second pie crust, sealing and crimping the edges. Cut vents into the top crust, then brush with the beaten egg.

Bake for 40 to 50 minutes, until the crust is golden brown and the filling is bubbling though the vents. Let cool completely before serving, so that the filling can set and be cut neatly.

CHEDDAR APPLE PIE

LIKE DARCY AND Elizabeth or Lady Gaga and Tony Bennett, sometimes two seemingly incompatible things can go perfectly together when given the chance. The same goes for apple pie and cheese.

If you live in certain regions of the United States, particularly New England, you might know exactly what I'm talking about—in fact, this pairing might be your favorite way to eat apple pie. Or, more likely, you're not only shocked to learn this combo exists, but horrified.

While not exactly common, this dynamic duo of pie and cheese is widespread enough to have multiple iterations—sometimes the cheese is shredded and baked into the crust; other times, a slice of cheddar is laid atop a warm apple pie so that it slightly melts. Its roots, like apple pie itself, reportedly trace back to merry old England, where dairy-based sauces were added to pies as early as the seventeenth century. Cheese, too, was served at the end of meals just before or alongside the dessert course, a natural combination of savory and sweet (and a tradition that endures today on the dessert menus of many modern restaurants).

It's unsurprising, then, that Americans started eating their beloved apple pie this way as well, and by the nineteenth century it was a popular pairing. Curiously enough, a Brit once reported on the practice of Americans eating cheese with their pie, then circled back to its origins in his home country: In 1882's *Through America: Or, Nine Months in the United States*, Walter Gore Marshall wrote, "You have a triangular-shaped slice put on your plate, and (in some parts of America) if you do not want to be singular you will eat it with a bit of cheese, Yorkshire fashion."

This pairing was so popular that there was even a common phrase uttered by the masses: "An apple pie without cheese is like a kiss without a squeeze." (One woman used that phrase to describe the inconceivable idea of a Thanksgiving dinner without turkey in 1891.) In fact, the duo sparked such passion that it ultimately inspired some poetry—in 1896, American poet Eugene Field wrote "Apple Pie and Cheese," a fervent ode to this pie style that included the line "But I, when I undress me / Each night, upon my knees / Will ask the Lord to bless me / With apple-pie and cheese!"

Though many modern Americans might think of cheese and pie as a quirky, little-known delicacy, it reached national prominence for a time—when the phrase "American as apple pie" was starting to percolate in the first half of the twentieth century, it was often expanded to "American as apple pie and cheese."

Today, though, that national spotlight has waned, and cheese is served with apple pie mostly in New England and the Midwest. (*Southern Living* once ran a headline "Why Southerners Wouldn't Put a Slice of Cheese on Apple Pie.") Meanwhile, up north, there's a Vermont law that decrees citizens should make a "'good faith' effort" to serve apple pie "with a slice of cheddar cheese weighing a minimum of ½ ounce." (There's also a long-standing legend that such a law exists in Wisconsin, but it's been proven to be nothing more than a myth inspired by the state's fervent love of dairy.)

CHAPTER TWO

PUMPKIN PIE

WHEN WAS THE first time you learned about the origins of Thanksgiving?

If you're one of the millions of people who celebrate the holiday each November, did you discuss the parable of "the Pilgrims and the Indians" between bites of mashed potatoes, seated next to cousins around the family table? Did you learn about the holiday in school? Maybe your first-grade teacher taught you how to make those cute little turkeys out of your handprint and told you about a time long ago, when a friendly group of people wearing funny hats with belt buckles met an even friendlier group of people with feathers in their hair. Maybe some source—an aunt, a parent, a schoolteacher, a children's book—spun a story about a difficult winter, a very nice young Native American man, the magic of corn grown *with* beans at the same time (!), and of course, a lavish feast that brought together two groups of people from opposite sides of the world to give thanks for the blessing of a successful harvest and a bright future ahead.

Now, when was the first time you learned this story of Thanksgiving was all a lie?

Even though, thankfully, we're now more open about discussing and acknowledging the reality of the first Thanksgiving (if you can even call it that), we still cling tightly to the traditions of this holiday. And that, more than anything, applies to the food we eat. While certain dishes are associated with various American celebrations throughout the year (though I wouldn't shed a tear if fruitcake somehow faded away from the Christmas rotation), the stereotypical Thanksgiving menu remains firmly set and stubbornly universal in a manner unrivaled by any other holiday. From dry turkey to jiggly cranberry sauce to pillowy sweet potatoes, most Americans continue to collectively emulate our modern idea of a harvest feast every fourth Thursday of November, year in and year out. Even if almost all of that harvest bounty comes from the supermarket nowadays.

And though various treats abound, there's really only one dessert unquestionably associated with Thanksgiving.* Pumpkin pie has held its undisputed crown as the ruler of the dessert table for centuries, a dominant pastry dynasty. And why shouldn't it? It stands out with its silky texture, pungent spices, and rich, almost savory flavor. Of course, it's also made from a plant harvested in the fall, adding some welcome seasonality. And, perhaps most importantly, it's the kind of dessert you can make ahead and leave to hang while you try to figure out just what exactly a spatchcocked turkey is and whether or not it's worth your time.† Pumpkin pie, it seems, really is the perfect dish to close an annual Thanksgiving feast.

---

* Some people might take issue with this comment and argue that sweet potato pie is also an iconic Thanksgiving pie. Don't worry—there's more on sweet potato pie to come later in this book.

† If you're wondering, it's a turkey split along its backbone and flattened out, and it's very much worth your time.

Like the reality of the holiday, however, the story of pumpkin pie is not necessarily a feel-good narrative. In addition to being coopted and melded into a whitewashed, sanitized narrative of Thanksgiving, pumpkin pie's overall proliferation has erased its Indigenous American origins and the culinary influences of the dish; in the end, it's a journey that reflects the overall erasure of Indigenous people's struggle from the falsely celebratory myth of Thanksgiving.

BEFORE PUMPKIN WAS a vital ingredient on the Thanksgiving table, it was a foundational food source for the Indigenous people who lived across North America. In fact, squash—the broader category under which pumpkin falls—very well might be the *first* foundational food source domesticated for human consumption in the Americas. As chronicled by Cindy Ott in her book *Pumpkin: The Curious History of an American Icon*, domesticated squash seeds can be traced back eight thousand to ten thousand years ago in Oaxaca, Mexico, which is two thousand years before the earliest domesticated corn or bean seeds can be dated. Admittedly, it's difficult to trace the specific lineage of pumpkin, as multiple layers of nomenclature, language translation, and historical documentation tend to blur the line between various squash varieties; often, little distinction can be parsed beyond just, well, "squash." Adding to this is the fact that the ancestors of the pumpkin we know today were different than the broad, hearty plants into which we like to carve jack-o'-lanterns each October. Early pumpkins were small, only around three to four inches (7.5 to 10 cm) in diameter. Over time, various Indigenous communities used their agricultural skill to breed the plants and yield larger, sweeter varieties more in line with what we know today (though not quite the same).

The diets of various Indigenous tribes throughout North America differed by region and were composed of local food sources. Regardless, a large portion of communities along the Eastern Seaboard relied on corn, beans, and squash as the core of their diet, and the three plants came to be known as the "three sisters." This grouping was emphasized by the fact that the three crops grew incredibly well together, flourishing in a symbiotic relationship. Beans grew by climbing the tall, sturdy stalks of corn as if they were trellises. Meanwhile, squash propagated on the ground between stalks and helped retain moisture in the soil. As French explorer Samuel de Champlain observed of certain Indigenous agricultural practices in 1605, "With this corn they put in each hill three or four Brazilian beans, . . . which are of different colors. When they grow up, they interlace with the corn, which reaches the height of from five to six feet; and they keep the ground very free from weeds. We saw there many squashes, and pumpkins, and tobacco, which they likewise cultivate."

Pumpkin, in particular, was valued in precolonial America because it grew and propagated easily, and like other hard winter squashes, it could be stored to last throughout the winter. The plant was just one of many varieties of squash that Indigenous people cultivated, and it wasn't particularly prized above other squashes and gourds. Nevertheless, it was eaten by people across North America. By the late fifteenth century, when European colonizers began arriving in waves from across the sea, pumpkin was being grown by the Iroquois in present-day New England, the Mandans of the Great Plains, the Ojibwas near the Great Lakes, the Cherokee in the Southeast, and as far away as the Cahuillas and Pueblos in the sunbaked lands of the Southwest. Indeed, almost all early accounts of Indigenous customs written by white colonizers after their arrival mention cultivated squash and pumpkin.

Since squash was grown and eaten by Indigenous tribes for thousands of years, it's no surprise that the plant was revered enough to take on a spiritual significance. Squash found its way into creation myths, festivals, and ceremonies long before its descendant pumpkin pie became a key figure in Thanksgiving celebrations. One Iroquois creation tale depicted the Great Spirit as a woman walking the earth; with each step, squash grew on her right, beans on her left, and corn in her footprints. Similarly, other tribes viewed corn, beans, and squash as the daughters of Mother Earth. Seneca and Huron oral traditions described squash sprouting from the abdomen and head of a sacred being. Meanwhile, squash was celebrated in many festivals and ceremonies, such as the Iroquois's annual feast of the squash or the Green Corn Ceremony of the Iroquois and Cherokees. The plant occasionally took on something of a practical use in these ceremonies as well; according to accounts attributed to Chief Gibson of the Seneca by Frederick W. Waugh, pumpkin seeds were among the crop seeds used as wagers in a game during a spiritual harvest ceremony.

Despite its widespread proliferation, and the very distinct reality (largely ignored by all those people sailing in from Europe) that Indigenous people lived across the entirety of North America, we'll focus primarily on the foodways and traditions of Indigenous tribes in the Northeast, such as the Wampanoag, Iroquois, and Powhatan. This region was the site of some of the first interactions between the English and Indigenous people (at settlements like Jamestown and Plymouth), as well as the location of the "First Thanksgiving" and the myth that propagated from there, which initially took root in the mid-Atlantic and New England.

When it came to actually eating all the pumpkin Indigenous people cultivated in the region, you could find it just about any which way you wanted it: boiled, baked, mashed, dried, fried, baked into bread, and more. And since there was no wheat in North America before the arrival of Europeans, Indigenous tribes relied on corn as their primary grain, meaning corn and pumpkin were often prepared together by tribes in the Northeast, like in corn and pumpkin bread or hominy. And of course, this absence also means that there was no pumpkin "pie" that existed in Indigenous cuisine prior to contact with Europeans. Not to mention, sugar and spices weren't available in North America, so the traditional sweet tastes most modern Americans are used to wouldn't have been incorporated into the Indigenous diet. (Wrote one European on Indigenous people he had encountered in Massachusetts and Rhode Island: "They will not taste sweet things.")

As a result, pumpkin was originally almost an exclusively savory food. Thanks to Canada's favorite condiment, maple syrup (or a rudimentary precursor, like the much-less-sweet maple sap), pumpkin could potentially have been gussied up with a little sugary flair by tribes in New England, though that's largely the extent of any dessert-like iterations. (Interestingly enough, honeybees didn't reside on the continent until introduced by colonists; one account claims the Iroquois referred to them as "English flies.") Of course, like with literally everything about Indigenous life, that would all change with the arrival of Europeans on American shores.

The entire trajectory of world history altered in 1492, when Christopher Columbus sailed the ocean blue and landed in the New World, on a piece of land he wrongfully identified as India. Columbus's landfall resulted in the deaths of up to 90 percent of the Indigenous population in the Americas over the course of the next few centuries, largely due to a deadly combination of disease and violence. The catastrophic loss of tens of millions of Indigenous persons was a genocide of the cruelest order.

For those Indigenous people who did survive, the European invasion still affected their entire way of life, including the way they ate. These effects are best summed up by the Columbian Exchange—in short, the transfer of foods, crops, and livestock among the Americas, Europe, and Africa. The term, however, is rather misleading. "Exchange" implies a peaceful, voluntary trade, engaged in for mutual benefit, but of course there was nothing voluntary or peaceful about it. Nevertheless, the impact of this geographical shakeup was enormous. Some of the most important crops and livestock introduced to the Americas included cows, pigs, sugarcane, wheat, and coffee. Meanwhile, American crops brought back across the Atlantic Ocean included corn, potatoes (they're not Irish after all!), and of course, pumpkin, among many others.

The Columbian Exchange is the very reason we are now able to eat and enjoy pumpkin pie, a cultural mashup of native North American pumpkin, European wheat, and Canary Island (and later, Caribbean) sugar. But when you peel back the layers of this seemingly charming embodiment of cross-cultural exchange to examine the deeper implications of European colonization in the Americas, is it really worth it?

Spoiler alert: It isn't.

MORE THAN A hundred years after Columbus set foot on land that was definitely not India, the *Mayflower* pulled into Plymouth Bay following a jaunt across the Atlantic that lasted sixty-five days. The ship made landfall in 1620, depositing 102 (woefully unprepared) people onto New England soil. Bearing wide-eyed optimism and a somewhat terrifying religious fervor, they, quite simply, had no idea what they were in for. The group had traveled to the New

World not just in search of religious freedom and the opportunity to live freely as Protestants, but with a more fanatical drive to establish a religious theocracy.

It wasn't the first English settlement on the continent: Jamestown, down south in Virginia, had been around since 1607. You're likely familiar with Jamestown from the Disney film *Pocahontas*. You're also likely familiar with the fact that the film doesn't exactly get a gold star for historical accuracy. After a series of wars—in which the Virginia Company at one point called for "a perpetual war without peace or truce" that would prevent the Powhatan "from being any longer a people"—the English colonizers all but extinguished the Powhatan. This tragic cycle would be repeated up and down the East Coast, including at the site of America's beloved Thanksgiving celebration.

We all know the Pilgrims up in Plymouth Bay had a difficult first winter in 1620—that's what the Thanksgiving fable tells us, after all! But what is typically obscured from the legend is just how difficult it was, and the measures to which the Pilgrims resorted as a result. With few supplies or resources, the small Pilgrim settlement suffered from devastating starvation; only about half of the original 102 people survived. The group became so desperate for food that they resorted to eating dogs, cats, rats, and mice.* What's more, the colonists raided nearby Indigenous graves and storage houses in pursuit of corn. Wrote one of their leaders, Edward Winslow, "There was also a heap of sand . . . newly done, we might see

---

* And in once instance, even each other. Reportedly, one man killed, salted, and ate his wife! (Unsurprisingly, he was executed for the grisly deed. It's never a good idea to keep a murderous cannibal around, no matter how resourceful he might be.)

how they had paddled it with their hands—which we digged up, and in it we found a little old basket, full of fair Indian corn."

The Pilgrims stuck it out, though, refusing to return to England in the spring with the *Mayflower*, and you've got to give it to them—they were a hardy set of people. And they knew it: One Pilgrim wrote, "It is not with us as with other men, whom small things can discourage." Of course, it wasn't just sheer stubbornness that enabled them to stick around. It was the local Wampanoag tribe.

One thing to note—the Pilgrims of the *Mayflower* weren't the first Europeans the Wampanoag had dealt with. Years earlier, in 1614, British captain Thomas Hunt had kidnapped members of the tribe and stolen them back to Europe to be sold into slavery. And like countless other Indigenous tribes, the Wampanoag had been devastated by disease from exposure to European colonizers. So when the *Mayflower* arrived in Plymouth Bay, the Wampanoag had reason to be both nervous and skeptical. In the end, their chieftain Ousamequin was inclined to ally with the Pilgrims—despite the horror they had already wrought on the Wampanoag—because he believed the Englishmen could be useful in his tribe's ongoing conflict against the Narragansett tribe to the west. Many of his people, unsurprisingly, felt differently.

Ultimately, they were right.

Ousamequin signed a treaty with the Pilgrims in 1621, which eventually turned out to be nothing but a piece of paper, but it started things off on the right foot between the Wampanoag and the religious fanatics who suddenly wanted to live on their land. The Wampanoag engaged with the Pilgrims via a member of their tribe named Tisquantum, also known as Squanto, who knew English because, and this is important, *he had been one of the people kidnapped by Captain Thomas Hunt in 1614.* (He had returned from

Europe to North America after a long and winding journey that lasted years.) Tisquantum shared agricultural methods like planting and fertilization with the colonists, which proved crucial to the survival of the Pilgrim settlement. As a result, they had a successful harvest in 1621, which consisted of corn, peas, and barley (reportedly for beer-making, because evidently that's where their priorities lay after HALF OF THEM STARVED TO DEATH). Suddenly, the Pilgrims were able to do a noteworthy little thing known as feeding themselves.

It's true that the Pilgrims and the Wampanoags celebrated together in the fall of 1621, though details on the exact proceedings are scant. Pretty much the only description we have of what we like to think of as "Thanksgiving" comes from the account of that same Edward Winslow who recounted raiding Indigenous settlements to steal food. Which should tell you something. Supposedly, Governor William Bradford invited Ousamequin (known by the Pilgrims as Chief Massasoit because apparently they had to have their own special name for everything) and his people to a three-day celebration consisting of much feasting. Approximately ninety members of the Wampanoag tribe showed up, bearing five deer to contribute to the festivities. However, it wasn't all warm fuzzy feelings: The celebration included rifle demonstrations by the English—just a little classic dinner-party paranoia.

A celebration of thanksgiving also wasn't a super unique thing at the time, either in Indigenous or colonist tradition. Many tribes in the region, including the Wampanoag, already held celebrations of thanks throughout the year, including the Maple Dance, the Planting Feast, and the Green Corn Celebration, hosted in gratitude for the first harvest. The English colonists, meanwhile, had previously had their own little shindig down in Virginia in 1610, when the Jamestown settlement held a celebration in honor of the arrival of an English ship bearing supplies and food following a harrowing winter. Not to mention, the Pilgrims themselves sometimes held thanksgiving celebrations, although in keeping true to character, these were typically somber affairs marked by extensive prayer and fasting (boring!).

The elephant in the room is, of course, one simple question: What did they eat in 1621? Besides the deer, there was reportedly turkey (shocker!), corn (of course), and even beer (your favorite football-loving uncle would have fit right in). There was not, however, pumpkin pie. Though there is no confirmation as to whether or not there was any pumpkin at all, it is likely that squash was present in some form, very possibly pumpkin. If so, the pumpkin would have been prepared in a way closely aligned with Indigenous culinary methods, rather than European ones, given that ingredients like wheat, butter, and spices were still missing from Plymouth. In other words, the first pumpkin dish served at the first Thanksgiving was almost certainly a direct descendant of Indigenous cuisine. Indeed, even the vegetable's name came from them—according to the Wôpanâak Language Reclamation Project, the word "pumpkin" is descended from the language of the Wampanoag people: the original word, "pôhpukun" (ponh-pu-kun), means "grows forth round."

So how, then, did the very sweet and very English pumpkin pie become the de facto dessert of the Thanksgiving table? Like Thanksgiving itself, the pie underwent its own journey of American mythmaking to result in a product almost entirely divorced from its Indigenous roots and the feast between the Plymouth Pilgrims and Ousamequin's Wampanoag tribe.

Part of the reason Thanksgiving is so misleading is because it entirely ignores what came after the autumn of 1621. Many accounts will have you believe that, after breaking (corn)bread together, the Englishmen and the Wampanoags lived in harmony. If you're skeptical of such a tidy story and have even the smallest grasp of American history, you might assume that it wasn't all so merry. What's much harder to swallow and too frequently ignored, however, is the fact that just a few decades later, the Massachusetts colonists and the Wampanoag—led by none other than Ousamequin's son Metacomet—engaged in all-out war that devastated the local Indigenous population. During the conflict known as King Philip's War (the colonists called Metacomet King Philip—once again with all the special names), the violence perpetrated by the colonists was brutal. Mere decades after the Pilgrims had been saved from the brink of starvation by his father's assistance, Metacomet was beheaded and drawn and quartered, with his head carried to Plymouth on a pike and mounted for display. Whatever mutual goodwill that existed in 1621 clearly didn't last long.

The concept of Thanksgiving was also coopted in Massachusetts for a much more sinister purpose shortly after the initial feast between the Wampanoag and Pilgrims of Plymouth Bay. In 1637, following the Englishmen's brutal massacre of thousands of members of the local Pequot tribe, including women and children, Governor William Bradford (the same one who invited the Wampanoags to feast in 1621) declared "a day of thanksgiving and celebration for subduing the Pequots."

While European colonists were killing Indigenous tribes, spreading disease, and settling on Native land, they were also eating a lot of pumpkin. The squash was readily adopted into the colonial diet, often referred to as "pompion" in early accounts. Edward Ward, an Englishman traveling throughout New England in the late 1600s, observed that "pumpkin porrage" was a favorite dish and wrote that pumpkins "were the chief Fruit that supported the English at their first settling of these parts." (Ward, meanwhile, did not discuss the ways in which Indigenous people supported the English at their first settling of those parts.) And according to *New-England's Plantation* author Francis Higginson in 1630, "This Countrey aboundeth naturally with store of rootes of great varietie and good to eat. . . . Here are store of Pumpions, Cowcombers, and other things of that nature which I know not."

Pumpkins weren't just common; they were necessary. For the same reasons Indigenous people valued the squash—its easy cultivation and propagation—so too did the English settlers gravitate toward the vegetable. One colonial song likely traced to 1630 went, "Instead of pottage and puddings and custards and pies / Our pumpkins and parsnips are common supplies / We have pumpkins at morning and pumpkins at noon / If it was not for pumpkin, we should be undone." Notice that according to this little ditty, pumpkins were *replacing* pie, not populating it. At the time, pumpkins were typically prepared by boiling them into a stew or porridge, which mirrors the way Indigenous people used the squash. Emulating Indigenous agricultural methods as well, colonists grew pumpkins in the corn crops they cultivated. One Maine farmer's five-acre farm was "all set with corn and pumpkins" in the spring of 1634. Just as they had seized the very land on which those pumpkins grew, white settlers readily seized Indigenous crops and cuisine for their own purposes.

It wasn't long, though, before pumpkin began to be Anglicized in the colonial kitchen and transformed into something much more Eurocentric. One 1671 cookbook, *New-England's Rarities*, shared a recipe in which pumpkin was prepared in "the Housewives' manner," i.e., just like baked apples, with butter and spices like ginger. Which, as we know from our pie journey in the previous chapter, means that it was a replacement for a popular British ingredient not even native to North America. Later, in 1770, the book *Travels into North America: Containing Its Natural History, with the Civil, Ecclesiastical and Commercial State of the Country* explicitly laid out the difference between Indigenous pumpkin preparations and European ones. Indigenous tribes, the book asserted, "boil them whole, or roast them in ashes." Meanwhile, "the French and the English also slice them . . . when they are done they generally put sugar on the pulp." Most tellingly, the book added that "some [Europeans] make puddings and tarts of pumpkins."

Indeed, according to Cindy Ott, further mentions of pumpkin pie began cropping up sparingly in colonial records throughout the eighteenth century, signaling how the English-style preparation gradually began to gain a foothold in the kitchen. And what's more, the brutal trade system organized by European merchants—which was built on the back of enslaved labor—meant that eventually the main spices we associate with pumpkin pie were soon available on the shores of New England as well. With the addition of non-native spices like cinnamon, nutmeg, ginger, cloves, and allspice, most of which were imported from the West Indies, colonial pumpkin pies and tarts became even further divorced from their North American origins.

Just like with apple pie, things weren't official until Amelia Simmons, our favorite plagiarizing colonial orphan and the author of *American Cookery*, said they were. As you (hopefully) remember, her primary goal in publishing America's first cookbook in 1796 was to ground English cooking practices in indigenous ingredients to reflect the way "Americans" (of European descent, of course) really ate. So it's no surprise, then, that pumpkin pie was included in the text. In fact, you could convincingly argue that her pumpkin pie recipe was really much more representative of "American" cuisine at the time than that apple pie I made such a big deal about last chapter.

The inclusion also notably established pie as a common preparation for pumpkin, plus solidified its use in sweets and desserts, as opposed to savory applications. In other words, the pumpkin pie recipe in *American Cookery* standardized a European interpretation of pumpkin completely divorced from its Indigenous origins; what's worse, it codified pumpkin pie as purely *American*, when in fact the only real cuisine native to North America was the one prepared by tribes like the Wampanoag and Powhatan. The myth of European descendants being "true Americans" had already begun, and pumpkin pie was there to prove it.

The symbolism goes even further. Throughout the eighteenth century, white settlers stigmatized pumpkin as a rustic, unsophisticated vegetable (so much so that "pumpkinhead" was used as a term of ridicule—biting!); therefore, by transforming this primitive squash into a refined, European-style sweet delicacy, Simmons asserted a symbolic mastery of the wild North American land. And—if you take things a step further and draw the all too obvious line—its people.

LEAVING *AMERICAN COOKERY* behind and entering into the nineteenth century, both pumpkin pie and its bedfellow Thanksgiving shed their (sometimes dubious) historical ties and became emblems of manufactured American pride. You see, the thing about American culture at the time was that, well, it didn't really *exist*. The English, French, and Dutch who had colonized North American shores were part of cultures whose roots stretched back centuries. Meanwhile, the people of the very young United States could claim one (rather impressive!) revolution, and that was about it. So naturally, many American people went about fixing that, using food and holidays to codify particular American ideals and values. This trend included pumpkin pie.

Those values often emphasized old-fashioned standbys like family and farm life. The timing wasn't a coincidence, either; as American life became more urban, fast-paced, and modern during the nineteenth century, people turned to nostalgic values like these as a way to hold on to the golden past. This all happened to suit pumpkin particularly well. Because it was extremely common, particularly humble, and never grown as a cash crop, pumpkin came to be strongly associated with an idealized New England and visions of bucolic rural life, as documented by Ott in *Pumpkin*. No less than Henry David Thoreau, the poster boy of natural idealism (even if his mom still did his laundry while he lived at Walden Pond), used pumpkin to represent the wholesome value of simple living, asserting, "I would rather sit on a pumpkin and have it all to myself than be crowded on a velvet cushion."

Naturally, pumpkin pie followed suit. Leaning heavily on nostalgia and ideals of wholesome family values, the dish became inextricably associated with New England farm life, so much so that many pumpkin pie recipes published in other parts of the country were labeled "New England Pumpkin Pie." Which I personally would call successful branding.

As early as 1818, John Palmer wrote in the *Journal of Travels in the United States* that "one or two dishes are peculiar to New England, and always on the table, toast dipped in cream and pumpkin pie." Later in 1833, a letter to the editor in *American Farmer* stated, with quite a bit of admirable snark, "Having recently traveled through the 'Land of Steady Habits,' or 'Pumpkin Dominion' (I mean the New England States), there was scarcely a family but what, in the article of diet, when forthcoming at stated periods, would bring up the rear with a company or platoon of pumpkin pies."* And in her landmark work *Rural Hours*, a document of Northeast life, Susan Fenimore Cooper wrote, "Yesterday, the first pumpkin-pie of the season made its appearance on the table. It seems rather strange, at first glance, that in a country where apples, and plums, and peaches, and cranberries abound, the pumpkin should be held in high favor for pies." She notably added, "this is a taste which may probably be traced back to the early colonists."

At the same time that pumpkin pie was becoming a sweet symbol of rural American pride and New England identity, the holiday of Thanksgiving was developing along very similar lines. Though it supposedly originated with the Plymouth harvest gathering all the way back in 1621, Thanksgiving wasn't celebrated as a national holiday until over a century and a half later in 1789, when George Washington declared a day of thanksgiving to be celebrated on November 26 at the request of the first Federal Congress. The proclamation was an important step in the creation of a national identity, coinciding with the formation of the new country. Though it wasn't celebrated annually until the Civil War, Thanksgiving became a common occurrence in American households. Drawing broadly from the vague outlines of the original Pilgrim feast, Thanksgiving represented agrarian bounty and communal gathering. Very much unlike the 1621 gathering, Thanksgiving also evolved to encompass family and spending time with loved ones.

So while pumpkin pie naturally became linked with Thanksgiving because of its association with the harvest and early colonial foodways, there was another reason the dish became so embedded

---

* I truly don't know why the author was so bitter—a platoon of pumpkin pies sounds fantastic.

in the holiday—it represented the same values of a newly forming, European-based American identity.

This all really kicked into gear over the course of the nineteenth century, when Thanksgiving evolved from a sporadically celebrated holiday to a widespread canonized event, and pumpkin pie evolved right along with it. Already by 1834, *American Farmer* stated, "If Thanksgiving in Massachusetts go not off with éclat, it will neither be for the want of a good proclamation . . . nor for lack of squashes, which every body knows are converted into what is by a figure of speech called pumpkin pie." The poet John Greenleaf Whittier notably cemented the relationship in his Thanksgiving poem, "The Pumpkin." According to Whittier, "on Thanksgiving day, when from East and from West / From North and from South come the pilgrim and guest . . . What calls back the past, like the rich Pumpkin pie?" He wished, quite dreamily, "And thy life be as sweet, and its last sunset sky / Golden-tinted and fair as thy own Pumpkin pie!" It's also not a coincidence that Whittier only referenced the Pilgrims and their "guests" in his poem.

And around the same time, Lydia Maria Child (author of *The American Frugal Housewife*) published her still-famous poem "A New-England Boy's Song about Thanksgiving Day" (better known as "Over the River and Through the Woods") a bucolic, family-oriented ode to Thanksgiving that culminates with "Hurra for the pumpkin pie!"

Perhaps most importantly, a woman named Sarah Josepha Hale featured pumpkin pie prominently in the Thanksgiving spread in her 1827 novel, *Northwood; or, a Tale of New England*, calling the "celebrated pumpkin pie" an "indispensable part of a good and true Yankee Thanksgiving." This book wasn't just another example of pumpkin pie's prominence on the Thanksgiving table; Sarah Hale, as it turns out, went on to become the editor of the hugely influential *American Ladies' Magazine* (later *Godey's Lady's Book*) and also the single greatest Thanksgiving enthusiast our nation has ever seen.

Hale was convinced that America needed an autumn holiday—up to this point, the only two national holidays were Washington's birthday in February and Independence Day in July—and thus launched a campaign for a national Thanksgiving Day in 1846, using her prominence as a magazine editor to basically turn her pages into a Thanksgiving propaganda leaflet the likes of which would have made Joseph Stalin proud. She wrote passionately about the holiday every autumn, like in an 1859 editorial in *Godey's Lady's Book* in which she postured, "OUR THANKSGIVING UNION.—The last Thursday in November—will it not be a great day in our Republic?" Another year, in 1860, she wrote, "We must advert once more to this grand object of nationalizing Thanksgiving Day, by adopting, as a permanent rule, the last Thursday in November in all the States . . . If all the States and Territories hold their Thanksgiving on that day, there will be a complete moral and social reunion of the *people* of America in 1860."

A true ringleader, Hale enlisted other magazines to take up the cause, and many began to publish Thanksgiving-related content as well. She also spent years writing to presidents, congressmen, and governors, requesting they establish a Thanksgiving Day in November, until Abraham Lincoln finally caved and did so in 1863 to promote national unity in the midst of the Civil War.

From there, the insidious myth of the humble Pilgrims and benevolent "Indians" took root, entwining itself with the defining narrative of Thanksgiving until the two were inseparable. By the late 1860s, Northern writers were linking Thanksgiving with the Pilgrims in stories for newspapers and magazines; by the 1870s, school textbooks promoted the sanitized narrative of the "First

Thanksgiving." The narrative was also included in *Standish of Standish: A Story of the Pilgrims* by Jane G. Austin in the late 1880s. The book was entirely fiction, though that seemed to fly above quite a large number of people's heads; many Americans seized upon Austin's story of an abundant feast, and the imagery reappeared in children's literature, books, art, magazines, and more. The tale became so embedded in American lore that the Pilgrims eventually became a symbol of national heritage used in schools to help the flood of immigrants in the late nineteenth and early twentieth centuries assimilate to an American identity. And just like Thanksgiving, pumpkin pie was upheld as a symbol of authentic American virtue used to promote national identity, as evidenced by its titular role in the famous cookbook by Henriette Davidis, *Pickled Herring and Pumpkin Pie: A Nineteenth-Century Cookbook for German Immigrants to America.*

It wasn't all harmless cookbooks or novels, either. In one particularly harrowing account, pumpkin pie was served as part of an 1892 Thanksgiving celebration at the Hampton Institute, a school in Virginia founded with the colonial-minded goal of educating Indigenous children and Black Americans. One Seneca girl was made to recite the story of the Pilgrims' first Thanksgiving for an audience; another Winnebago boy was quoted as saying, "I am thankful that by the help of the white race, the Indian and negro races are advancing in civilization and Christianity." In truly disturbing fashion, pumpkin pie and Thanksgiving were used by the Institute as tools to assimilate Indigenous children *into their own country.*

Elsewhere, the *St. Louis Globe-Democrat* declared in 1884 that the pumpkin "is known to have been the early comrade of the Pilgrim Fathers and was a constant companion of the pioneers who followed the star of empire westward. It was a friend in need to the patriots who fought the Revolution." One writer for the

Emporia (Kansas) Daily Gazette called pumpkin pie "national discs of delight" in 1895. Perhaps most wildly, the *Kansas City Journal* believed pumpkin pie was so patriotic and nobly American that it warded off *treason*, declaring that "When properly made the pumpkin pie is the embodiment, so to speak, of peace on earth and good will toward men. No man ever plotted treason or formulated dark damnable designs while filling his system with a genuine New England pumpkin pie."

By the twentieth century, pumpkin pie had become the de facto standard dessert for a Thanksgiving feast, largely because the nostalgic, humble ideals of the pie and the holiday so closely aligned. In his 1906 *Pacific Monthly* article "The Golden Pumpkin Pie," John L. Cowan put it plainly when he wrote, "Surely a Thanksgiving dinner without pumpkin pie would be an empty sham and a hollow mockery." Pumpkin pie appeared everywhere from the Waldorf's 1908 Thanksgiving menu to holiday feasts at hospitals during the Great Depression to Thanksgiving dinners sent to American military troops in the 1940s. In 2000, *Martha Stewart Living* asserted, "For many, without pumpkin pie, it's just not Thanksgiving." And perhaps most tellingly, the first Thanksgiving edition of *Time* after the September 11 terrorist attacks featured a pumpkin pie with an American flag smack dab in its middle on the cover. I'm not sure it gets much more stereotypically patriotic than that.

Many of us now eat pumpkin pie and celebrate Thanksgiving each year without much of a thought, even if we've begun to acknowledge the limitations of the prevailing Thanksgiving myth more readily. But for the Indigenous people who have suffered centuries of oppression as a result of settlements like Plymouth Bay, Thanksgiving means something entirely different. And those scant nods toward the reality of history simply aren't enough.

Despite the fact that one of the most popular Thanksgiving dishes stems directly from Indigenous foodways, there are members of the Indigenous community who don't currently eat pumpkin pie at the end of November. Instead, some gather in Plymouth on the fourth Thursday of the month to commemorate the National Day of Mourning, a reminder of democide by European colonizers and the American government, theft of Native lands, and the ongoing oppression and suffering of Indigenous people that has been held since 1970. Others make their way to Alcatraz Island for Unthanksgiving Day, also known as the Indigenous People's Sunrise Gathering. Held since 1975, the ceremony honors the Indigenous people of the Americas and their rights, serving as a direct counter-celebration to the traditional American Thanksgiving.

The idea that Thanksgiving represents a national feast of American gratitude and unity, hinging on the shared consumption of similar foods, doesn't fit with the reality of the Indigenous experience. Nor does pumpkin pie. Over the centuries, Thanksgiving and pumpkin pie have ultimately become tools of assimilation—for a culture and history that wasn't even native to North America, one that itself was fabricated.

This makes pumpkin pie, admittedly, a difficult thing to swallow (some pun intended). Can non-Indigenous Americans pop open a can of Libby's and bake a pumpkin pie, chock-full of spices and ingredients forced onto North America by colonizers, and feel good about it? Can Thanksgiving be celebrated without perpetuating a false myth and causing harm to Indigenous people?

Honestly, I'd say no. But I'm also not the right person to answer this question. I spoke with Durwood Vanderhoop—a member of the Wampanoag tribe in Aquinnah, Massachusetts, and a language instructor, singer, and artist specializing in tribal cultural arts—about this question, and he shared his personal reflections on Thanksgiving more broadly. For a good part of his life, he celebrated Thanksgiving and ate pumpkin pie alongside his relatives, before reevaluating the holiday's narrative and complicating its simplistic story when he attended the National Day of Mourning while in college.

He spoke about the way the prevailing myth of Thanksgiving should be interrogated, as well as the personal importance he places on finding joy and comfort in his Native community. I'll leave you with his words:

> Looking at the realities around us, it can be really exhausting to look at our poor condition, our inability to remain in our homelands, the loss of our homelands, the systemic genocides, or other things that have happened as a result of colonization. And there's the other side, where sometimes we just want to be able to celebrate and be with family, and be thankful for each other. I have tended to sometimes just want to be with my family on Thanksgiving, but I think now, more than ever, there is discussion about the whole Thanksgiving myth. . . . We all love to eat and share in our community. The Thanksgiving holiday allows for that to happen. . . . Many of us do that and are thankful for that, but we are also much more able to talk about the things that some of our ancestors have persevered through. And to educate more of our young ones about why they should be a little skeptical of that whole notion around Thanksgiving to begin with.

MAPLE PUMPKIN PUDDING
(OR, A CRUSTLESS PUMPKIN PIE)

An entire book about pie . . . and this isn't even a pie recipe! Instead, it's more of a baked pudding. Or you could also think of it as a crustless pie. Most crucially, it's made with all precolonial ingredients, meaning nothing that arrived here as a result of European settlement: pumpkin, maple syrup, corn, and pecans. If you do make it for a holiday, use it as an entry point to discuss why certain traditional recipes (like classic pumpkin pie) look the way they do, and what that legacy means for the people who live in America in both the past and the present.

   1½ cups (173 g) pecan halves
   ¾ cup (180 ml) pure maple syrup, plus more for drizzling
   1¾ cups (420 ml) pumpkin puree
   2 tablespoons cornstarch
   1½ teaspoons allspice
   1 tablespoon vanilla extract

Preheat the oven to 325°F (165°C). Line a baking sheet with parchment paper.

   In a medium bowl, toss 1 cup (115 g) of the pecans with ¼ cup (60 ml) of the maple syrup until fully coated. Spread into a single layer on the prepared sheet. Bake for 10 minutes, then let cool while you prepare the filling.

   Increase the oven temperature to 350°F (175°C). In a food processor, combine the remaining ½ cup (58 g) pecans with 1 cup (240 ml) water and process for 1 to 2 minutes. In a large bowl, whisk the pecan milk from the food processor with the remaining ½ cup (120 ml) maple syrup, the pumpkin, cornstarch, allspice, and vanilla. Pour into a 9-inch (23-cm) pie pan, and use an offset spatula or the back of a spoon to smooth the top. Sprinkle the pecans in an even layer over the surface of the filling. Use your fingers to slightly press the pecans into the filling.

Bake for 40 minutes, until set. Let cool completely. You can serve now, or place in the fridge for a few hours, until completely chilled. Serve by slicing or scooping. (An additional drizzle of maple syrup is a nice touch!)

CHAPTER THREE

MOLASSES PIE

MOLASSES ISN'T A super common ingredient in today's kitchen. Aside from digging out that half-used jar from the back of the pantry once a year to bake up some too-dry gingerbread, most people don't rely on it in their regular cooking. Such relative obscurity, however, is only a recent development. As it turns out, molasses has been consumed in the United States for centuries. With a rich, nuanced flavor, bold sweetness, and a surprisingly high amount of nutrients, the dark syrup served as an everyday ingredient in households throughout American history, particularly prized on the Eastern Seaboard all the way from New England to the Deep South.*

It emerged as a vital staple as far back as the first days of the United States, becoming one of the country's primary sweeteners before the country itself even became official. (It helped that it was also the primary ingredient used to distill rum. It helped a whole lot, in fact.) According to the research of historian and foodways scholar Frederick Douglass Opie, one anonymous source writing

---

* Don't worry—I promise we'll make it out West eventually! (Skip ahead to Chapter Six if you're anxious.)

around 1730 observed, "Molasses is generally used throughout all the Northern Colonies, and at our Fisheries, in brewing their Beer, and the poorer Sort, who are very numerous, eat it with their Bread, and make Puddings of it." (The source might have been referring to hasty pudding, a type of charmingly named porridge made from oats or cornmeal and also served with butter or milk.)

Later, in the nineteenth century, molasses was valued as a cheap, easily available alternative sweetener, as it was produced in sugar-making regions like Louisiana and the Caribbean as a byproduct in the sugar refinement process. By 1820, for instance, the price of crude sugar was half that of refined sugar, the latter of which could equal up to 14 percent of a skilled worker's daily wages. Though all manner of cooks used the widely sold product in their cuisine, this affordability particularly endeared molasses to cooks producing food in kitchens that might not exactly have overflowing cabinets. What's more, the ingredient appealed to lower-class families because it allowed them to easily raise the caloric content of their food without expensive staples like dairy and meat, a handy if extremely dubious nutritional decision. Opie has written of its import, asserting that "molasses has been one of the three Ms of the diet of southern common folks, along with meat (salt pork) and meal (corn meal)."

It wasn't just hard-pressed families who relied on it, either. One Civil War soldier, Leonard C. Ferguson, noted in his diary that molasses was a regular feature in the meager rations provided to him while he was imprisoned by the Confederacy in South Carolina. Indeed, molasses became especially prized during the Civil War because blockades meant refined sugar from Louisiana and neighboring states was rationed and unavailable elsewhere in the country.

Molasses, especially back then, was about as versatile as Gary Oldman's acting range, used in savory applications as much as sweet. To name just a few uses for its unique flavor and sweetness:

It could be simmered alongside beans, folded into a cake, drizzled directly on top of biscuits, or stirred into porridge. And of course, it was baked into pie. And when it came to pie, there were multiple ways to deploy the rich, sticky syrup. You could find it in a pure, straight-up molasses pie cradled by a classic butter crust and buttressed by eggs, butter, and—why not?—more sugar. At the same time, it was frequently used as a complementary sweetener in everything from apple to pumpkin pies, taking the place of more expensive refined sugar.

Many nineteenth-century Southern cookbooks included recipes for pure molasses pie that reflected its particular popularity in the region, especially, for whatever reason, in Virginia. These include 1838's *The Virginia Housewife*, 1879's *Housekeeping in Old Virginia*, and the 1938 recipe collection *The Williamsburg Art of Cookery*, which shared a molasses pie recipe (it was technically listed, quite hilariously, as "molaffes" pie) attributed to a housewife from 1837. Even the venerable periodical *The Southern Planter*, a stereotypically named and very influential agricultural journal published in Virginia in the decades before the Civil War, featured a molasses pie recipe in 1858. The author emphatically declared, "This is decidedly the *best* substitute for apple pie."* (For the record, this same molasses pie recipe, snarky sidenote and all, was also published in another farmer's guide, *The Maryland Farmer*, in 1866.)

And when molasses became such a savior in the lean years of the Civil War, molasses pie was a common sweet treat at a time when dessert had all but disappeared from family tables. (These wartime

---

* I can't tell, but something about this feels like a backhanded compliment? Also, molasses and apple pies are literally nothing alike? ALSO, this recipe called for "six tablespoonfuls of good vinegar," which seems like an awful lot, plus it directed readers to mix the filling and *then* "cover with a rich paste." I don't know, I guess that's what happens when agricultural journals publish pie recipes.

limitations also directly influenced a curious pie that appears as the subject of a chapter later in this book.) One Shenandoah Valley woman, Emma Cassandra Riely Macon, recalled baking and eating molasses pie in her book, *Reminiscences of the Civil War*:

> The molasses pie recipe, whose chief recommendation . . . was cheapness, was as eagerly sought out as that for the cake. These pies were nothing but molasses or sorghum and lemons stewed together and baked in pastry. So easily made that only three minutes were required to prepare them, so the recipe said. I suppose the lemons were intended to insure a rapid fermentation of the molasses.*

In the Deep South of Louisiana, where domestic molasses was produced on sprawling plantations, the unrefined syrup also thrived. In his extensive 1885 compilation of Creole cuisine, *La Cuisine Creole: A Collection of Culinary Recipes from Leading Chefs and Noted Creole Housewives, Who Have Made New Orleans Famous for Its Cuisine,* author Lafcadio Hearn included a recipe for Molasses Pie, as well as, immediately following, a recipe for Richer Molasses Pie that included both molasses *and* sugar, as well as more eggs and butter. In case, you know, you were feeling indulgent enough for something a little richer than a pie made from straight syrup.

But let's not stop at just the South! Molasses pie could also be found on the dessert table well beyond the region, as demonstrated in the 1857 tome *Miss Leslie's New Cookery Book*, published in Pennsylvania and promising "wholesome and palatable food where economy is very expedient." True to its titular promise to provide

---

* No, I don't know why one would want to ferment their molasses, but I'm intrigued.

recipes for cooks who either wouldn't or couldn't spend their precious money on food, the book bore a molasses pie recipe, as well as a molasses pudding recipe calling for "West Indian Molasses." (We'll get to the significance of this particularly descriptive name shortly.) Interestingly enough, the recipe also declares that the molasses filling should be baked into a double-crusted pie. Not only did this differ from most versions of the dish, but it also departed from Pennsylvania's storied molasses pie iteration: shoofly pie. One of the most well-known examples of Pennsylvania Dutch cuisine and a descendent of European baking traditions, the single-crusted, crumble-topped shoofly pie is a separate, distinct version of molasses pie with a culture and origin all its own, hence the reason it's not really part of this main molasses pie narrative—sorry, shoofly!

Molasses pie was so ingrained in American baking that it even got something of a presidential shine; a recipe for Molasses Pie was shared in *The White House Cook Book,* originally published in 1887, to which Mary Todd Lincoln supposedly contributed, though to be honest the explicit connection between this particular molasses pie recipe and the sixteenth president remains unclear. (Interestingly enough, Abraham Lincoln also reportedly patronized a Washington, DC, bakery owned by the father of prominent molasses and sugar industry figure Isaac W. Taussig. There's obviously not a lasting menu from this nineteenth-century bakery—at least as far as I can find—so who knows if molasses was used there, but I like to imagine Lincoln chowing down on some molasses pie anyway, especially given his reported sweet tooth.)

But despite molasses's previous widespread prominence, molasses pie itself has unquestionably declined in the past century. Following a drop in sugar prices after World War I, molasses lost its popularity and receded to the background of national cuisine alongside other alternative sweeteners, like maple syrup. Today, the syrup is typically only used in dishes that call for its specific flavor, and anyone baking a pie with it does so out of fondness, not necessity. As a result, molasses pie can easily be classified as more of a niche dessert, one typically found in devoted regions like the South and rarely mass-produced. Eating a slice now, particularly for those with strong personal or geographic connections to the dish, may conjure something of a nostalgic reminiscence. Indeed, the dish harkens back to a time when molasses sustained generations spanning all the way back to the early colonies with its dependence, versatility, affordability, and accessibility.

Except . . .

Molasses is not a fruit. Nor a vegetable. Nor any other food product that can be grown naturally. It must be created—produced from sugarcane stalks that rise from the earth. And as things turn out, the very virtues that made molasses so useful to cooks throughout the centuries—the distinct affordability and accessibility that made it so appealing in homemade pie—come back to how it was created. And *that* story . . . well, that story isn't nostalgic or sweet at all.

It is, on the other hand, absolutely necessary to tell.

THE SUGARCANE FROM which molasses is made was first brought to the English colonies in 1619—the same year the first enslaved Africans were delivered to North American shores. The sugarcane ultimately failed, as the Mid-Atlantic region of the early colonies didn't provide the right growing conditions to successfully cultivate the crop. The systematic enslavement of Africans, on the other hand, did not.

This small note in history represents the story of sugar, and by extension, molasses. It is interwoven with that of slavery, and the forced labor of millions of enslaved persons on sugar plantations and in sugar mills spanning from Brazil to Jamaica to the Missis-sippi River. And without this enslaved labor, molasses wouldn't have been produced in such large quantities or been available in so many places across the United States. Without the free servitude of enslaved persons, it would never have been so cheap and, by exten-sion, molasses would never have been made into pie.

It all started, as so much death and pain and destruction did, with Christopher Columbus's arrival. Bearing sugarcane seedlings from the Canary Islands off the coast of Africa, he introduced the crop to the New World along with everything else he brought across the sea with him, like plants and guns and, of course, disease.

The sugarcane took quickly to the warm, tropical climates of the Caribbean and South America, literally sowing the seeds of a forthcoming sugar revolution. The Spanish drove the initial boom of sugar in the New World, pioneering sugarcane production, milling, processing (including the extraction of both molasses and sugar crystals), and the system of enslaved labor that fueled it all on islands like Cuba, Jamaica, and Puerto Rico. Like a racehorse bursting out of the gates with a little too much enthusiasm, that Spanish lead initially puttered out, and the Dutch, English, French, and Portu-guese came right behind to capitalize on the enormous opportunity for wealth that New World sugar promised. At that point in history, sugar was a luxury product in Europe because it was difficult to produce in bulk, so it promised some pretty high profits for those who could bring the sweet stuff back to the Continent.

The European powers carved out their sugar empires from the mainland of Central and South America—including Mexico and Brazil—as well as the Caribbean sugar islands of Barbados, Cuba, and others. The British, in particular, took control of several islands in the West Indies in the seventeenth century, such as Jamaica in 1655. Sugar was the foundation of the British economy on the island,

and molasses, though not the primary good produced, played an integral role. One solicitor to British sugar colonies testified to the importance of the molasses trade in supporting the overall Caribbean sugar industry:

> It is well known to every one concerned in the Sugar Trade that the Profits of the Planter depend upon the Vent which he finds for his Rum and Molasses for if Sugar only and no Rum or Molasses could be produced from the Sugar Cane it would hardly pay the expense of Culture and making[,] consequently as the Vent of Rum and Molasses is stopt or increased the Sugar Colonies . . . must thrive or decline.

But the commodity crop was incredibly resource-intensive to produce—both planting the sugarcane and processing it into crystalized sugar and molasses to trade. One of the key resources needed to make it all work? Labor, and lots of it.

To solve this problem, the British and other European nations decided to just get as much labor as possible . . . for free.

In order to successfully turn a profit with their sugar ventures, British planters resorted to the widespread importation of enslaved Africans to work the sugar plantations of Jamaica and additional islands in the West Indies. In Barbados, another British colony, the small Black population skyrocketed to fifty thousand by the end of the seventeenth century, at which point they vastly outnumbered the white islanders and accounted for three-quarters of the total population. Meanwhile, 662,400 enslaved Africans were brought to Jamaica, mostly for sugar. By 1753, the British were stealing an average of 34,250 Africans each year. And they weren't the only ones engaging in the barbaric practice. Across the New World, nearly eleven million Africans were enslaved as European nations vied to fill their coffers in pursuit of "white gold." (That number doesn't even account for the people who perished on the Middle Passage.) In pursuit of the purity and power of sweetness, Europeans engaged in a practice utterly ugly and grotesque.

For those who did survive the harrowing journey across the sea, the work that awaited Africans stolen from their homeland— the harvesting of sugarcane and milling of sugar and molasses— was horrific. One English sailor, referring to the enslaved Africans destined for West Indian sugar plantations, attested, "They have a more dreadful apprehension of Barbados than we can have of hell." *And that apprehension was for good reason!*

Working the sugar plantations was exhausting and dangerous, following a regular pattern of planting, cultivating, and harvesting the cane for milling. In the sugar mill itself, enslaved laborers fed the harvested cane into grinders, powerful machines that extracted the sweet juice from the tough stalks. This juice was then continuously boiled down in a series of vats, until what was left was raw crystalized sugar, like what we're familiar with in our cooking and baking. Meanwhile, a viscous brown syrup was left over after the crystals formed—this byproduct, still plenty sweet on its own, was molasses.

Viewed as nothing more than equipment to produce sugar and molasses, like the mills and vats themselves, enslaved workers were just as easily discarded and replaced in the name of efficiency. Truly, that sailor wasn't far off in the slightest when he likened the conditions to hell.

And beyond the terror of the actual work, enslaved persons were often forced to toil under cruel, inhumane overseers whose punishments far exceeded even the pain of the plantation labor. One sugar plantation overseer in Jamaica, Thomas Thistlewood, punished an enslaved man by gagging him and locking his hands, then covering him with molasses and exposing him naked to flies and mosquitos all day and night. Even when they weren't worked to death making it, molasses still became a source of agony for enslaved persons, no matter how sweet its taste.

By the late seventeenth century, the sugar and molasses produced in the West Indies had found a booming market in the English colonies. In particular, a robust trade network developed between Barbados and Rhode Island—the New England colonists sent products like cider, pork, and butter to the West Indies, and in return, they received shipments of rum, molasses, and sugar. This successful system expanded into a profitable global trade network—a little old thing known as the Triangular Trade, which spanned from Africa to the Caribbean to America, illustrating how deeply intertwined slavery and molasses truly were.

In the New England colonies, molasses emerged as quite a handy substance, used in the production of the two things every New Englander desired: food and rum. The fact that molasses enabled the distillation of rum was, unsurprisingly, a *huge* factor in its popularity in the colonies. Remember, these were the same people who brought apples with them from England to make sure they could brew cider! And planted barley the second they arrived in their new homeland to ensure a ready supply of beer! Of course they hoarded molasses without a second thought about the people who produced it. If it led to alcohol, who cared?

Despite colonists' ample thirst, molasses was also incredibly useful in the kitchen. The cane sugar that initially arrived in the colonies from the plantations of the West Indies was too expensive for everyday cooking, so its cheaper byproduct, molasses, became the primary sweetener in cooking and baking for New Englanders. This widespread use laid the foundation for the molasses pies that would follow in the years and centuries to come.

The whole molasses trade with the colonies became so profitable that the British government tried to cash in by passing the Molasses Act of 1733, which put a tax on molasses imported from the West Indies to the colonies. Devoted to their beloved molasses (and rum), New Englanders were so pissed off by the Act that it became part of the unfair taxation system that led them to, you know, launch an entire revolution for independence. I mean, they really liked eating and drinking! (*Especially* drinking.) What else were they supposed to do?

Though the sugar plantation boom started in South and Central America and the Caribbean, with the products subsequently imported into the colonies, it wasn't long before sugar production itself spread to taint North American shores as well. Because why trade for the stuff when you can just make it yourself? As early as the late seventeenth century, some English farmers moved from the West Indies to the North American mainland and brought the brutal system of the sugar plantations with them to establish a similarly structured version in the South.

Though the crop was grown throughout the South—including Alabama and Virginia—it was in Louisiana, in particular, where the heart of domestic sugar production soon emerged. Sugarcane was first planted in New Orleans by French Jesuit priests in 1751 (ironic that men of God got the whole sugar thing going down on the bayou), and plantations eventually sprung up all along the Mississippi River between New Orleans and Baton Rouge, where the rich soil was ideal for growing sugar. The raw sugarcane could typically be processed in mills right on the property, with the subsequent crystalized granules and molasses packaged into barrels and shipped to New Orleans. From the port city, the sweet stuff could be distributed all over.

So brutal was enslaved life on sugar plantations in Louisiana that at one point the enslaved population had a *negative* birthrate—that means more Black people died on the plantations than were born. Ceceil George, who was enslaved on a sugar plantation in Louisiana, described the never-ending toil: "Every body worked, young and old, if you could carry two or three sugarcane you worked. Sunday, Monday, it all [sic] the same . . . it like [sic] a heathen part of the country." Slave revolts erupted in protest to such harsh brutality, including the German Coast Uprising in 1811, which was one of the largest such revolts in American history.

And beyond the South, far from the plantations infamous for their backbreaking enslavement, the "free states" continued to perpetuate the whole system. These states' ready and rapid consumption of slave-produced goods, including molasses, fueled the labor system from which they came. Overall—though many Northerners would probably have liked to get up on their high horse and deny it back then—the entire country's sweet tooth was complicit in upholding this practice, including every single pie (molasses or otherwise) that was baked and savored in the era.

ENSLAVED PEOPLE NOT only had to deal with molasses in the field, but also in the diet—both their own, and that of their white owners. Since molasses was considered a rough, basic food—literally leftovers of circumstance—it frequently showed up in the diets of enslaved people. The formerly enslaved Betty Cofer, speaking of other enslaved people, recalled: "They only had ash cakes [corn pone baked in ashes] without salt, and molasses for their dinner." Meanwhile, the weekly rations of Henry Brown, an enslaved man in South Carolina, included a "quart o' molasses." Recalled formerly enslaved Fannie Clemons, "And sugar—we did not know about that. We always used sugar from molasses." Even as far back as the days of the Trans-Atlantic slave trade, slavers sometimes flavored the water given to enslaved Africans on the boats of the Middle Passage with molasses.

Beyond the basic rations provided to enslaved people, molasses also made its way into the plantation kitchen. There, enslaved cooks incorporated molasses into the food they prepared for white tables, a departure from the prevailing white preference for refined granulated sugar, which was considered more upper class. By cooking elegant dishes with molasses, enslaved chefs changed the Southern white perception of the ingredient and made it more enticing to rich white palates of the region.

After the Civil War nominally ended the production of slavery-produced molasses (though the sharecropping that continued for decades afterward certainly extended to the sugarcane fields), molasses—and by extension, molasses pie—continued to retain a foothold in national cuisine for another half century, particularly in regional Southern cuisine. It also retained its air of frugal practicality; for instance, it popped up in 1871's *Mrs. Porter's New Southern Cookery Book, and Companion for Frugal and Economical Housekeepers*, which specifically called for "West Indian molasses."

One 1889 tome, *The New Dixie Cook-Book* (the rebranding of "new" not-so-subtly aligning with a postwar, post-slavery region) even included molasses pie among recipes designed to help white housewives struggling to adjust to a new way of life; it was specifically dedicated "to the mothers, wives and daughters of the 'sunny South,' who have so bravely faced the difficulties which new social conditions have imposed upon them as mistresses of Southern homes, and on whose courage and fidelity in good or ill fortune the future of their beloved land must depend."

In addition, the dish later appeared with a somewhat patriotic alignment in 1918's *"Win the War" Cook Book*, published by the St. Louis County Unit Woman's Committee Council of National

Defense. The book provided a recipe for Brer Rabbit Ole South Molasses Pie (referring to the Brer Rabbit Molasses brand), which promised to be "a Southern pie that will make any cook proud." Around the same time, in 1917, molasses pie retained its deep-rooted Louisiana ties by appearing in *The New Orleans Federation of Clubs Cook Book*, in a fairly standard recipe made with sugar, molasses, eggs, butter, and flour. Quite tellingly, too, not one but *two* recipes for molasses pie were included in the 1912 cookbook *Favorite Southern Recipes*,* both submitted by women from Alabama.

And, of course, Brer Rabbit Molasses tried to cash in on this legacy by promoting molasses pie in ads for its product, encouraging bakers to "get the real Southern flavor in your goodies," which included what they referred to as "'lasses pie." A 1921 ad for the product in *Ladies' Home Journal* that featured an illustration of molasses pie mused, "Recipes were passed along, copied carefully—but what became of that celebrated 'Louisiana plantation flavor'?—Ah! That had come from something all the recipes called for, from something that practically went out of existence for years—from the home-made molasses." Brer Rabbit Molasses, the ad explained, was meant to "revive this bygone delicacy of [the founders'] plantation days." In addition to pie, it could also be used to make treats like "Ole Mammy Cookies" and "Plantation Cakes."

It should come as no surprise that even as cookbook authors, chefs, brands, and housewives celebrated the Southern lineage and long-standing tradition of molasses pie in the twentieth century, they largely ignored and erased its inextricable link to slavery. Like much of antebellum Southern culture—such as "moonlight and

---

* This particular cookbook, it feels worth noting, bears a distressingly problematic illustration on the cover with an offensive caricature of a Black "mammy" figure in the kitchen alongside a smiling, rosy-cheeked white female cook.

magnolia" plantations and reformatted slave markets—molasses was recast as a charming, nostalgic bit of heritage that should be preserved as America barreled into modernized, fast-paced times. The brutal reason for its widespread popularity, meanwhile, was basically buried.

Frederick Douglass called out this tendency early; in 1870, he wrote, "The South has a past not to be contemplated with pleasure, but with a shudder. She has been selling agony, trading in blood and in the souls of men. If her past has any lesson, it is one of repentance and reformation." But while an idealistic myth of the South's past grew common in the early twentieth century, such omissions of molasses's true legacy aren't simply a thing of the past, either—the second volume of *The Oxford Encyclopedia of Food and Drink in America*, published in 2004, does not mention the role of slavery or the labor of enslaved people in its entry on molasses, instead only referring to "slaves" twice while reciting the profitability of the Triangular Trade.

Like so many relics of our nation's history, it's necessary to contextualize the use and consumption of molasses and molasses pie when dining today. True, the molasses bottle we pluck off a supermarket shelf was not made by enslaved laborers toiling in dreadful conditions. But the very reason that jar of syrup is on an American shelf in the first place—or that pie recipe is tucked into the folds of an old cookbook you might be referencing—is because of the legacy of enslavement embedded in North American history, one that continues to reverberate in every part of American life, society, and governance.

This legacy doesn't mean molasses can't, or shouldn't, be used today. But failing to acknowledge this painful lineage can make even the sweetest pie taste bitter.

MOLASSES PIE

Adapted from *La Cuisine Creole* by Lafcadio Hearn

MAKES ONE 9-INCH (23-CM) PIE

Just a fair warning: You won't enjoy this pie if you don't like molasses. If you *do* like molasses, however, you'll find this to be a striking way to indulge in its dark, smoky, almost salty flavor. Cut small slices—it's incredibly rich!—and serve with a big dollop of whipped cream or a scoop of vanilla ice cream to balance out the richness.

1 All-Butter Pie Crust (pages 12–13)
1 cup (240 ml) unsulphured molasses (not blackstrap)
1 cup (200 g) granulated sugar
3 large eggs
4 tablespoons (½ stick/55 g) unsalted butter, melted

Preheat the oven to 425°F (220°C). Line a 9-inch pie pan with the prepared crust. Trim excess dough and crimp the edges. Place in the refrigerator while you make your filling.

In a large bowl, whisk together the molasses, sugar, eggs, and butter until smooth. Pour into the prepared crust.

Bake for 15 minutes. Reduce the oven temperature to 350°F (175°C) and bake 50 to 55 minutes more, until the filling is mostly set but still slightly jiggly in the center. Let cool completely before serving.

CHAPTER FOUR

SWEET POTATO PIE

WHEN THE NATIONAL Museum of African American History and Culture opened in 2016 in Washington, DC, food played a key role in programming. Unlike the soggy sandwiches and dry cookies found at most museum cafeterias, the museum boasted carefully curated cuisine at its Sweet Home Café. Designed in tandem with the museum's programming, the menu was created with the input of legendary culinary historian Jessica B. Harris and reflected the Southern Black experience. So naturally, one of the most classic dishes in the Black American culinary canon, sweet potato pie, was on the menu.

And people had some thoughts.

The pie, it turned out, was made with the addition of ginger. Which might not seem like a big deal—ginger is a warming ingredient, after all, and pairs well with other flavors in the pie—but to many, it's not traditional. And when it comes to a beloved dish like sweet potato pie, whose legacy spans generations, it's all about tradition. Esteemed Black foodways historian Michael Twitty put it pretty clearly while speaking to journalist Tracie McMillan for NPR: "You don't play around; you do what the mamas did."

As McMillan reported, enough diners spoke up about the sweet potato pie, both online and in person, that the Sweet Home Café eventually tweaked its recipe to align with more traditional tastes. Innovation might have been fun at first, but it was clear that when it came to sweet potato pie, there was to be no more playing around.

It's notable, of course, that sweet potato pie was on the menu in the first place—selected as an embodiment of the Black American experience at the country's flagship African American museum. Because, as was so tellingly revealed in this good-natured dustup over ginger, sweet potato pie means a great deal to many Black Americans, especially those with roots in the South. It's something their mothers made, and their grandmothers, and their ancestors before them. The pie is a deeply rooted tradition with personal and cultural nostalgia.

But beyond that, sweet potato pie also embodies the historic legacy of the Black American experience, as painful and redemptive as it has been. It was inspired by and born from West African cuisine, rose to prominence because of enslaved chefs who prepared it for others to eat, then was ultimately reclaimed and liberated by Black cooks in freedom. In many ways, sweet potato pie is one of the most powerful culinary touchstones our country has to offer, and as a result, it's no coincidence the dish has endured to remain every bit as potent today as it has been in the past few centuries. Sweet potato pie is a goddamn culinary icon.

It didn't start that way though. It started humbly, steeped in pain.

To talk about sweet potato pie, we need to first talk about yams. Real yams, not the ones we refer to with the muddied lingo of the holiday table. *Real* yams are West African, and they are absolutely not the same thing as sweet potatoes. In fact, the two tubers are completely different plant species that come from opposite sides of the world (which is the whole point, actually). Sweet potatoes are a New World crop that originated in Peru; remnants have been found in Peruvian caves from as far back as 8000 BCE. Yams, on the other hand, come from the Old World and are thought to date all the way back to the Jurassic Era. They're a starchy, lighter-colored tuber with passing similarities to sweet potatoes, and they have long been eaten as a staple food in West African cuisine.

Though the two vegetables share similar characteristics, it's actually due to linguistic confusion that they are so often referred to interchangeably. Enslaved Africans called sweet potatoes in America by an African word that sounded like "yam," muddying the waters separating the two plants; the exact linguistic roots are unclear, but it could be either the Gullah word "njam," Senegal "nyami," or Vai "djambi." The first recording of the American use of the word "yam" dates to 1676.

Stolen from their home by white slave traders and forced across the world in brutal conditions, enslaved West Africans were cast adrift in a culinary abyss upon their arrival in America. Cut off from the foods with which they were familiar, they were forced to use North American stand-ins for West African ingredients. One such substitution was sweet potato. Grown prolifically across the South—particularly in Georgia, Virginia, and the Carolinas—the tuber boasted characteristics similar to starchy West African root vegetables like cassava, plantain, and, of course, yams. As a result, enslaved Africans employed sweet potato as a passable substitution for such common staples, incorporating it into their adapted American diets, according to Black foodways scholar Adrian Miller. Emulating the styles of meals enjoyed in their homeland, for instance, West Africans could use sweet potatoes as the main starch in a meal, served alongside a sauce or stew of vegetables or fish.

It also helped that sweet potatoes were easy to propagate, and thus appeared in the rations many enslaved Africans received from white slaveholders. Frederick Douglass Opie shares in *Hog & Hominy* that in South Carolina, for example, enslaved rations included sweet potatoes among crops like rice and corn. Enslaved people used such rations to prepare simple meals, but limited by the scarcity of the food provided—both in quantity and diversity—many took matters into their own hands and turned to alternative food sources to supplement their diet.

The most aboveboard version of this practice came through the cultivation of small gardens, which enslaved people tended to in the small pockets of time they found when they weren't performing work for white masters, according to Harris. It's no surprise that sweet potato could often be found in such gardens, with its passing similarity to West African culinary tastes. Despite the limited time and energy enslaved persons had to devote to their gardens, they were often a success; so much so, in fact, that there are reports of masters purchasing vegetables from these plots. Which maybe sounds slightly, I don't know, not too bad . . . until you realize that sometimes the currency offered by these white customers was the privilege of a visiting pass to do something as basic as leave the property.*

In other cases, enslaved people turned to more, ahem, clandestine methods to source food. Harris writes in *High on the Hog* that foraging and hunting were common practices. Resourceful enslaved people supplemented their diet with hunted wild game, such as opossum and fish, and foraged plants like wild garlic and ramps.

* Not-so-fun fact: Thomas Jefferson reportedly purchased sweet potatoes grown by his enslaved laborers in their garden plots at Monticello.

Enslaved cooks transformed these meager rations, as well as food they tended in their gardens, into nourishing, if simple, meals—demonstrating a forced culinary ingenuity stemming from unavoidable scarcity. (For reference to just how impressive this cooking was, Swedish traveler Fredrika Bremer tried enslaved persons' cooking in Charleston and declared, "I must confess I have seldom tasted better or more savory viands.") Common hallmarks of enslaved diets included pork, greens, and cornmeal. Cheap, low-quality meat would be cooked for a long time, which broke down connective tissue to turn tough meats tender (the foundation of barbecue!); salt pork was also instrumental to season greens cooked for extended periods of time until tender.

Opie writes that when it came to sweet potatoes, enslaved cooks would often roast them in ashes, or, drawing on West African culinary traditions, perhaps use sweet potatoes like bread. In another example of white people eternally cribbing Black culture, white masters in Virginia followed suit and consumed the orange tubers in the same way. Frederick Law Olmsted, while visiting a Virginia tobacco plantation, recounted a meal eaten around the white dinner table: "But one vegetable served—sweet potato, roasted in ashes, and this, I thought, was the best sweet potato, also, I ever had eaten." It's more than likely Olmstead was left in the dark as to the inspiration for such a delicious meal.

Unsurprisingly, sugar was in short supply in the diets of enslaved persons. Solomon Northup, who was captured and sold into slavery in 1841 and whose story is depicted in *12 Years a Slave*, described the rations he and other enslaved persons received thus: "Each one receives, as his weekly allowance, three and a half pounds of bacon, and corn enough to make a peck of a meal. This is all—no tea, coffee, sugar and with the exception of a very scanty sprinkling now and then, no salt." One enslaved woman in Appalachia, Harriet Miller, resorted to stealing molasses and sugar (for which she was whipped by her mistress). And Booker T. Washington reportedly never saw dessert growing up, so that when he once encountered his mistresses eating cakes, he described the cakes as the most desirable thing he'd ever seen.

This lack of sugar means that sweet potato pie, in the classic form we typically think of today, wasn't part of the regular diet of enslaved persons. But! That doesn't mean they never ate it. And like, well, just about everything we put in our mouths, it's pretty significant when and how enslaved Black Americans did so.

For the most part, enslaved Black people only ate sweet potato pie or other desserts during holidays or celebratory occasions. According to Solomon Northup, pies were a treat enjoyed during the special feasting of Christmas and holidays; he described tables with "every manner and description of pies" during such celebrations. He added, "Only the slave who has lived all the years on his scanty allowance of meal and bacon, can appreciate such suppers. White people in great numbers assemble to witness the gastronomical enjoyments."

In addition to possible feasts provided by white masters, holidays and other occasions like barbecues were also the rare instances in which enslaved people were bestowed extra time and rations with which to cook (though still probably not that much time and not that much food). The result of such additional resources was sometimes pie, or at least a close approximation. Enslaved cooks made cobblers out of fruit that had been foraged, or used leftover pie dough scraps from the plantation kitchen to craft desserts. One woman, Caroline Farrow, described a celebratory supper that featured "good potatoes and pumpkin pies," which she described as the "best eating ever." Another man, Gus Feaster, recounted a barbecue for which enslaved women prepared "pies, cakes, and custards."

Emma Virgel, an enslaved Black woman, explicitly referenced the sweet potato pie made by her mother in her recounting of a corn-shucking celebration among the enslaved population, adding, "Jus' thinking 'bout dem pies makes me hongry, even now." These unique iterations of sweet potato pie were some of the first versions of the dish created in the newly born Black American food tradition. They were almost always as basic as possible, with no spices for flavor and likely nothing other than the tuber itself for sweetness, given the little access to sugar. Overall, these pie characteristics are emblematic of the conditions in which Black Americans lived at the time, and they represent the intense scarcity that defined the beginnings of the Black American experience, born in the shackles of enslavement.

BUT WHILE THE pies that enslaved persons ate were important, the ones they *didn't* eat are just as significant. The simple, humble pies of corn-shucking celebrations and holidays weren't the only ones enslaved persons made—they were just the only ones they had the pleasure of consuming themselves. Far from the humble cooking spaces of the enslaved quarters, in the well-appointed kitchen of the plantation house, enslaved cooks encountered sweet potato pie on a regular basis. Except these desserts looked a whole lot different.

As you well know by now (yawn), pie originally arrived in America and on Southern plantations from British and European food traditions. Interestingly enough, pies made with sweet potatoes were already present in these cultures, although they were regarded as an upper-class English dessert because imported sweet potatoes were rare and very expensive, a somewhat hilarious prospect. (Husband of the Year[s] King Henry VIII allegedly enjoyed sweet potatoes, including baked into pies, and believed they were an aphrodisiac. Maybe the starchy orange tuber is to blame for . . . ahem, you know. *Everything*.)

In the American South, however, the vegetable grew in abundance and was very much *not* a rare or expensive ingredient. With similarities in preparation to early pumpkin pie, sweet potato pie naturally became a common and accessible dessert enjoyed across the region. American versions of the pie, sweet potato pudding, or both appeared in the nineteenth-century cookbooks *The Virginia Housewife*, *The Kentucky Housewife*, and *The Carolina Housewife*, indicating their prevalence in Southern households (and cookbooks with extremely uncreative titles).

These new cookbooks fall into the next phase of American recipe writing, in which cookbooks were written with a distinct regional focus instead of the broader national one espoused by our girl Amelia Simmons of *American Cookery* fame. And when it came to Southern regional recipes, the framework in which they were written and cooked was very distinct indeed.

Authored by Mrs. Lettice Bryan and featuring "nearly thirteen hundred full receipts" (!), 1839's *The Kentucky Housewife* was a tome dedicated to the art of managing a household; it set out to help genteel women "discharge each devolving duty with care and precision, fulfilling the station of a housewife indeed, and not a wife only." Inspiring stuff! Of course, the key point here is the *management* of a household—the all-important duty to oversee housework being done, and not to actually do it yourself. Because, after all, someone like Mrs. Lettice Bryan had people for that.

"Have established rules for domestics and slaves to be governed by, and fail not to give them such advice as is really necessary to promote their own welfare as well as your own," she advised in her book's introduction. Mrs. Mary Randolph, author of the highly influential *The Virginia Housewife* (considered to be America's first regional cookbook) was in a similar situation, also referring to "slaves" in her introduction and probably writing under the assumption that her audience would have the labor of Black men and women to rely upon.

So, needless to say, it's pretty safe to assume that Mrs. Bryan and Mrs. Randolph were not in fact the ones carrying out much of the real work in their households and kitchens, nor were most of their readers. The real workers—and the people actually baking—were enslaved Black people.

In *The Kentucky Housewife*, Bryan included a recipe for a rather luxurious sweet potato pie. Her pie recipe is seasoned heavily with "butter, sugar, cream, nutmeg and cinnamon," and is directed to be served "with cream sauce or boiled custard" AND grated sugar over top. As in many well-off Southern households, enslaved chefs were probably the ones to prepare (and develop) such sweet potato pies, and with its overload of sugar, cream, and spices, there was quite a bit more abundance in such a dish than, say, the ash-roasted sweet potatoes of enslaved kitchens.

Slave owners hungered for sweet potato pies like Bryan's (or, to be more accurate, sweet potato pies like those of her chefs), and they relied on enslaved labor to produce them. Pie was so important in plantation kitchens that most white households required pie-making skills from every cook that worked in their kitchens. In fact, pastry chefs were considered one of the most valuable of enslaved professions, next to carpenters, and their talent and skill distinguished them from mere cooks. According to author Betty Fussell, "In the Carolinas slaves were often sent to the eating houses of Charleston for training in the Anglo-French arts of cookery, arts they were expected to pass on to the next generation."

Despite such extensive and clearly visible training, white masters viewed the incredible culinary skills of enslaved chefs as natural, inherent talents to which they were genetically predisposed—racially charged stereotypes that have continued to endure for centuries. As shared by Harris in *High on the Hog*, an 1880 issue of *Harper's* magazine declared, with absolutely unbelievable sincerity, "The Negro is a born cook. He could neither read nor write, and therefore he could not learn from books. He was simply inspired; the god of the spit and the saucepan had breathed into him; that was enough."

Though enslaved chefs toiled in the kitchen, not in the backbreaking fields, preparing meals (including pies) was not an easy position. White mistresses still abused them—accounts of such mistreatment include white women spitting into leftovers so enslaved chefs couldn't supplement their meager diets with extra food, or meticulously weighing ingredients to ensure Black chefs and cooks didn't eat a single bite. Harris shares the experiences of one enslaved woman, Mariah Robinson, who recounted the inherent dangers of daily kitchen work, such as the burns chefs suffered when scorching pots would spill. It was under these conditions that the legacy of Southern sweet potato pie originally flourished.

Unlike enslaved quarters, where cooking was done in limited indoor facilities during cold winter months or outdoors over a fire in the heat of summer, plantation house kitchens were fully furnished and equipped. The place where so many enslaved chefs labored to produce sweet potato pies and other delicacies for white consumption was typically a separate structure, built apart from the main house in case of fire. The floors were usually brick or stone to be easily washed, and the dominant feature was the fireplace, where most of the cooking was accomplished. In such spaces, Black chefs toiled with no recognition or compensation to produce mouthwatering pies that would go on to become foundational in Southern cuisine.

Like so much of the Southern and national culinary canon, a dish like sweet potato pie simply wouldn't exist the way we know and love it today without the knowledge, skill, and labor of enslaved Black chefs. The irony that this pie was defined and perfected by Black chefs who were barred from actually eating it is a vital thread of that legacy.

Through prominent cookbooks like *The Kentucky Housewife* and *The Virginia Housewife*, white housewives obscured and excluded the contributions of Black chefs, receiving all the credit and profit for the work. As Marcie Cohen Ferris writes in *The Edible South*, "Ignoring [enslaved chefs'] intellectual hand in the creation of the distinctive cuisine of the South, particularly on the printed page, was the same denial of African Americans' humanity that whites had honed since slavery's introduction to the southern colonies."

Additionally, Black chefs historically taught their craft orally, in large part because they were systematically denied access to resources teaching them to read and write, and thus this teaching and knowledge wasn't preserved in most historical records—something Toni Tipton-Martin has written of in *The Jemima Code*. Therefore, the pie recipes that were made and consumed in white households, both before and after the Civil War, were in most instances a result of forced Black labor; the ultimate credit taken by white women, and their resulting denial of ownership to Black chefs, was another form of racial oppression perpetuated in the South.

SUCH SYSTEMIC OPPRESSION eventually began to shift with the publication of Black-authored cookbooks, which finally took ownership over sweet potato pie by presenting the knowledge of such a dish directly from Black authority. Such cookbooks came in the years and decades following the Emancipation Proclamation, which is obviously not a coincidence. They represented a new period of Black American life, one in which freedom and independence, if still elusive, were now possible.

The first such cookbook was *A Domestic Cook Book: Containing a Careful Selection of Useful Recipes for the Kitchen*, authored by Malinda Russell and published in 1866—making it, quite extraordinarily, the oldest known published cookbook written by a Black woman. Russell's book represented the transformation of Southern Black chefs from anonymous, frequently enslaved laborers to free citizens using their culinary talents to succeed in society, and her own story embodied a similar narrative arc.

She was born in Tennessee to "one of the first families set free by Mr. Noddie of Virginia"; in other words, her birth literally ushered in the new generation of free Black Americans leaving behind the shackles of slavery. When she was nineteen, she embarked for Liberia with a traveling party (so badass), but before she could leave the country, her plans were shattered when she was robbed in Lynchburg, Virginia. With her money gone, she hunkered down in Virginia, eventually marrying and birthing a son while using her domestic skills to earn money as a cook and washerwoman.

It was in Virginia that Russell really deepened her knowledge of cooking and baking, all thanks to Fanny Steward, a local Black cook. And get this: According to Russell, she cooked "after the plan of the 'Virginia Housewife,'" almost surely the very cookbook Mary Randolph had published.

Russell became a widow while her son was still young, after which she moved back to Tennessee to run a boarding house, then a pastry shop. In this way, Russell followed the trail blazed by many free Black pastry chefs before her—women like Phillis Hill, Frances Carly, Nancy Golding, and Susan Jackson, who owned property and businesses in Savannah, Georgia, as early as the 1820s—who used their highly valued pastry skills to achieve economic independence and freedom when such basic rights were systematically denied to the Black population by white society.

Despite her success, Malinda Russell did have some seriously bad luck when it came to crime—in 1864, she was robbed yet again, after which she decided it was time to hightail it out of the South once and for all. As she wrote, she and her son "followed a flag of truce out of the Southern borders." Probably a very smart move, for quite a number of reasons. She ended up settling in Michigan, which is where she eventually published *A Domestic Cook Book* and thus changed our country's publishing history.

Her cookbook demonstrated a keen mastery of cooking and baking, with complex dishes included alongside more traditional Southern favorites. But perhaps most noteworthy (at least for our very specific purpose) was the recipe she published on page 23: Sweet Potato Slice Pie.

To be honest, the recipe itself isn't much. It's directed to be "made in the same manner as above," in reference (presumably) to the preceding recipe for Slice Apple Pie, and calls for the addition of brandy, vinegar, lemon rind and juice, and sugar to taste. Russell advises that it be eaten "with sauce," though just what kind of sauce, exactly, is not specified. Baker's choice? What's more notable is that her recipe differs from the custard-style sweet potato pies that we typically know today—it's a "slice" sweet potato pie, a different version that's been mostly lost to time.

With her familial origins in enslavement and subsequent birth and career in freedom, Russell embodied the post-slavery trajectory of many Black Southerners. In addition, her authorship of a sweet potato pie recipe three years after the Emancipation Proclamation, credited to and profiting a Black woman for the first time in American cookbook history, was nothing short of radical.

It signified Black people's reclamation of sweet potato pie for their own purposes and enjoyment, a foundational touchstone in Black American foodways.

Similar to Malinda Russell, Abby Fisher also reclaimed sweet potato pie and rightfully rooted it in Black culinary knowledge with her book, *What Mrs. Fisher Knows About Old Southern Cooking*, published in 1881 (and originally thought to be the first American cookbook written by a Black author, before *A Domestic Cook Book* was rediscovered). Fisher was actually born into slavery in South Carolina, before moving out West from her residence in Alabama to San Francisco; it was in California that she eventually published her cookbook. As she reveals in her introduction, Fisher could neither read nor write—neither of which stopped her from sharing her thirty-five years of experience in a book. (Which, I can now personally attest, is downright incredible.)

True to its title, Fisher's cookbook is indeed an extensive, evocative portrait of Southern cooking. Though few details exist about her life in the South, Fisher makes several references to plantation life in her cookbook, indicating the likely roots of her skill. And, given this background and purpose, it was therefore inevitable that she included a recipe for sweet potato pie. Her method makes the more well-known custard-style pie, with the unusual (and delicious-sounding) addition of orange:

> Boil the potatoes soft; peel and mash fine through a cullender while hot; one tablespoonful of butter to be mashed in with the potato. Take five eggs and beat the yolks and white separate and add one gill of milk; sweeten to taste; squeeze the juice of one orange, and grate one-half of the peel into the liquid. One half teaspoonful of

salt in the potatoes. Have only one crust and that at the bottom of the plate. Bake quickly.

(The clear, distinct, and very authoritative "bake quickly" is my favorite part of that whole thing.)

The publication of Black-authored cookbooks like *A Domestic Cook Book* and *What Mrs. Fisher Knows* epitomized the trajectory of Black American life during Reconstruction. Now, Black culinary knowledge and labor were wielded independently of white folks. The production and consumption of sweet potato pie by Black families, beyond the pages of these cookbooks, embodied this new way of life.

In the decades following the Civil War, Black Southerners were no longer restricted to partaking in sweet potato pie during special occasions, as they had been permitted according to the whims of their white masters. And they weren't forced to settle for brutally basic approximations like the ash-roasted sweet potatoes of the enslaved persons' quarters, either. At the same time, these post-war sweet potato pies weren't crafted in a fancy, robustly stocked, (white-owned) plantation kitchen. They were simply prepared, it's true. But unlike the pies crafted by enslaved chefs, they were baked by Black hands for Black mouths—a foundation that has continued to stretch through the centuries.

In this way, baking a classic dish like sweet potato pie was almost a radical act, a culinary assertion of independence and autonomy. And indeed, this was the new reality Black families were carving out for themselves across the South, despite the staunch efforts of white people who just wanted things to go back to (their own personal) "normal."

Of course, Emancipation was neither a smooth nor complete process. Generations of racism, as we well know, are impossible to stamp out with some signed papers. As Frederick Douglass wrote, the Black Southerner "was free from the individual master, but the slave of society. He had neither money, property, nor friends." Nevertheless, Reconstruction ushered in a new era of life for millions of Southern Black people. Some formerly enslaved people took new names, abandoning those imposed by their white masters and making a clear mark between the old way of life and the new.

After the Civil War, the Southern agrarian economy shifted from plantation slavery to tenant farming and sharecropping. With little economic recourse, many Southern Black people became entangled in sharecropping systems that were only marginally better than actual enslavement. For those Black Southerners who remained in the region after the war and continued to provide for themselves through agriculture, food access remained limited due to the poverty that still defined much of their lives.

In the sharecropping system, in particular, most food was substandard and minimally nourishing—sometimes it was even hard to come by. As a result, cooking practices became defined by simple ingredients, straightforward cooking techniques, few tools, and a focus on stretching limited resources. Staple ingredients included sweet potatoes, corn bread, collards, and pork. (There are even accounts of dried and ground sweet potatoes being used to make a substitute for coffee!) If these sound familiar, there's a reason—this diet was similar to that of enslaved Black people. Other holdovers from the antebellum diet included hoecakes and johnnycakes.

For many Black people in the South, access to sugar and other basic baking ingredients was limited, as well. And to make things even worse, poverty wasn't the only limiting factor; straight-up discrimination sometimes made it hard for Black Southerners to purchase baking ingredients at white-owned establishments.

According to Anne Yentsch, "being poor and black made it impossible to buy the ingredients to bake a cake at some stores."

And here is where we finally get into the age-old divide, one influenced by class and tradition and heritage and sugar: cake versus pie. (You can probably guess which side I fall on.) In this case, the difference becomes notable because of ingredients; as Yentsch writes, cake requires much more specialized baking ingredients than pie—baking powder, baker's chocolate, vanilla extract, nuts, coconut—which were expensive and difficult to attain in the South at that time. With its adaptability and accessibility—all you needed were ingredients for a crust and a filling, which could be made from the most basic foraged or harvested produce—pie may have been an easier dessert to create on a regular basis. Cheap, flavorful, and abundant, sweet potatoes were a particularly natural fit.

As more Black farmers acquired their own land from 1890 to 1910, families became increasingly self-sufficient, bolstering Black pride and self-esteem. They supported themselves and their community through gardens and orchards, as well as by raising livestock like chickens and hogs. Their meals reflected this new reality—humble and simple, but plentiful and pleasurable.

Iconic chef Edna Lewis grew up in a Black agricultural community that embodied such a lifestyle. She was the granddaughter of formerly enslaved people who took the plot of land bequeathed to them by their former owners and turned it into a close-knit, successful Black community in Virginia appropriately named Freetown. (This was a common occurrence—in the decades after the war, many formerly enslaved people banded together to form all-Black communities, sharing land, crops, schools, churches, and more.)

At Freetown, there was a school for the community's children, a nearby general store, and an abundance of food to be grown, foraged, and hunted. And there was pie. (Of course there was!) Lewis's grandmother Mama Daisy prepared sweet potato pies in an old stove; meanwhile, in her landmark book, *The Taste of Country Cooking*, Lewis presents many different recipes for pie, including classics like sweet potato pie. Her recipe calls for sweet potatoes, sugar, cinnamon, nutmeg, salt, eggs, vanilla, butter, and milk, served in a lard-based crust that reflects the agricultural community in which she was raised.

In Freetown, as in so many other independent Black communities, sweet potato pie was a symbol of the simple abundance created by Black inhabitants—access to butter and lard to make pastry, as well as sweet potatoes grown and harvested in garden plots. Resources were limited and hard work was necessary, yet Freetown is an example of the new lives Black Southerners created for themselves in the uncertain landscape of post–Civil War America.

And finally, you can't talk about sweet potatoes in America without mentioning George Washington Carver, the great Black inventor and agricultural scientist whose extensive research on the orange tuber and its amazing versatility boosted its popularity. Naturally, he had his own sweet potato pie recipes, though one of them was a slice-style pie similar to Malinda Russell's recipe, a noticeably different version than custard-style pies. It was Sliced Potato Pie, featuring thin circles of sweet potato rather than a smooth blended filling:

> Line a deep baking dish with a rich sheet of pastry. Parboil the number of potatoes desired. When two thirds done remove the skins, slice lengthwise, very thin, cover the dish to a depth of 2 inches, sprinkle with ground allspice and a dash of ginger, cloves and nutmeg. To a pie sufficient for six people, scatter around the top in

small pieces a lump of butter the size of a hen's egg; add one teacupful of sugar and ½ teacupful of molasses. Add ½ pint of cream, dust a little flour over the top sparingly; cover with hot water, put on upper crust, crimp edges and bake in a moderate oven until done. Serve hot, with or without sauce.

Though it originally developed with close ties to slavery, sweet potato pie became such a potent symbol of Black American foodways because its story is much more complex, and ultimately redemptive. Despite the fact that the first iterations of the dish were tasted amidst enslavement, sweet potato pie was eventually reclaimed by Black populations to become a powerful touchstone of identity and tradition. Prepared by Black chefs and eaten frequently in Black households, sweet potato pie has evolved to become a potently nostalgic dish and a pillar of Black American cuisine.

Just be careful about playing around and adding any ginger to it.

ABBY FISHER'S SWEET POTATO PIE

*Adapted from What Mrs. Fisher Knows
about Old Southern Cooking*

MAKES ONE 9-INCH (23-CM) PIE

Quickly skim the ingredients below, and you'll notice a crucial missing element: spices. Unlike most of today's sweet potato pie recipes, Abby Fisher's didn't include any cinnamon, nutmeg, coriander, or other spices (and certainly not ginger!). The result is a pie with pure, unadulterated sweet potato flavor, accented by a slight note of orange. When I baked it for my family, they declared it the best sweet potato pie they'd ever had.

1 All-Butter Pie Crust (pages 12–13)
1 pound (455 g) sweet potatoes
1 tablespoon unsalted butter, melted
¼ teaspoon salt
¼ cup (60 ml) milk
½ cup (100 g) granulated sugar
Zest and juice of ½ orange (about 2 tablespoons)
2 large eggs, separated

Preheat the oven to 425°F (220°C). Line a 9-inch (23-cm) pie pan with the prepared crust. Trim excess dough and crimp the edges. Place in the refrigerator while you make your filling.

In a large pot of water, boil the sweet potatoes until soft, about 15 to 25 minutes, then peel and mash through a colander (or mash with a fork) while they're still hot.

In a large bowl, combine the sweet potatoes, butter, salt, milk, sugar, orange zest and juice, and egg yolks and mix until smooth.

In the bowl of a stand mixer, whisk the egg whites until soft peaks form. Gently fold the egg whites into the sweet potato mixture until just combined. Pour the filling into the prepared crust.

Bake for 15 minutes. Lower the heat to 350°F (175°C) and bake for 25 to 35 minutes more, until the filling is mostly set but still jiggles in the middle. Let cool completely before serving.

CHAPTER FIVE

PECAN PIE

NAPOLEON WAS IN trouble. (Yes, *that* Napoleon.) He wanted to conquer lands across the world, but that also meant feeding his army in lands across the world—in places as far away (and decidedly not France) as Egypt.

So he did what any great leader would do. He tried to find someone smart who could solve this problem for him.

The French emperor put out a call for innovations in food preservation to feed his army, launching a competition in which the winner with the best idea would receive twelve thousand francs. A victor was eventually crowned: Nicolas Appert, who introduced the brand-spanking-new process of canning in *L'art de conserver pendant plusiers années toutes les substances animales et végétales* in 1810. (I'll save you the trip to Google Translate—it means "the art of preserving all animal and plant substances for several years.") No longer would food spoil during transportation or grow rotten shortly after harvesting. With Appert's new process, fruits, vegetables, and other ingredients could be hauled all over, delivering a meal with just the pop of a lid.

And that is how we got pecan pie.

Okay, obviously not directly. But Appert's invention of canning at the turn of the nineteenth century laid the foundation for what would eventually become an industrialized American food system. And that shift to mass-produced, commercialized goods—which started in the mid-nineteenth century before hitting its stride at the turn of the twentieth century and completely defining our food system in the modern age—did, in fact, lead to pecan pie. At least, it led to the pecan pie most of us know today. Honestly, it's most likely the reason many of us even know and bake pecan pie at all. Otherwise, the dish might have remained an obscure, niche regional staple forever (like that underground band your hipster cousin always tells you about while stressing that you need to listen to their early stuff).

Like most heartwarming underdog stories, pecan pie had fairly humble origins before making it big and becoming a star. Surprisingly, the pie didn't really crop up in America until the nineteenth century, despite the long history of pecans in the United States. The nut is native to the North American continent, and it was an important food source for many Indigenous people as far back as thousands of years ago. In fact, the nut's name most likely comes from the Algonquin word "paccan," which refers to a nut that needs to be cracked by stone. Like so much else related to Indigenous food origins, that history's been pretty much erased.

Pecans were cultivated by white people once they settled onto the continent, and there are accounts of Thomas Jefferson growing them at Monticello. He even recommended them to his pal George Washington, and they were installed amongst the crops of Mount Vernon. Despite this clear fondness for the nut, commercial pecan production didn't really take off until around 1847, when an enslaved man known only as Antoine (the Beyoncé of pecans) invented a way to graft pecan trees. Introduced on the Oak Alley plantation in Vachery, Louisiana, Antoine's game-changing invention quickly spread across the South, launching lucrative pecan cultivation in states like Georgia and Texas, which would eventually become hot spots for growing the nut.

Once this commercial pecan market sprang up, the nut started to become available everywhere—by 1867 you could find pecans sold in New York markets through the winter and spring. Beyond common city markets, pecans were also exhibited at fairs and festivals all over, like the World's Columbian Exposition in Chicago in 1893.*

As the nut grew more popular, people started to use it more and more in their kitchens. Including, for some, in pie. Key word there—some. Though people across the country enjoyed pecans by the latter half of the nineteenth century, there really aren't that many accounts of people baking them into pie, which is really quite shocking, when you think about everything else they were willing to sandwich into a pastry crust by this time, like crackers (more on that in a later chapter). References to pecan pie started showing up in Texas cookbooks in the 1870s and 1880s, localized in the heart of American pecan country. There's some argument that pecans were also incorporated into pie by French cooks in New Orleans, given the culinary traditions and agriculture of the region. But though pecan pralines were certainly a thing, there's not too much evidence to back up that pie link.

Pecan pie certainly started to gain some steam toward the end of the century—in 1886, *Harper's Bazaar* declared: "Pecan pie is not

---

* At one point in 1902, a particularly clever girl discovered a new way to reach the elusive pecans at the top of a tree; she plopped into a hot-air balloon anchored by a bunch of men and shook out all the previously out-of-reach nuts at the tip-top. This isn't actually that relevant to the influence of pecans in American diets, but I mean, how could I not mention that?

only delicious, but is capable of being made 'a real state pie,' as an enthusiastic admirer said." According to this account, the pie was made by boiling pecans in milk, then draining the pecans and adding to a custard. If desired, a cook could apparently add a meringue, a flourish not typically included in today's pecan pies.

Another early recipe featuring a meringue was published in 1897 as Texas Pecan Pie in *Ladies' Home Journal*. Shared by the vaguely named Mrs. M. B., the recipe went as follows:

> One cup of sugar, one cup of sweet milk, half a cup of pecan kernels chopped fine, three eggs and a tablespoonful of flour. When cooked, spread the well-beaten whites of two eggs on top, brown, sprinkle a few of the chopped kernels over. These quantities will make one pie.

So it's clear that pecan pie was being baked and eaten in Texas and other areas of the country by the turn of the century, even if the dish wasn't widely known. This timeline also means that one woman's claim to have invented Texan pecan pie around 1913 was absolutely untrue. But despite a clear paper trail to refute her claim, she sure had a wild and completely true-sounding story to back it up.

According to Vesta Harrison, who recounted the tale while being interviewed by historian Sue March, the idea for the previously unheard-of dish known as pecan pie came to her in a dream the night before her first day of cooking school in Fort Worth. After waking from the prophetic dream, which should go down in history with the likes of Constantine and his cross, Harrison claimed to have said, "I don't know, but I'm gonna mess up something making a pecan pie." (In Texas vernacular, this was presumably a good, determined sort of thing.) She went on to make a sorghum syrup pie, added a cup of pecans, and there you go—Texas pecan pie! Her revelatory recipe went on to win $500 in a cooking contest.

Even if this wasn't actually the first pecan pie recipe (it definitely wasn't), the fact that Harrison hadn't been exposed to pecan pie—even in Texas!—and thus believed it to be original suggests how isolated and regionalized the dish was up to that point. By the 1940s, however, beloved cookbooks like *Joy of Cooking* were sharing recipes for pecan pie, making it a dessert that had received national renown in all corners of the nation. And that dramatic spike in popularity can be attributed to the rapidly commercialized food system that had been developing ever since the first French soldier popped open a can of perfectly preserved peas. Specifically, it was because of one particular commercial product that was introduced to the American public as part of a radical reshaping of what they ate and how they ate it: Karo Corn Syrup.

Karo Corn Syrup was introduced to the American consumer in 1902, and, trust me, we'll get back to that date in a little bit. But first, we're going to Europe, to catch up on a little history of how, exactly, Karo even arrived on store shelves, and why it embodied a century-long evolution in American eating.

After canning kicked off in France, it spread to other European nations and into England, one of the key hubs for American immigration. Thus, it was only a matter of time before it found its way into the States. And originally, canning and food preservation spread into the US not through necessity, but rather, luxury—like sending turtle soup across the pond, for instance (of all the fancy food you could send to show off . . .). Soon enough, of course, people realized it was good for a whole lot more than a soup made from reptiles.

Naturally, the practice of food preservation became a useful tool in American households, even if people had no idea how it actually worked (seriously—they were hazy on the science but didn't let that stop them from canning). It caught on both at home, with home canning practices, and in the marketplace, where new canned products started to become available. This availability beyond a homemaker's kitchen was a key shift toward an eventual food system dominated by packaged products.

Hardship begets hunger and necessity, so it's no surprise that canned foods proved particularly useful during the Civil War, and there's evidence that canned goods were present in Union camps; one soldier wrote a letter home to his wife on the back of a Borden's Condensed Milk label, surely the height of romance. Canned foods were also handy in the great migration west as explorers and pioneers took their covered wagons to the horizon, though canning was still relatively new and small-scale at this time.

As actual food preservation evolved in America over the course of the nineteenth century, food also became more industrial in other ways, mostly as a product of the large-scale social evolution that occurred in the latter half of the century. Before industrialization reshaped all aspects of American life, not just food, family was the defining social unit. A majority of families lived in rural locations, and they supported themselves by growing and producing almost everything they needed, whether by eating it directly or trading in the marketplace. With the outbreak of the Industrial Revolution, this entire way of living shifted. Families moved to cities, and men (and women!) took jobs in factories instead of in the fields.

Meanwhile, mechanization spread from textile factories and steel mills into agriculture. Whereas the ingredients families cooked with had been localized and seasonal for pretty much the entirety of American history—making them the original farm-to-table evangelists—the debut of the Transcontinental Railroad in 1869 opened the country's biggest new grocery store: the West. The extensive plains and verdant valleys west of the Mississippi were suddenly an agricultural business, and, baby, they were ready to make some sales. Thanks to this extensive railroad and its nifty refrigerated cars, fruits, vegetables, grains, and more could be easily transported from thousands of miles away straight to cities and towns in the East for the first time in history.

Suddenly, food wasn't grown in the backyard garden or traded for at the market down the road, but rather purchased in a store from producers far, far away—things like wheat from the Great Plains, beef from the Southwest, and lemons from California. It was totally game-changing.

Unlike, say, an old man intent on growing the perfect tomato, industrialized farms were (and very, very, *very* much still are) defined by principles like, among others, specialization, standardization, and vertical integration. You know, all the stuff that would make a kid in an MBA program foam at the mouth. So agricultural products turned into commodities that used mechanization to maximize profit from the field. And in tandem to this burgeoning system of industrialized agriculture, the food industry continued to innovate in other ways beyond farming.

For instance, stores started selling baking powder—"one of the first chemical products in food," according to the *Encyclopedia of Food and Drink in America*—to go with that cheap new refined flour from the plains; the product enabled women to more efficiently bake up quick bread, pies, and cakes in their home's wood stove. The 1890s also saw the introduction of dry cereals, which went on to replace hot cooked breakfasts for many families (although I am still shocked it was able to replace bacon). Overall, food prices dropped so that the masses of people who had moved into cities for industrialized jobs could afford dinner purchased from the store.

Products also started placing an emphasis on branding to better stand out in an increasingly nationalized and cluttered marketplace.

Though it wasn't technically food, it's notable that the Smith Brothers secured official trademarks in 1866 for the cough drops they sold and marketed in glass jars, pioneering the use of packaging to brand a product for a consumer's benefit. This practice would become widespread in the food market soon enough. Around the same time, Henry Crowell of Quaker Mill Company started to pioneer "saturation advertising" by launching plenty of absurd promotions (he got an ad for his oats on the White Cliffs of Dover in England) and bogus health claims. Such stunts would be echoed by other food brands (though maybe not as extreme as the cliffs propaganda). Royal Baking Powder, for example, spent a mind-boggling $500,000 on advertising in 1893—more than $15 million (!) in today's dollars.

And there were new tools, too! Like the pressure cooker, which provided an entirely new and efficient way for women to cook at home when it became available in 1874. The transition away from open-hearth cooking to indoor coal- and wood-fired stoves was another huge gain for homemakers, as was the introduction of indoor plumbing, which had one or two benefits beyond cooking.

After the champagne bottles popped to ring in the new century on January 1, 1900, the changes ushered in during the previous decades steadily continued as the twentieth century revved up, and processed food became more and more prevalent. But canned foods were hiding a dark secret . . .

They were low-key getting a ton of people sick because, um, actually it turns out that people hadn't *completely* figured out how to successfully preserve food just yet. Somewhat important elements like, I don't know, sanitation were still very much in question, and as a result the risk of spoilage and getting sick was distressingly high. Many people were worried about eating canned and preserved foods for the very reasonable fear that they just might kill them, which needless to say dampened their enthusiasm.

The unease was also more general; one contemporary journalist wrote that many women saw the transition to a "large-scale corporation food-industry" as "new and mysterious, and therefore disquieting." Eventually, the disquiet grew so feverish that Congress passed the Pure Food and Drug Act in 1906, signaling the extent to which commercialized food was starting to influence the American table (and marketplace).

IT WAS INTO this fracas that Karo Corn Syrup boldly entered.* The product was invented by the Corn Products Refining Company of New York and Chicago, and, as mentioned, hit the market in 1902. It predated the introduction of Coca-Cola, Cracker Jack popcorn, and Jell-O, all wildly influential food brands in their own right that hit the shelves slightly later—a hundred years into the future, our diets are still impacted by the changes of this era.

No one really knows where Karo's name came from; some say it's because the inventor's wife's name was Caroline, while others claim it stemmed from an earlier brand name, Kairomel. A liquid sweetener like honey or maple syrup, the product didn't crystalize when heated, making it particularly useful for dessert and candy-making. As the name implies, it was derived from cornstarch, making it a byproduct of the massive (in both literal size and influence) corn industry that would come to define the Midwest and also basically everything we eat today.

It wasn't the first time such a sweetener had been introduced; attempts to turn corn into sugar like a much-sweeter

---

* Just a note: Sugar is a preservative that pretty much kills a lot of the gross stuff that might get you sick, so it didn't suffer from the whole "this food might not actually be edible" problem that packaged produce and meats faced.

Rumpelstiltskin date back to the 1700s, when Americans were seeking a substitute for molasses after the passage of the Molasses Act of 1733. In 1865, New York's Union Sugar Company introduced the industrial conversion of cornstarch to sugar; the following decade, the American Glucose Company advanced the process. But with Karo, corn syrup soon became consolidated under a single brand.

Before the nationally distributed and branded Karo stocked store shelves, cooks sourced corn syrup for pies and candies by refilling jugs from barrels at the local grocery store. These regional corn syrup brands varied, unlike the new uniform, consistent, packaged version that Karo made available in "friction-top tins." And while the new product was undoubtedly useful for anyone curious enough to pick up a sample, the brand rose to prominence not on good old-fashioned word of mouth, but rather because of savvy marketing, a key hallmark in the coming age of commercialized food.

Almost as soon as it debuted, Karo ran full-page ads in *Ladies' Home Journal*, which was *the* definitive source for all things homemaking. Prominent ads proclaimed that the syrup was a wholesome sweetener option, despite the fact that this was, uh, far from true. But hey, who said marketing ever had to be 100 percent honest? Or even slightly honest at all? One ad claimed Karo was "a pure clear wholesome syrup made of the grain of the corn and retaining the full nutriment of this most nutritious of all cereals." Often, it was promoted as "The Great Spread for Daily Bread." (As someone with a massive sweet tooth, even I can point out that toast spread with corn syrup does not sound appealing in the slightest.)

In 1910, the company launched a massive and unprecedented $250,000 publicity campaign designed to make Karo a household name—a staggering cost amounting to more than $7 million today. As part of this marketing blitz, the company decided to teach people how to use its product by distributing free cookbooks chock-full of

Karo recipes. And, boy, did the *Karo Cook Book* deliver. First of all, the brand wisely stayed in the *Ladies' Home Journal* lane by hiring Emma Churchman Hewitt, former associate editor of the *Journal*, to write the cookbook. The result was a fifty-page wonderland boasting "120 Practical Recipes for the Use of Karo Syrup." In her introduction, Hewitt claimed the syrup was "wholesome, sustaining, higher in food value than other syrups and more digestible," and shared her completely unbiased opinion that "I find that it imparts a flavor not to be obtained from any other sweet. It seems to blend more naturally with every other article of food."

The cookbook included plenty of notable facts, such as the little tidbit that "thousands of people eat Karo freely who cannot digest other sweets" (which does not make an ounce of sense) and "men at hard labor . . . find they can go further on a diet of bread and Karo than almost any other ration." It also omitted some pretty telling stuff, like any awareness for racial equity with the inclusion of a recipe for "Jim Crows" (YIKES) and, on a much less offensive scale, pecan pie. That's right! The *Karo Cook Book* had a whole section titled "Pastry & Puddings" that shared recipes for Mince Pie, Pumpkin Pie, Squash Pie, Karo Pie, Cranberry Pie, Lemon Pie, and Orange Tart . . . but no pecan pie. Despite the glaring absence, the cookbook clearly defined the influential new syrup not just as an incredibly versatile pantry staple—chapters ranged from Vegetables to Breads and Muffins—but also a valuable ingredient in pie production.

According to the cookbook, Karo sold sixty million cans the year before publication, and with the ongoing marketing push those numbers only continued to grow. The syrup popped up as an ingredient in cookbooks sold across the country, beginning as early as 1909 with mentions in cookbooks published in California, Illinois, and Massachusetts. Throughout the next decade, Karo was listed in plenty of other cookbooks spanning the nation from the East to West Coasts.

So on the one hand, it's obvious that the product's enthusiastic marketing worked—people all over the country were buying and baking with Karo, and, quite notably, the product was so well known that it was explicitly called out by cookbook authors, a landmark move in an industry where brand names hadn't previously really been a thing. But despite the 120 different uses put forth in 1910's *Karo Cook Book,* almost all of the Karo recipes in these cookbooks were for divinity candy or some variation, like Divinity Fudge or Divinity Frosting.*

Karo's journey over the next few decades coincided with an ongoing increase in processed food consumption in American households. By 1920, the largest manufacturing industry in America in terms of earnings wasn't steel, automobiles, or even textiles . . . it was food processing. Food processing! Was beating out steel! It's truly hard to grasp. Consequently, food prices dropped, making it more affordable for the masses. So, somewhat unsurprisingly, between 1914 and 1928 workers consumed an average of two more pounds of food per day, along with more refined sugar, bread, and starch products. These developments were aided by improvements to home and cooking technology, like the introduction of gas, oil, or electric stoves to replace coal and wood stoves.

Such changes dovetailed with the continued rise of women's magazines (like Karo's favorite billboard, *Ladies' Home Journal*),

* What is this divinity stuff, you ask? It was an early-twentieth-century confection whose primary ingredient was corn syrup. Recipes were included in Karo cooking brochures, so we can likely chalk up the popularity of the candy and its appearance in all those cookbooks to Karo's marketing. Which also explains why the syrup was so widely used in the recipe—those advertisements were working! In a way, divinity candy walked so that pecan pie could run.

which became fertile advertising grounds for packaged products to appeal directly to the housewives who were doing the shopping and the cooking. Because housewives *were*, in fact, doing more of the shopping and cooking—at this time, domestic labor shifted from being performed by paid and unpaid servants to the housewife herself. So naturally, she was constantly on the lookout for products and recipes that would make her life easier (and her husband happier, if these advertisements were to be believed).

Like many other packaged foods, Karo recognized and targeted these women with its branded recipes, well-placed advertisements, and wholesome message of health. And by all accounts, Karo was incredibly successful at it. But it wasn't until it slipped its syrup into the most quintessential American homemaker dish that Karo Corn Syrup truly became a lasting culinary icon. That's right—we're talking about pie.

The Karo pecan pie finally hit the scene in the 1930s, several decades after Americans had overcome their (rightful) fear of packaged food to embrace industrialized products wholeheartedly into their diets. The story goes that the wife of a corporate sales executive dreamed up a nifty little recipe that would put Karo Corn Syrup to use. It called for corn syrup, sugar, eggs, vanilla, and pecans, all baked up in a pie shell. It was, quite obviously, a pecan pie, one that distinguished itself from the regional versions pockmarked across the states. And eventually, it became *the* pecan pie, eclipsing the individual heritage recipes kept tucked away in kitchens and memories across the country to become the definitive version of this dish.

I want to take a quick sidebar to note that, as brilliant as this employee's wife might have been, it's pretty likely this wasn't the first time Karo had actually been used in pecan pie. In 1931, the student publication *Ward-Belmont Hyphen* (of Ward-Belmont College in Tennessee) published this fun little anecdote in its "Club Chatter" section:

> Was Hortense ever surprised Monday night after discovering that the club business she was called down to the Agora House for turned out to be a dinner! Well, the expression on her face told the story pretty plainly . . . The 'eats' consisted of chili, potato salad, hot rolls and butter, karo-pecan pie, and coffee. Three young ladies on campus will tell you if you ask them that preparing a meal isn't the simplest thing in the world, especially making coffee. However, they will also add that 'all's well that ends well,' surprise parties not excepted. *

And even before this wholesome little surprise party, a pecan pie made with Karo was published in 1925 in *800 Proved Pecan Recipes: Their Place in the Menu*, a collection of pecan recipes meant to reinvigorate pecan consumption after it fell flat following World War I. Tucked amidst a massive section on "Pecan Pies and Pastries," the book contained a recipe for Molasses Pie (ironically made without any molasses at all) from Mrs. Gus. O. Selbensen that called for "½ C. sugar, 2 T. butter, 2 eggs, 2 T. flour, ¼ t. salt, 1 t. almond extract, 1 C. white Karo syrup, 1½ C. chopped pecans." Other recipes abound: Mrs. Frank Herring shared her recipe for Karo Pecan Pie in Oklahoma's *Democrat-American* in 1931, a pretty conventional version similar to most recipes; in 1932's *The National Cookbook*, meanwhile, a standard recipe for Pecan Pie called for "1 cup Karo Syrup."

---

* I just love that out of everything they prepared for sweet little Hortense, the dish that gave them the most trouble was the coffee.

But truly, the under-the-radar presence of Karo Corn Syrup in pecan pie before Karo debuted its own official recipe to the world just goes to show you that their branded pecan pie recipe didn't become popular naturally—it became popular because it was marketed with a lot of money.

You've got to give the folks at Karo credit: They knew when they had a hit on their hands. They began folding Karo pecan pie into their prodigious marketing campaigns, and it soon became a signature piece of content used to usher the brand's corn syrup into home kitchens. Instead of snake oil–shilling proclamations about the wholesomeness of the product, Karo began printing its pecan pie recipe in advertisements and displays. One 1941 display ad in Texas's *Big Spring Daily Herald* took the pecan pie back to its roots, proclaiming:

> Surprise the Folks with Karo Pecan Pie Tonight . . . it's wonderful! Try this Texas favorite: 3 eggs, slightly beaten, ⅛ teaspoon salt, 1 teaspoon vanilla, 1 cup sugar, 1 cup Karo (Blue Label), ⅔ cup pecan meats, coarsely chopped. Mix together all ingredients, adding nut meats last. Pour into 9-inch pie pan lined with your favorite pie crust. Bake in hot oven (450 degrees F.) ten minutes, then reduce heat to moderate (350 degrees F.) and continue baking until a silver knife blade inserted in center of filling comes out clean.

Karo ran its recipe in the places where people (read: housewives) were looking for them, sharing a compelling dish directly with its target market. The recipe also eventually got printed right on the corn syrup's label, so that each package shipped out into the far-flung corners of the country spread the pie just a little bit further into people's homes. The marketing angle worked spectacularly, and pecan pie soon became synonymous with Karo Corn Syrup; in many cases, women's pecan pie recipes explicitly called for the specific product, like one handwritten iteration included in *The New Milwaukee Cook Book* in 1938. Sometimes, the brand was included right in the recipe name, such as *The Delta's Best Cook Book*'s recipe for Karo Pecan Pie (which, apparently, was important enough to include separate from not one, but two other regular pecan pie recipes also printed in the book).

On the back of Karo's national prominence, pecan pie also rose to stardom, launching to become a household name. No longer was it just a humble Southern staple, but rather a national darling. And like all celebrities, it inspired some pretty strong feelings on both sides of the divide. In 1942, author Marjorie Kinnan Rawlings shared her, um, *decisive* feelings about it, declaring that "fat men in particular are addicted to it." She added, "I have nibbled at the Utterly Deadly Southern Pecan Pie, and have served it to those in whose welfare I took no interest, but being inclined to plumpness, and having as well a desire to see out my days on earth, I have never eaten a full portion." Which, given that the product shilling the pie was literally sugar syrup, her incredibly blunt take isn't exactly wrong.

By the 1950s, when Karo was running recipes for pecan pie in *Better Homes and Gardens*, nearly every American from all four corners of the country had either enjoyed a slice of pecan pie, or at the very least knew what it was—a far cry from the days just few decades earlier when Vesta Harrison thought she had invented the dish in the very state in which it likely originated. The recipe was particularly beloved on holiday tables, associated with the harvest and cooler weather. In her famous *Southern Cookbook*, Marion Brown proclaimed it "the South's most popular pie." Karo kept up the marketing angle, too, continuing to share recipes like De Luxe Pecan Pie (which wasn't that different from most other pecan pies) into the latter half of the twentieth century. Today, the recipe for classic pecan pie still resides on the back of each bottle of Karo Corn Syrup.

OF COURSE, CORN syrup—and corn as a whole—has not only continued to be a part of our American diet since Karo made its splashy entrance onto the national scene. Now, the starch pretty much defines what we eat. Corn is the foundation of our processed food; it's used to make, well, pretty much everything, employed as a starch, meal, alcohol, and of course, sugar. As modern farming technology made corn production more efficient, and thus cheaper, food corporations used it to replace more expensive ingredients, driving their costs down and profit up (right along with calorie counts). Notably in 1985, Coca-Cola replaced cane sugar with corn syrup; it's now the most-used sweetener in processed foods.

It's even seeded international conflict: In 2001, a trade dispute blew up between the United States and Mexico when America started dumping excess corn syrup off on its neighbor to the south, flooding the Mexican market and damaging Mexican cane sugar producers' business. The whole affair ended up going before the World Trade Organization, where the dispute was settled in favor the Americans (because things were totally non-biased in any way whatsoever toward a global superpower).

So it's fairly fitting that corn syrup, perhaps the most industrialized of all commercial food products, was the ingredient that made one obscure pie go national and become a staple in American diets. For home cooks baking up pecan pie well into the twenty-first century, Karo is still pretty much the only brand you can buy in grocery stores, keeping that corporate hold strong to this day. You can break from these industrialized roots by replacing the corn syrup with sweeteners like maple syrup or sorghum syrup. Or embrace the legacy of this dish, pick up a bottle of Karo, and accept that, at the very least, it bakes up a damn good pie.

KARO PECAN PIE

From Karo Corn Syrup

MAKES ONE 9-INCH (23-CM) PIE

Syrupy sweet and deeply nostalgic, this is Karo's classic pecan pie recipe. You'll find plenty of pecan pie recipe spins out there—versions that include a dose of bourbon, or that ditch the corn syrup entirely (!). And there's a time and place for those . . . but this isn't it.

When it comes to the Karo, you can choose dark corn syrup for a deeper, more complex flavor; light corn syrup will be more neutral and allow the pecans to shine.

1 All-Butter Pie Crust (pages 12–13)
1 cup (240 ml) Karo Corn Syrup, light or dark
3 large eggs
1 cup (200 g) granulated sugar
2 tablespoons unsalted butter, melted
1 teaspoon vanilla extract
1½ cups (150 g) pecan halves

Preheat the oven to 350°F (175°C). Line a 9-inch (23-cm) pie pan with the prepared crust. Trim excess dough and crimp the edges. Place in the refrigerator while you make your filling.

In a large bowl, whisk together the corn syrup, eggs, sugar, butter, and vanilla until smooth. Stir in the pecans. Pour the filling into the prepared crust, then bake for 60 to 70 minutes, until the filling is mostly set. Let cool completely before serving.

DERBY PIE

PIE CAN DO a lot of things, but there's only one version that can get you sued.

In Kentucky, there's a certain style of pecan pie known as Derby Pie, made with either pecans or walnuts, plus bourbon (naturally), and chocolate. It's a pretty beloved classic in the state, not only because it's delicious and contains bourbon, but also because it honors the Bluegrass State's most famous annual event. What's more Kentuckian than the literal Kentucky Derby?

As much as Derby Pie is enjoyed, however, there's just one problem: Only one company is allowed to make it. Try it yourself, and you'll get slapped with a lawsuit.

A company called Kern's Kitchen has had a federal trademark on "Derby-Pie" since the 1960s. The eponymous Kern family officially started making the pie a decade earlier, in 1954 at their Melrose Inn in Prospect, Kentucky. The pie itself has always been a secret recipe—all the Kerns will reveal nowadays is that "premium chocolate and choice walnuts are folded into a decadent filling, then baked in a delicate crust." And as for the name that's launched a thousand lawsuits (there haven't been a thousand lawsuits), the

Kerns claim it was picked out of a hat full of suggestions from family members.

The pie proved a hit at the Melrose Inn, so much so that the family filed for state and federal trademark protection for the Derby-Pie trademark upon the advice of local restaurateur friends. Since then, its popularity has only grown: Today, Kern's Kitchen (the company eventually founded by the family) makes more than one thousand pies a day and sells over one hundred thousand a year. And in between all that pie-making, the Kerns track down anyone who might be selling a Derby Pie themselves.

Kern's Kitchen regularly doles out cease-and-desist letters to establishments selling anything called a "Derby Pie," reportedly sending one or two letters each week. One hostess working at an inn in Shelbyville, Kentucky, said her restaurant has to worry that Kern's might send in a plant to catch them calling their chocolate pecan pie "Derby Pie." After Science Hill Inn, another restaurant in Shelbyville, received a cease-and-desist letter from Kern's, a hostess claimed, "We were threatened." One Kentucky restaurateur got so fed up that the Kerns were trying to keep a state dish to themselves that he put up a sign at his establishment proclaiming "Have a piece of 'I Can't Call It Derby Pie' pie.'"

It's not just local restaurants that Kern's metes out their particular form of justice to, either. In 1987, the company sued *Bon Appétit* after the magazine ran a recipe for Derby Pie in its pages. The two ultimately settled their case in appeals court.

Many bakers in Kentucky feel the pie is a piece of their state and their community, and it shouldn't be owned by a single family. Kern's, however, doesn't seem apologetic, or concerned with the role pie can play in the collective culture of an American region (or, for that matter, the role the Kentucky Derby plays in, uh, Kentucky). On its company website, Kern's brags: "Kern's Kitchen has successfully enforced the Derby-Pie® trademark throughout the years against *Bon Appétit* Magazine, Sweet Streets Desserts and Nestle Foods to name but a few."

So don't get caught selling Derby Pie anywhere in the US, or they just might hunt you down and add you to that list, too.

CHAPTER SIX

CHIFFON PIE

PIE JUST SORT of seems like it's always been there.

And as you know if you've been following along thus far, it basically has. The dish has been made since ancient civilizations in the Mediterranean were enclosing meat in heavy olive oil–based crusts. And, as we know, pie was baked in the United States even before the Declaration of Independence was shipped off to England like the world's most formal breakup letter. The beauty of pie, and the reason it has become so interwoven into the fabric of American cuisine, is that it is endlessly adaptable, forgiving, and—in contrast to the towering layers of an elaborate cake—humble.

At least, that *was* the beauty of pie. Until one man came along in the 1920s and decided to shake up everything. His real name was Monroe Boston Strause, but he was perhaps better known as "The Pie King." (Apologies to my potential future husband, whose would-be title has already been claimed.) In Los Angeles, a growing city unbound by historical tradition, Strause pioneered a new meringue-based dessert that embodied the shifting cultural landscape of the West in the '20s: the chiffon pie, a refined, polished, and delicately airy confection that snubbed the sturdy practicality of traditional custard and double-crusted pies.

Pie, as we've covered thus far, usually evolves over time. But with chiffon pie, things were different. Here was a dessert that arose not because of the convenience of circumstance or availability of ingredients, but rather from the sheer inventiveness, creativity, and ambition of its creator. It was an origin that mimicked the time and place in which this pie was born: California in the 1920s.

The '20s were a decade of profound change across the country, beyond just the pastry-verse. In addition to flappers and speakeasies, gangsters and jazz, a nation firmly rooted on the East Coast began to look West. With the rise of Los Angeles and the emergence of Hollywood and the film industry as a potent force with landmark movies like *The Jazz Singer* and the shift to "talkies," a new American center of culture began to take shape. One that was, for the first time, on the Pacific Coast.

The chiffon pie similarly filtered beyond the West and throughout the country to become a staple in daily lives, arguably hitting the mainstream when its recipe was published in *Joy of Cooking* in 1931. Today, it's a common genre of pie found in bakeries and cookbooks pretty much everywhere. All thanks to one very important man.

Like most legendary royals—King Arthur, Princess Mia Thermopolis—the Pie King started from humble origins. Monroe Boston Strause was born to Midwestern parents, real "salt of the earth" people as he described them, who had escaped the frigid plains of the Midwest to start a new life in California. There they eventually married and started a family consisting of the future pie prodigy Monroe and his two older sisters, who grew up surrounded by the doers and dreamers of LA.

This sun-soaked childhood differed greatly from that of his parents, who were born in Garrett, Indiana, and Ironton, Ohio.

Monroe's parents' journey to California was part of a larger migration west in the early decades of the twentieth century, during which the nation collectively realized that constant sunshine and 72-degree weather every day was probably a better way to live than dealing with lake-effect snow and frigid temperatures half the year. With the Southern Pacific Railroad connecting the region to the rest of the country, millions of people, including Strause's parents, decided to hightail it across the country and move to California—a significant internal migration movement that proved instrumental in shifting the balance of the US beyond its historical urban centers.

Between 1910 and 1920, Los Angeles grew faster than all other West Coast cities combined; after another decade, Los Angeles was the fifth-largest city in the entire country. And unlike the major metropolises in the East, Los Angeles developed as a modern city, one built for cars (so many suburbs) and industrialization.

However alluring the Pacific Coast might have been, the western boom didn't happen entirely organically. Like most social trends, the move was fueled by advertisers, businessmen, and other people motivated by the desire to make money. The image of Southern California as a wonderland of natural beauty, plentiful business opportunity, good weather, and exotic lifestyle was explicitly fueled by commercial developers looking to make a quick buck. The whole thing was essentially a booster campaign, one that Collier's called out in 1915 when it dubbed Los Angeles "The City Advertising Built."

There was also an unmistakable xenophobic element to the growth of LA. As cities on the Eastern Seaboard accepted more and more immigrants flooding in from foreign shores, white people grew increasingly frantic that the beloved country they had established on the homeland of Indigenous people was turning into something far too ethnic for their tastes. California, with its shiny aura of the new and untapped, presented itself as a haven far from the immigration problems that plagued the rest of the country (despite its clear Spanish and Mexican influence). Charles Lummis, one of the many boosters who peddled an idealized narrative of Southern California life to attract new residents and business, called it "Eden for Anglo-Saxon home-seekers."

The one goal that united these dauntless internal migrants was the same one that had been luring Americans westward since the days of the great Gold Rush over half a century prior: the material dream of a better life. California was dubbed the "Land of Opportunity," a place where you could achieve your wildest (and most expensive) dreams. As historian Hilary Hallett has written, "Many of these youthful strangers from someplace else shared . . . a willingness to use their economic and imaginative resources to chase new desires in the City of Dreams." Such opportunity applied to any industry: oil (the oil boom of the era, off which George Getty made his massive fortune, was dubbed "Oildorado"), shipping, and quite obviously, entertainment. It could even apply to pie-making.

From pastry to pictures, that pursuit of prosperity often meant rethinking convention to blaze a bright new path to glory. This approach was most obviously applied to the film industry, where entertainment titans were capitalizing on the success they'd had developing an American film industry in the 1910s to reach even higher in the '20s.

During the decade, Adolph Zukor of Paramount developed the foundation of the movie studio system, while Fox Film broke ground on a brand new 450-acre studio lot in Hollywood. Across the country, glamorous "picture palaces" were constructed to play films to the masses, and as soon as 1922, Los Angeles was estimated to produce 84 percent of the movies made in America to solidify its status as the "Film Capital of the World." In 1929, the whole cinematic boom was celebrated with the first Academy Awards ceremony.

In 1927, a journalist wrote that in Los Angeles, "anything seems possible; the future is yours, and the past?—there isn't any." Raised in such a place, Monroe Boston Strause was bound to apply the same expectation of wild possibility to the profession he was thrust into and eventually chose: pie.

Strause's father was reportedly a flour miller, an occupation the younger Strause supposedly ventured into before pivoting into baking. That pivot came as a result of his uncle Mike, who operated a wholesale pie business that Strause went on to join in 1919 when he was a teenager. There, his most formidable challenge soon arose in the form of cakes, the greatest enemy of pie. You see, housewives were finding cakes much easier to make at home, possibly due to more standardized equipment and the availability of commercial ingredients. This mounting competition led the young Strause to dig deep and get creative. His greatest ambition: Innovate pie.

Though his creativity was indisputable, there was another key to his success. Strause approached pie-making as a scientist, a stark departure from the adaptable, free-form approaches that so many bakers (especially women) had traditionally used for their desserts. This methodical approach was something he prided himself on— he thought that housewives "tend to be too slipshod for scientific pie-making." Just how dedicated was he to this method? Well, he went so far as to call his recipes "formulas" and approached pie-making like an inventor or mathematician seeking to write the perfect equation. As Strause's publishers described in his book, *Pie Marches On*: "He has reduced pie baking to an exact science and measures each ingredient with the care of a pharmacist."

As a pie "scientist," Strause was particularly opposed to volume measurements, relying instead on more accurate weight measurements for all of his ingredients and recipes (something that also suited his work in a professional bakery working at scale). As he once grandly proclaimed, he believed "the tea cup and teaspoon are the greatest enemies to a good pie." Strause also obsessively experimented to land on a final recipe, and at one point made 150 different versions of cherry pie to find the right one. With all the drama of a good diva, he once derided a common method for thickening fruit filling by scoffing, "I'm afraid my vocabulary is too limited to provide a sufficiently appalling description of such a product (I hesitate to call it pie)." The pettiness, it must be noted, was truly admirable.

In all, his methods deviated from the previous reputation of pie as rustic, humble, and easily adaptable. Much like the rest of California industry, Strause abandoned old, quaint ways tied up in tradition in favor of a bold, inventive approach. He emphasized breaking away from established, routine, and accepted means of baking pies in favor of new methods to improve the dessert.

So with a deep desire to create a new, modern pie that would inspire people to abandon cake, establish his skill, and satisfy his own personal pie preferences, Strause began the '20s hard at work in the lab . . . erm, the kitchen. He zeroed in on one specific, and highly personal, problem: cream pies. The thing is, he hated them. He found them too thick and heavy, and lambasted their resemblance to cornstarch-thickened pudding. Like the best deep-rooted grudges, his went all the way back to childhood; as legend has it, Strause once ate so much cornstarch pudding as a kid that he made himself sick and studiously avoided the dish as a result. So he set out to invent a new, signature version of the common dish.

In the end, he came up with the chiffon pie, a new style that would go on to bring him fame and fortune across the country. The filling featured egg whites beaten until voluptuous and stiff, then gently folded into a base of cornstarch-thickened cream. Unlike the drab, gloopy puddings he so detested, this pie filling was delicate and ethereal, with plenty of volume for a show-stopping presentation. When she saw it for the first time, Strause's mother declared that it "looks just like a pile of chiffon," crowning it with its iconic name.

Like Hollywood, Strause's new pie was also emphatically focused on appearance, pioneering a new pie style in which the filling was piled higher in the middle than on the sides, creating a round, dome-like shape—Strause wrote that it was "a distinctive feature of the true chiffon pie and adds greatly to its eye-appeal." So long to mundane custards and rustic lattice designs; this pie not only tasted good—it looked good, too. The pie's crust was yet another notable first, as it was likely one of the earliest official itera-tions of graham cracker crust, which, as a journalist later wrote, yielded "a shell light, crisp, and tender—the ideal mate for chiffon."

We have ample recordings of the first airplane flight, or the exact moment a man stepped on the moon, but this particular leap in human ingenuity is less documented; we don't know the exact date chiffon pie made its debut, as most coverage of the pie's inven-tion fails to mention the precise date. One profile of Strause from the '50s claimed he invented it in 1928, while the *Los Angeles Times* asserted that he debuted it in 1926. Either way, it was amidst the Hollywood boom. And like the leading men and ladies on the silver screen, it went on the become a star, skyrocketing in popularity—and bringing the man who invented it right along with it. By the '30s, when Strause wrote his book, he commented that "today chif-fon pie is known to people in every walk of life; and is probably the most talked of and highest publicized of all pies." (Modesty and understatement were not his strong suits.)

Whereas traditional baked-fruit pies might have been con-sidered dowdy—the realm of those same housewives Strause dismissed—his chiffon pie was elegant and refined, just like the world of Hollywood outside his door in Los Angeles.* And Strause didn't merely suggest such a connection—he specifically promoted it. In the opening pages of his book, he included a photograph of silent film star Mary Pickford along with an orange chiffon pie. In the image, he stands with a rather large pie cradled in both hands; in truly over-the-top fashion, the dessert is at least twice the size of a typical nine-inch dish. Mary, dressed in a classy black dress and triple strand of pearls, smiles beatifically as she dips her fork into the billowy whipped cream that crowns Strause's pie. With her coiffed curls and striking makeup, she appears every bit the movie star. The caption, meanwhile, boasts, "Mary Pickford, America's Sweetheart, tastes a delicious orange chiffon pie presented to her by the author." Of all the pies in all pages that Strause authored (and boy, there were a lot—chiffon was just one of his many pastry creations), it's no surprise that the one specially prepared for an icon of Hollywood was his own iconic chiffon.

It wasn't just the glamour of Hollywood that Strause embodied in his approach to pie, either. One of the key elements in the growth of the film industry throughout the 1910s and '20s had been the shift from small-production companies to massive corporations who prided themselves on efficiency and consistency. With his mathematical measurements, precise approach, and emphasis on scaling up pie production business (later in his career, Strause

---

* Chiffon pie's launch also aligned with a shift in American cuisine to "feminine" food early in the twentieth century; in other words, dainty dishes that featured things like cream, whipped egg whites (sound familiar?), and gelatin (notably, later incarnations of chiffon pie would be thickened with gelatin instead of cornstarch, as Strause made it). Chiffon pie's appearance in the 1920s was a natural extension of this trend, and likely very much informed by it (no matter how original Strause wanted to believe he was).

boasted to a reporter that he had designed a pie plant in St. Louis that could make 100,000 pies in one day), the Pie King took one or two cues from the studio executives who populated his city.

Beyond Strause's chiffon pie, other examples of his creations reflected the changing trends and social landscape of the era. Perhaps his second-best-known pie was the black bottom pie, which featured a chocolate base with additional fillings piled on top. In his book, Strause wrote that it was "the most sensational pie that has even been introduced, and is one of the outstanding originals of the writer." High praise, indeed! Now, you would think the pie's name came from its chocolate base, but according to the *Los Angeles Times*, there was more to it: "It came from the Black Bottom Dance which was the rage in the early '20s." The dance was the same kind of swinging, Jazz-Age jaunt as the Charleston, and the pie itself capitalized on that modern, freewheeling sense of daring with its name.

Despite the popularity of the black bottom pie and other pastry inventions, Strause ultimately built his entire career on the fact that he invented the chiffon pie. It was his masterpiece, the signature dessert upon which he hung his (chef's) hat and the foundation of a lucrative profession.

Except . . . what if he didn't invent it?

In 1925, the book *800 Proved Pecan Recipes: Their Place in the Menu* included a recipe titled Chiffon Lemon Pie made with pecans, credited to a Mrs. Hannah Breckenridge. The method for preparing went as follows:

Add lemon juice and grated rind to water and boil. Beat egg yolks well and add 5 T. sugar and 1 T. water. Stir boiling lemon juice and water slowly into egg yolks. Return to double boiler and cook until thick. Cool. Beat 2 egg

whites very stiff and add 4 T. powdered sugar. Fold into
other mixture and pour into baked crust. Brown slightly
in oven, remove and add meringue made from remaining egg white, sugar, and pecans. Return to oven to
brown slightly.

It differs slightly from Strause's method, but still uses beaten
egg whites to achieve a lofty, airy texture characteristic of the chiffon pie. It's even named the same thing! And Mrs. Breckenridge
wasn't the only one whipping up chiffon pies at that time—in April
1926, the American Women's Club of London included details on
how to make lemon chiffon pie in its magazine, among other distinctly American favorites like molasses cakes and divinity fudge. So
much for Mrs. Strause's off-the-cuff exclamation of pure delight that
named her son's newest invention. Unless it's all just a coincidence?

Since the date of Strause's chiffon pie invention is somewhat
unclear, and the identities of Mrs. Breckenridge and those particular London ladies are lost to time, it's difficult to parse out an exact
series of events or culinary inspiration. The entire concept of multiple discovery, after all, is based on the idea that inventions and
discoveries happen at the same time completely independent of
each other: A little-known scientist named Elisha Gray filed a caveat
to later apply to patent the telephone on the same day Alexander
Graham Bell filed his own application for a telephone patent, for
instance. The same thing could have easily happened with pie.

Did Strause steal the idea for the chiffon pie from a cookbook
meant to promote pecan sales in the years after World War I, or a
magazine made by American women living in England? Given how
straight-up obsessive he was about inventing pies, I'd say it's safe to
assume no. Though who can really know for sure? One thing that's
clear is that Strause wasn't quite as much of a renegade as he might

have led people to believe: According to Jean Anderson in her book *American Century Cookbook: The Most Popular Recipes of the 20th Century*, "Fluffy unbaked pies debuted in the early 1920s as 'souffle' or 'gelatin' pies. . . . Knox Gelatine's 1915 booklet, *Dainty Desserts for Dainty People*, features gelatin 'sponges,' 'marshmallow puddings,' and 'marshmallow creams'—the airy mixes that would one day emerge as chiffon fillings." Anderson also traced airy, delicate gelatin pie fillings to *Good Housekeeping* as early as 1922.

Overall, what this coincidence really reveals is the extent to which Strause actively engaged in his own mythmaking, spinning a story of discovery and invention that mimicked the grand tales being told on the movie screen and in business offices across Los Angeles during the same years he toiled in the kitchen. (He even embellished his origins in the profession: He once quipped that he started making pies because, "One time a guy threw a pie in my face. It tasted so good I just started baking them." Which, given the fact that his uncle literally owned a pie business, seems less than likely.) In many ways, he actively used his pie to make himself into a star.

And he really did become a star. Eventually, Strause's pie business expanded to become one of the biggest in the West, and people desperately sought his pie expertise. He traveled around the country to teach hotels and restaurants how to make the dish himself, intent on keeping the recipe a secret. When it did eventually leak, the chiffon pie was so well known that it didn't matter: The Pie King had officially been crowned.

The chiffon pie also started to get some local press, discussed frequently in the *Los Angeles Times* starting around 1929. By that year, many folks were writing in to the paper's "Practical Recipes" column to request the recipe for lemon chiffon pie, a version of which was shared in the paper's pages. (Once again, there's no way to be entirely sure it was Strause's pie to which they were referring, but still . . . the geography, at least, matches up.) And once the '30s rolled around, multiple businesses in LA were hawking the dessert; in 1935, lemon chiffon pie was sold at Ralph's Grocery, one of Southern California's most prominent supermarket chains.

As his pie became more and more famous, so too did Strause. By breaking away from established means of baking pies, Strause basically became a culinary celebrity in America, decades before the twenty-first-century pastry chef Dominique Ansel would chart a similar course with his invention of the viral Cronut. Strause also followed the same path as the movie industry, which easily weathered the storm of the Great Depression (more on that in the next chapter) to reach a golden age in the 1930s, some of the peak years of the major studios who dominated the industry. It was also a decade in which the Pie King thrived.

After selling his original business at a profit, Strause became a national "pie consultant." He taught classes and led lectures; he opened factories and developed new ways to ship his products. In Chicago, he entered a pie contest against over 2,500 other pies— and, to no one's surprise (least of all his own), won.

It seems absurd, even for me, to say this about a pie-maker, but he really was like a movie star. He had glowing profiles written about him, and crowds of people turned up for his speeches and demonstrations. He said absurd, vain things like, "I have a good complexion and marvelous digestion," which he credited to a steady, though moderate, diet of pie. More than the glitz and glamour, he also embodied the kind of splashy showmanship and affinity for publicity that the businessmen and advertising executives who built LA had favored. The accounts of his pie performances are numerous, including the time he baked a pie twenty-four feet in diameter for newsboys in Los Angeles, or when he made the largest lemon chiffon pie in the world (clocking in at three feet in diameter).

He never stopped inventing, either, including a technique to ship frozen pies that he initially developed for World War II. In 1939 Strause published his book, *Pie Marches On*, and in the foreword his publishers declared, "Monroe Boston Strause has indeed every right to the title of 'The Pie King.' Every baker in the United States or Canada or wherever he is known acknowledges him as such." His success brought fortune as well; one profile in the *Globe and Mail* declared that he made "a bank president's salary out of pie."

Sadly, given his clear desire for public notoriety, Strause eventually faded from the spotlight and into obscurity. By the late 1950s, the profiles trickled to a standstill, and the dashing pastry stunts either ceased or went unrecorded. His pie influence waned, and perhaps most notably, his association with (and self-asserted ownership of) chiffon pie disappeared. Perhaps he was boxed out by food corporations who made chiffon pie so public that there was no more room for a story about how one man had claimed to invent an entirely new genre of pie.

In the '90s, the *LA Times* called Strause "probably the last pie celebrity in our history." But even more important than being the last, he was the first. The first to invent a number of influential pastry creations, and the first to promote pie-making as a scientific venture built on the back of innovation and experimentation. As the Roaring Twenties exploded with glamour and modernity, and Los Angeles dictated American culture from a new coast on a shining sea, the Pie King shook up the pastry world with a spark that continues to glow to this day.

LEMON CHIFFON PIE

Adapted from *Pie Marches On* by Monroe Boston Strause

MAKES ONE 9-INCH (23-CM) PIE

In his book, Monroe Boston Strause recommended readers "take the doctor's advice in reading this prescription." In other words, read the recipe before making it. He advised bakers to read the recipe through no fewer than three times to ensure success (though between you and me, you can probably get away with twice). And of course, use metric measurements if you can—it's what the Pie King would have wanted.

For the crust
¼ cup (46 g) shortening
4 teaspoons (12 g) all-purpose flour
⅛ teaspoon salt
1 cup (100 g) graham cracker crumbs
4 teaspoons (20 ml) corn syrup
4 teaspoons (20 ml) warm water

For the filling
4 large egg whites
¾ cup plus 3 tablespoons (186 g) sugar
¼ cup (28 g) cornstarch
3 tablespoons (45 ml) fresh lemon juice
1 cup (240 ml) water
1½ teaspoons lemon zest
½ teaspoon salt

Whipped cream, for serving

MAKE THE CRUST: Preheat the oven to 425°F (220°C). In the bowl of a stand mixer, beat together the shortening, flour, and salt. Add the graham cracker crumbs and beat until thoroughly mixed.

In a small bowl, combine the corn syrup and warm water until the syrup is dissolved. Pour into the graham cracker mixture and mix until a dough forms.

Pat the dough out into a 9-inch (23-cm) pie pan, covering only the bottom of the pan—the crust doesn't go up the sides. Bake for 10 minutes, until the edges of the crust are browning slightly. Remove from the oven; the crust will still be quite soft, but will harden as it cools.

MEANWHILE, MAKE THE FILLING: In the bowl of a stand mixer, whisk the egg whites and ¼ cup (50 g) of the sugar to stiff peaks. Add an additional ¼ cup (50 g) of the sugar and beat until it disappears. (This will take only a few revolutions of the machine.) Set aside.

In a small bowl, dissolve the cornstarch in the lemon juice. Set aside.

In a medium saucepan over medium heat, combine the water, the remaining 7 tablespoons (86 g) of the sugar, the lemon zest, and the salt. Bring to a boil, then whisk in the cornstarch and lemon juice mixture. Cook over medium heat, whisking constantly, until the mixture noticeably thickens; this should occur very quickly.

Immediately pour the cooked lemon mixture over the beaten egg whites and carefully fold in until completely combined.

Pour the filling into the prepared crust. Use a spatula to shape the filling, making the center higher than the sides and giving it a dome shape. Allow to cool completely. Top with whipped cream before serving.

KEY LIME PIE

MONROE BOSTON STRAUSE'S reported invention of the graham cracker crust was important for a lot of classic pie recipes, key lime pie being one of the foremost among them (though it must be noted that there are plenty of purists who advocate for a traditional pastry crust in key lime pie instead). But while the provenance of this classic pie's crust can be traced without much fanfare, the origins of the tangy green dessert are actually the subject of some fervent debate.

You'd automatically assume key lime pie was invented in Florida, right? After all, it is the state pie, and tucking into a slice is basically Tourist Activity #1 while visiting the Keys. And that does align with the pie's local origin story. As legend has it, the pie was invented by a Floridian woman known only as "Aunt Sally" around 1869, when she dreamed up the dish in the kitchens of Key West's Curry Mansion while working as a cook for millionaire William Curry. Like the best legends, however, this story has never been verified, and according to Key West historian Tom Hambright, Aunt Sally makes for a compelling story, but it's hardly fact.

So what's the truth? Pastry chef Stella Parks laid out an alternate theory in her 2017 book, *BraveTart*. According to her research on the origins of key lime pie, the dish likely got its start far from the tropical islands of Florida. Instead, she traced it to the cold urban jungle of New York City.

Parks identified a 1931 recipe for Magic Lemon Cream Pie—a sweetened condensed milk pie strikingly similar to key lime pie, just with lemons instead of limes—that was created by the Borden Company (of condensed milk fame) in New York. She suggests that company advertising caused the recipe to proliferate and eventually make its way to Florida, where residents swapped the lemons for key limes. It's a very logical story that nevertheless has received backlash from Key West locals and key lime pie historian David Sloan, the author of the 2013 book, *The Key West Key Lime Pie Cookbook*.

These aren't the only theories: There's also local lore that traces the rough foundation of the pie back to the nineteenth century. According to Hambright, coastal sponge harvesters in the 1890s were tired of eating fish while out on the water, so they decided to switch up their diet with a new treat: lime juice, sweetened condensed milk, eggs, and old bread. They'd soak the stale bread in the canned milk, then top with island eggs and key lime juice to create a mixture that jelled. Notably, the base was supposedly Cuban bread, a reflection of the island's geography.

That geography is also likely the reason sweetened condensed milk is so foundational to the classic key lime pie recipe. Because fresh milk and refrigeration were largely unavailable in the Keys until the 1930s due to the islands' isolation, sweetened condensed milk became essential.

Regardless of the exact origins of the pie and the debates that have sprung up around it, it was clearly being made in Florida by the mid- to late 1930s. One 1936 *Miami Herald* article called the key lime pie a "Conch contribution to American cookery worthy of the Cordon Bleu." And in 1937, the *Orlando Sentinel* wrote about a baker by the name of Jefferson Bell who "makes a Key lime pie that causes Winter visitors to get out their note books."

Sadly, key limes don't really grow on the island like they used to, back when they were a big commercial crop in the nineteenth century. A hurricane and changing trends knocked them out beginning in the 1920s, and now the local pie tourists to the Keys enjoy is either made with regular limes or key lime juice that's been shipped to the islands.

CHAPTER SEVEN

MOCK APPLE PIE

SOMETIMES, A PIE is notable not because of what it contains, but rather, because of what it lacks. Like, for example, an apple pie made without any apples at all.

Wild, right?

The mock apple pie is a curious concoction that's arguably the most unique pie in this book. Instead of apples in the pie filling, it uses . . . crackers. Turns out that, ground to pieces, coated in spices and sugar syrup, and tucked beneath a pastry crust, plain crackers make a surprisingly effective filling substitute for apple pie. It's hard to believe that it all really works. Indeed, with a mushy brown filling, the dish looks different than most apple pies you're likely familiar with. But heavily spiced, darkly sweet, and with an unmistakable fruit tang, it does not resemble a bunch of ground-up crackers. Miraculous yet true, the dish tastes just like baked apples.

It's a fun novelty and a good joke, and, speaking from personal experience, it makes a hell of a party trick. (A rousing game of "guess what this pie filling is made of" is the perfect icebreaker.) But though on the surface it may appear to be little more than a quirky recipe, the dish is actually a powerful example of the skill and ingenuity housewives have been forced to display during times of immense struggle in American history.

Mock apple pie is most closely associated with the Great Depression, when economic disaster forced enterprising home cooks to get real creative, real quick. But in reality, the pie first came to prominence in another uncertain and catastrophic time, though it was one plagued by war, not stocks. During the Civil War, Southern households faced ingredient scarcities caused by blockades, rationing, and damaged crops. As a result, they were forced to adapt their kitchens to accommodate a new culinary reality.

One of the dishes they turned to was an ingenious little number known as the "mock apple pie," or sometimes just "cracker pie." The pie actually already existed both in and beyond the region, popping up in various periodicals and cookbooks before the outbreak of the war. One example is the 1857 news publication *Brookville American*, which described it as "an excellent substitute when apples are scarce." That same year, the *Saturday Evening Post* shared a recipe for the pie, noting, "As apples are very scarce in many sections of the country, I think the housewife will find the following recipe for making an apple pie out of crackers, very acceptable."*

In addition, a food blogger known as "Crazy Pie Lady" (with whom I now want to be best friends) discovered a letter dating to 1858 from Henderson, Texas, in which a woman named Sue Smith wrote to her friend Bet, "I have learned to make a new kind of Pie I think you all would like them they taste just like an apple pie make

---

* Now, I'll say what you're probably thinking: It does seem kind of curious that apples were so unavailable people had to start making pies out of crackers instead. I mean, apples literally grow on trees, and many Southerners did, after all, live in agricultural communities. But who am I to argue with the *Brookville American*? Plus, it often wasn't availability that made apples difficult to access, but rather price.

some and try them see if you don't love them . . . Take a teaspoon heaping full of tartarlic [*sic*] acid and dissolve it in water a teasp [*sic*] full of sugar and stir it in the acid then take cold biscuit or light bread and crumble in it." Remarkably, this method is quite similar to the mock apple pie that would endure for over a century after Sue first passed it along. Of particular note is the acid—almost all mock apple pies contain some form of acid, like cream of tartar or lemon juice, which is the real secret to making the filling taste like fruit. Don't be surprised to see it in the recipes mentioned throughout this chapter.

Interestingly, the pie wasn't isolated to the South, or even the East Coast. One cookbook published in California, *How We Cook in Los Angeles*, shared a recipe for California Pioneer Apple Pie reportedly from 1852 (though the book itself was published in 1894), which was made from soda crackers. The woman who shared the recipe noted, "The deception was most complete and readily accepted. Apples at this early date were a dollar a pound, and we young people all craved a piece of mother's apple pie to appease our homesick feelings." Nostalgia, convenience, and thrift, all wrapped up in one tasty package. Another woman, Elizabeth Storrs of Emporia, Kansas, turned to cracker pie to feed her guests, who reportedly "wondered by what magic she could provide green apple pies when there wasn't a bearing apple tree within 50 miles."

But though it appears to have been a handy hack for Midwest settlers and pioneers in the mid-nineteenth century, mock apple pie's true time to shine came a bit later. During the war, mock apple pie likely rose to prominence when it was published in 1863's *Confederate Receipt Book*, the only cookbook to be published in the Confederacy during the war. There, it was described as "Apple Pie Without Apples," and the recipe itself was straightforward: "To one small bowl of crackers, that have been soaked until no hard parts remain, add one teaspoonful of tartaric acid, sweeten to your taste, add some butter, and a very little nutmeg."

Written to help Southern white families cook and eat when ingredients were scarce (its subtitle literally noted that it was "adapted to the times"), the recipe book contained many other dishes and tricks suited to wartime, such as Artificial Oysters, Method of Curing Bad Butter, Substitute for Coffee (made with acorns), and Preserving Meat without Salt.

During the war, the mock apple pie spread not only through the *Confederate Receipt Book*, but also by other means. In her book *Reminiscences of a Soldier's Wife*, Ellen McGowan Biddie wrote about the high cost of food she faced in wartime, following up by adding, "Perhaps I might give a couple of recipes that we used, showing how one can get along without either milk or eggs." One of those recipes? Apple-pie, without Apples, which she credited to Mrs. Coolidge, a woman who ventured out onto the frontier in 1850—a lineage that reflects the western-bound mock apple pie recipe shared in *How We Cook in Los Angeles*. Biddie's directions went as follows: "Soda crackers soaked in water, and warmed until soft, but do not break too fine; add essence of lemon and sugar and a great deal of nutmeg; bake in pastry, with a top crust to the pie." Her review was enthusiastic: "You will feel sure it is apple-pie (if you do not make it yourself)."

It's particularly notable that women even bothered to make apple pie when ingredients like dairy and wheat (or at least the money to pay for them) were scarce, and when there were no apples to begin with. Especially since this dish is a dessert—great to have, but not exactly necessary for one's health or survival.

It's clear that to these wives and mothers (and by extension, their families) apple pie was worth going out of one's way to bake and eat, even in its shabbily adapted form. During a time of earth-shattering upheaval, a freshly baked apple pie, or even an imitation of the dish, kept a culture and way of life alive and preserved a sense of normalcy. As white Southerners' carefully constructed (and, ahem, problematic) world dissolved around them, this, at least, proved to be something they could hang on to. Even for those beyond the region, this familiar dish was a thread connecting them to their homes and memories, and a balm for homesickness. Amelia Simmons would be proud her apple pie had become such a powerful cultural symbol! (Though she'd possibly be horrified at the new cracker-based version of the dish, having written her whole cookbook as an ode to cooking with local ingredients and all that.)

In its later incarnations, mock apple pie would be baked under notably different conditions and in much more modern environments. But that deeper power—the ability to conjure an air of normalcy even as life radically changes—would remain part of its appeal.

MOCK APPLE PIE stuck around after the Civil War. I mean, you don't simply ditch such a fun and inventive dish. It continued to be published in various cookbooks under a variety of creative names. *Housekeeping in Old Virginia*, for instance, included a recipe for Soda Cracker Pie when it was published in 1879. The pie also later appeared in *Favorite Southern Recipes* in 1912 (that same cookbook with the offensive "mammy" image on the cover, if you recall from our molasses pie chapter), where it was named Cracker Pie and called for the addition of raisins (gross). And it also popped up outside the South, such as in *The Kitchen Companion Cookbook* published just after the war in 1869 in Philadelphia. So the pie never really disappeared in the decades after the Civil War, but in a thriving world where such kitchen shortcuts weren't exactly necessary, its usefulness deteriorated. It took the devastating economic crisis of the Great Depression to revive such a desperate form of baking.

At that point, we all know what happened: In 1929, the stock market crashed, plunging millions of American (and international!) families into dire economic straits. The worldwide GDP plummeted, and the American unemployment rate skyrocketed to over 20 percent. Across the United States, and beyond American borders, the gears of a functioning economy ground to a devastating halt. The subsequent fallout was not pretty.

The effects of the Great Depression crept slowly and inexorably into every facet of life. In the kitchen, it was impossible to ignore. Herbert Hoover may have referred to the country's "abundant harvests," but in reality, families were struggling to put food on the table as they dealt with crippling unemployment.

Suddenly, the threat of starvation haunted American families, many of whom were unused to dealing with the stark reality of food insecurity. In 1933, one report found that over a million people in New York City were completely dependent on public funds for support like food, while up to an additional million were "barely existing." For many suffering families, the effort to simply obtain food was all-consuming, and it forced many to get creative to feed themselves and their loved ones. One aid worker observed, "The myriad ways in which a family, its entire attention concentrated on food—just food—succeeded in obtaining it constitutes abundant evidence of the ingenuity and perseverance of these people."

Breadlines and soup kitchens drew crowds that stretched around the block, sometimes numbering in the thousands. Many struggling Americans relied on neighbors or roommates to pool their food resources. Hooverville residents scavenged for food scraps. Rural families canned weeds for the winter. In Louisiana, Black plantation tenants fed themselves from the livestock feed. One child recalled eating dog food.

Even those who weren't under the direct threat of starvation had severe challenges in the kitchen. Studying unemployed families at the time, E. Wight Bakke wrote: "Economy was chiefly exercised through the curtailing of expenditures involved in the normal pattern of food supply." Among the changes, fresh fruit was cut from families' diets. Said activist Oscar Ameringer, "Millions of children . . . , on account of the poverty of their parents, will not eat one apple this winter."

Unlike the rural economies of the nineteenth-century South, families of the Great Depression could find their cupboards empty of apples but full (well, maybe not *full*) of pantry staples and processed crackers instead. One woman in coal country recounted how many local families relied on the Red Cross to supply groceries, which consisted of "flour, lard, beans, salt, and sugar. No milk was provided, whether fresh or canned, and no fruit or vegetables." And recall, if you will, the rapid encroachment of processed food upon the American diet that had been taking place in the decades leading into '30s. Not only were simple processed foods like crackers widely available, but they were also cheap—especially one specific brand of cracker, introduced during the decade and specially marketed to appeal to families facing economic crisis. But more on that in a second.

The limited availability of fresh fruit and the dependence on cheap processed food staples clearly supported the case for the reintroduction of mock apple pie into the American diet at this time. So too did the new cooking and baking habits of American women. Like Ellen Biddie during the Civil War, many housewives were forced to get inventive in the kitchen to expand their limited supplies. They stretched resources to the absolute maximum, using oily margarine wrappers to grease pans or making one meal's leftovers last across the course of a week. Meals were simple; as one

Wisconsin woman recalled, "Every family knew what it was to live on bread and Wisconsin gravy." (Wisconsin gravy, if you're curious, was a simple mixture of flour, water, salt, and pepper.) Families got resourceful when it came to stocking their pantries. Remembered one woman, "Butternuts were for the picking if you were smarter than the squirrel." Faced with meager supplies, housewives made do with what they had to put nourishing meals on their family's table.

Needless to say, the challenge required creativity. In her cookbook, *Stories and Recipes of the Great Depression*, Rita Van Amber praised "the mothers who cooked those meals out of nothing and made them taste so good." That creativity was almost otherworldly; she added, "as a result of the constant need the women became near magicians in their large kitchens, out-performing in putting meals on the table."

The difficulty of cooking at home was a nationally recognized problem. To help guide struggling housewives with their new domestic burden, a national figure stepped up. A fictitious character springing from the minds at the federal Bureau of Home Economics, Aunt Sammy (so-named because she was meant to be Uncle Sam's wife, though if you think too hard about it that doesn't really make sense) was a spokeswoman and radio personality who debuted on the radio in the '20s, chatting regularly about domestic duties to something like five million listeners in her regular show, "Housekeeper's Chat." As circumstances evolved throughout the '30s, she spoke directly to housewives keeping afloat during the Depression, offering insight on how to cook when there really wasn't all that much to cook with. Her advice often involved the kind of tricks and menu substitutions that fit comfortably alongside the mock apple pie, such as tomato-juice cocktail instead of oyster stew for the Thanksgiving table, or a mock duck consisting of a creatively rolled and stuffed flank steak.

Aunt Sammy's radio show started to fade away in the mid-'30s, but before that she shared insights on how to make every scrap of food count and how to use ingredients that saved precious time, effort, and money. Doing so quickly became a hallmark of Depression-era cooking. Another example of this necessary ingenuity that started popping up in home kitchens? Substituting packaged crackers for apples in pie, of course.

It was finally time for this pie to shine yet again! In home kitchens defined by cheap ingredients and creative substitution, the mock apple pie once more could be a useful way to re-create the familiar staples of the family table, even during a time of severe want. To be honest, it's unclear if the pie was "rediscovered" during this era, or if it was something that had always been known but not as popular until it became practical. Either way, it's remembered by Americans as being most closely associated with this decade, even if that's not the true story of its origin.

Despite how strongly mock apple pie is linked to the Great Depression, there actually aren't that many direct accounts of the pie itself from this time period. Struggling families, of course, didn't have their on-the-fly recipes reflected in national cookbooks or publications, and, in that sense, it can be difficult to determine just what people were baking day-to-day.

But truly, this recipe's status as an icon of the Great Depression may actually be due to the public boost of a national food corporation (more on that in a second) and the myth that subsequently arose around it, and less to do with the overwhelming frequency with which it was made at the time.

Does that make it any less notable? I'd argue no, because overall, the mock apple pie fit squarely into the broader trend toward "mock" foods that naturally erupted during this period. Imitation foods were nothing new in American cuisine—recipes for things like mock turtle soup appeared long before the Great Depression (again with the obsession with turtle soup!)—but their usefulness made them extremely popular during the decade. Like the innovative tips for acorn coffee and the like included in the *Confederate Receipt Book*, the suggestions were both creative and confounding. One Minnesota community cookbook shared a recipe for Mock Turkey Legs and Mock Maple Mousse, for instance. Another cookbook, published in Cincinnati, offered a recipe for Mock Lobster Soup made, inexplicably, from a combination of pea soup, tomato soup, cream, milk, and sherry.

These mock recipes demonstrated the desire to reproduce classic favorites and the necessary shortcuts to do so. That desire, in fact, is key—these approximations of varied and distinct dishes were a way to keep the taste buds and the spirit alive, in addition to the body. Cheap, bulky staples like beans and rice might fill a person, but when they were constantly consumed meal after meal, did they really satisfy them? One popular folk song, "Beans, Bacon and Gravy," summed up the era's eating conditions this way: "Beans, bacon, and gravy / They almost drive me crazy," adding, "As for pies, cakes, and jellies, we substitute sour bellies." In the end, food was about more than just nutrition for many people, especially during such a stressful and emotionally turbulent time.

In particular, pie became a breeding ground for economically friendly adaptations. It is, after all, one of the most familiar and comforting dishes in the American diet. Not to mention that, like a true chameleon, the dish can shape-shift to circumstance and ingredients, and thus new trendy stars emerged beyond the mock apple pie. These include the mock mincemeat pie, an iteration meant to evoke the classic English-style staple, as in the community cookbook *Choice Recipes*. Another frequent meaty stand-in was chopped green tomatoes.

In addition, there was vinegar pie, a pantry-friendly dish often made with basics like eggs, sugar, vinegar, water, and butter. One community cookbook, *The Benkleman Cook Book*, included multiple recipes for vinegar pie submitted by various members of the community. Alongside those recipes were other thrifty desserts like Eggless Pumpkin Pie, Poor Man's Pie (notably made with apples, in direct opposition to the whole point of the mock apple pie), that old favorite Mock Mince Pie, and a recipe for Apple Pie Dessert made with only egg whites, flour, sugar, salt, baking powder, and nuts. There was even, apparently, a kidney bean version of pecan pie (!), in which, according to Southern foodways writer Kathleen Purvis, "the cheap beans take on the crunchiness of nuts."

These pies are specific examples of a broader genre of pies that emerged amongst the food shortages of the Great Depression. "Desperation pies," sometimes referred to as "nothing-in-the-house pies," were a popular staple in the 1930s, so called because they were made with just a few simple and inexpensive ingredients when there seemed to be—unsurprisingly—nothing in the house. Folklorist Emily Hilliard, who has written extensively on the anthropology of pie, describes nothing-in-the-house pies this way: "A genre of pie . . . that became popular during the Great Depression and, with a dose of ingenuity, were made from few, inexpensive ingredients. The name speaks to our practical home-baker sensibilities, roots in the history of pie, and appreciation for all the women and men, past and present, who have used their ingenuity and wit to make something delicious and beautiful with what they have."

Though all of these pies were widely baked and endure to this day, most of them sort of faded out of the rotation of everyday staple pies made with little thought and regarded without much fanfare. Vinegar pie, one might argue, is almost so basic as to not really be paid that much attention. The exception to this trend, however, is the mock apple pie, which is often cited as the quintessential "Great Depression pie." And one of the reasons mock apple pie stands out from these other Depression-friendly pies (besides being the most nifty) was that it got somewhat of a mainstream boost. It came, naturally, from a packaged cracker brand: Ritz Crackers.

Like all those desperation pies, Ritz Crackers were specifically attuned to fraught economic conditions—and related dietary habits—of the era. The popular product was introduced to the American market by the National Biscuit Company in 1934, still in the midst of the Great Depression and alongside a glut of packaged convenience foods continuing to flood American diets. Other low-cost products of the era included Miracle Whip (1930), Twinkies (1930), Honey Maid Graham Crackers (1934), and SPAM (1937).

These debuts also marked the emergence of supermarkets, which provided cheaper processed foods for families—things like prepared mixes, precooked meats, canned goods, bottled gravies, and more. Now I should note that America, as we know, was already trending toward processed foods; this simply continued that existing trend, spurred on by the immense economic challenges families faced.

Those folks running Ritz knew exactly how to appeal to households with little in their pantries and less in their bank accounts. Though the product was just a simple cracker, Ritz was marketed to struggling families as an inexpensive indulgence, with one 1936 ad promising, "see how they bring out hidden flavor in soups, salads, cheeses and even the plainest economy dishes." One newspaper advertisement boldly proclaimed that meals, spreads, drinks, and cheese "gathers glamour from Ritz." Even the name itself was meant to conjure decadence and wealth—reportedly born from a company-wide cracker naming contest, it's said to have come from Manhattan's posh Ritz-Carlton Hotel, naturally.

The cracker itself also evoked a little bit of extra indulgence. Unlike plain-Jane soda crackers (the original choice for mock apple pie; the dish was sometimes explicitly named Soda Cracker Pie in old recipe books), these were butter crackers, crispy and flavorful. And while the idea of a cracker being a luxury seems a bit funny—no matter how buttery it might be—I don't think many families were too picky back then. They'd take their treats where they could get them. And at an affordable nineteen cents a box, Ritz really was achievable for most consumers, especially since Nabisco was the only baking manufacturer who had the resources to produce and distribute nationally at the time.

Keeping in line with all the other food corporations shilling their product through recipes (remember, this is the same decade Karo debuted the legendary pecan pie), Ritz eventually starting printing recipes for mock apple pie on its labels. It's a bit unclear when this practice actually started. Most peg the year at 1935, one year after the crackers first hit shelves, but it's also possible it didn't happen until World War II, slightly after the Great Depression but still during a time of struggle, scarcity, and sacrifice. As such, it's fairly impossible to know just what exactly the first iteration of the printed recipe said, but here's one version that has appeared on Ritz packaging (date unknown):

Mock Apple Pie
NO APPLES NEEDED!
Pastry for two crust 9-inch pie
36 RITZ CRACKERS
2 cups water
2 cups sugar
2 teaspoons cream of tartar
2 tablespoons lemon juice

Grated rind of one lemon
Butter or margarine
Cinnamon

Roll out bottom crust of pastry and fit into 9-inch pie plate.
Break RITZ CRACKERS coarsely into pastry-lined plate.
Combine water, sugar and cream of tartar in saucepan; boil
gently for 15 minutes. Add lemon juice and rind. Cool. Pour
syrup over crackers, dot generously with butter or margarine and sprinkle with cinnamon. Cover with top crust.
Trim and flute edges together. Cut slits in top crust to let
steam escape. Bake in a hot oven (425°F.) 30 to 35 minutes,
until crust is crisp and golden. Serve warm. Makes 6 to
8 servings.

Regardless of when, exactly, the recipe made its first packaging appearance, its presence illustrates the extent to which mock
apple pie had become part of the mainstream culinary canon. Prior
to its debut on the Ritz Cracker box, mock apple pie had been a
sort of local legend. It didn't appear in mainstream cookbooks of
the era, nor did it really boost itself into the official cooking classics. (I mean, it *was* a pie made out of crackers, after all.) Rather,
it remained an underground sort of dish. It's possible there was
some sort of shame associated there—who wants to admit they
can't scrape together the ingredients for a classic apple pie?—or
perhaps it just hadn't reached the mainstream public. Either way,
the pie hit a new level when Ritz decided to use it to sell its products.

For many bakers, the pie's association with Ritz eventually
came to be its defining feature. The pie was sometimes referred to
specifically as Ritz Cracker Pie, like in the 1947 cookbook *Treasure
of Personal Recipes,* which included both a Ritz Cracker Pie and a

Ritz Date Pie with no crust. The Ritz Cracker Pie as shared in this cookbook, as a matter of fact, was made in a different way than most mock apple pies (with stiffly beaten egg whites), which means it's possible that Ritz was either tinkering with the classic recipe in some of its promotions, or, more likely, the idea of Ritz Crackers being baked into a pie had become so common and accepted by the mid-'40s that women were putting their own personal spins on the concept. Intrigued? Here's how it went:

> 3 egg whites, beaten stiff
> Gradually add ¾ cup granulated sugar. Beat well. Fold in:
> 20 Ritz Crackers, rolled fine
> ¾ cup chopped nuts

> Spread in buttered nine inch pie pan. Bake 35 minutes at 350 degrees. Top with whipped cream or ice cream.

Recipes like these also marked a change, because now the defining benefit of such a pie recipe wasn't that it tasted just like apples, it was that this pie made out of Ritz Crackers just tasted good, period. Which speaks a lot to the new ways of cooking and baking that American women were pursuing in the mid-twentieth century, something we'll dive into much more deeply in the next chapter.

In time, as World War II came to an end and life returned to normal, the overall need for mock apple pie faded, and the dish lived on mostly as a fond memory and occasional promotional device for Ritz. It's even been featured in marketing materials for the product into the twenty-first century, curiously lauded as a holiday recipe. (I love my family, and I love this pie, but if they ever served me a fake apple pie instead of the real thing while we're holding a once-a-year celebration, I'd riot.) But in a time of industrial food and global capitalism, the idea that one might ever need to swap crackers for apples just to be able to make a pie is somewhat old-fashioned. Even the economic crisis of the 2008 recession didn't cause people to resort to such means.

And yet, pie always finds a way. In the early days of the COVID-19 pandemic, in 2020—when life was suddenly turned upside down not by war, nor the stock market, but disease—the mock apple pie enjoyed a mini-resurgence among a number of other crisis recipes like water pie and cake pan cake, many of which can be traced to the Great Depression as well. The circumstances weren't entirely the same: It wasn't that people couldn't afford apples, but rather that they were too scared to venture outside for new ingredients for fear of a deadly virus. And even then, it's not that there was a particular *need* to make mock apple pie or other simple recipes like vinegar cake, another Depression-dessert that popped up again for a brief period of time. Rather, stuck at home, bored and terrified, home cooks engaged in a sort of historical cultural retrospection, looking to the past as a way to cope with the present. As one small news outlet rather succinctly reported about a local resident who suddenly found himself with a lot of time on his hands, "Ritz Cracker Mock Apple Pie [was] part of forced time-off creations."

In March and April 2020—when the panic and strangeness of quarantine was at its height—one food outlet ran a series on "historic dishes born from tough times that you can make at home," promising readers they could "use every last crumb with these feats of culinary creativity." Among those dishes featured were mock apple pie (duh!), sugar cream pie (another classic desperation pie), salt-rising bread (useful when there was literally no yeast to be found), and nothing soup (brilliant name). Of these historic dishes, one of the series authors, Luke Fater, wrote, "They're our ticket out of this mess. The better we are at staying home and stretching what ingredients we have, the sooner we can all get back out there and have someone else do the cooking. After all, it's not the first time we've faced down a situation like this. History has given us lessons. Now it's our turn to eat them."

RITZ MOCK APPLE PIE

Adapted from Ritz Crackers

MAKES ONE 9-INCH (23-CM) PIE

I know that, after all this, you're probably still doubting that the mundane collection of ingredients below can be transformed into a filling that comes anywhere close to apples. Have faith. It will work. And trust me, it'll be incredibly fun to have people try to guess what your pie is made out of. (No one will get it right!)

2 All-Butter Pie Crusts (pages 12–13)

2 cups (400 g) sugar

2 teaspoons cream of tartar

1½ teaspoons ground cinnamon

Zest of 1 lemon

2 tablespoons freshly squeezed lemon juice

36 Ritz Crackers

2 tablespoons unsalted butter, cold, cut into ¼-inch (6-mm) chunks

1 large egg, lightly beaten, for brushing the crust

Preheat the oven to 425°F (220°C). Line a 9-inch (23-cm) pie pan with one of the prepared crusts.

In a medium saucepan over medium-high, combine 2 cups (480 ml) water, the sugar, the cream of tartar, and the cinnamon and bring to a boil. Reduce the heat and simmer for 15 minutes. Stir in the lemon zest and juice. Remove from the heat and let cool for roughly 10 minutes.

Break the crackers into coarse pieces, then place into the prepared crust.

Pour the syrup over the crackers in the crust. Dot the filling with the butter.

Top the filling with the second pie crust, sealing and crimping the edges. Cut vents into the top crust, then brush with the beaten egg. Bake 30 to 35 minutes, until the crust is crisp and golden. Let cool until it's not too hot to handle, then cut and serve warm.

INDIANA SUGAR PIE

DESPERATION PIES CAME in all sorts of styles and flavors, united by their ability to provide pleasure with easily accessible ingredients. They were eaten across the country, but in the Midwest, one particular pie outlasted pure usefulness to become a sweet state symbol.

Indiana's sugar pie—affectionately known as Hoosier Pie—didn't originate during the Great Depression. Like mock apple pie, it was baked in the nineteenth century; in this case, the early 1800s. Some people claim the Shakers that settled in eastern Indiana first introduced the pie; others say it was the Amish in the northeast of the state; and still more people assert it was actually North Carolina Quakers who brought the recipe to Indiana. Either way, it's pretty clear the pie has been enjoyed since the early days of Indiana's history, possibly even before it officially became a state in 1816: One of the oldest recipes for the dish comes from *The Hoosier Cookbook*, which was technically first published in 1976 but contains a sugar pie recipe supposedly dating back to 1816.

Sugar pie is made with the most elementary of baking ingredients: flour, dairy, and sugar. It's a dead simple pie—filled with a sweet (duh) and creamy filling—but nevertheless enticing. As with our fake apple friend, the pie underwent a resurgence in prominence during the lean years of the Depression, when its simple and afford-able ingredient list made it a dinner table darling.

But its sweet star only continued to rise after the early '30s. Most importantly, one of Indiana's most famed sugar pie bakers started selling its wares just after this culinary crisis. Wick's Pies in Win-chester began making sugar pies in 1944 and hasn't stopped since; with a total pie count of ten thousand a day, the bakery is believed to be the world's largest sugar pie producer.

In addition to being called Hoosier Pie, sugar pie goes by a few other names throughout the state: sugar cream pie, transparent pie, and (my favorite) finger pie, since the filling can be mixed with just one's fingers. Steeped in nostalgia, the rich dessert is so embed-ded in the culinary traditions of Indiana that the Indiana Foodways Alliance has a Hoosier Pie Trail, mapping out places to enjoy this local delicacy.

With each stop at the dozens of establishments marked on the trail, you'll find a familiar pie with slightly different embellishments. Sugar, after all, is technically the only consistent ingredient in this widely baked pie. The dairy can be either milk or cream, and season-ings such as cinnamon, nutmeg, and vanilla rotate in and out based on preferences. Sometimes a thickening ingredient like flour or corn-starch is added. (For what it's worth, Wick's includes shortening in its recipe.) And, most controversially, an egg may be used. Some Indianans, however, claim that a filling made with eggs is actually a custard pie, and should *not* be called a sugar pie.

In Indiana, sugar pie is serious business . . . and all the sweeter for it.

CHAPTER EIGHT

JELL-O PIE

"AT LAST!" THE illustration proclaims, the two words a bright, eye-catching red that leaps out from the page. "A creamy-dreamy coconut pie you can make at home—in minutes!"

Attention: caught.

The pie in question looks classic enough. A circle of nondescript cream filling, garnished with a ring of whipped cream and a smattering of some unidentifiable red substance that might be sprinkles or might just be an illustrated artistic flourish. (Plus, the red goes well with the rest of the text on the page. Appearance, you know, really is everything.)

Other bits of text surround the pie. "A thrifty treat!" shouts one line. "Tastes homemade!" adds another. In an additional abuse of exclamation points, the dessert is described as "a luscious homemade coconut cream pie like you never had before!"

The orgasmically effusive praise makes sense, though. Because doesn't this solve everything in your life? Haven't you been agonizing over how to make a mouth-watering, irresistible pie for your family in your home kitchen, squeezed into the scant amount of time you have to bake? Isn't the pursuit of a perfect pie pretty much the main concern of your day-to-day existence?

Never fear: Jell-O is here to solve all your worries.

Because this luscious pie and over-the-top text comes, naturally, from an advertisement. An ad for Jello-O Coconut Cream Pudding & Pie Filling tucked into the pages of *Good Housekeeping* in 1951, to be more specific.

The filling, the ad assures, takes just five minute to make. All you need to do is add milk, and this big, beautiful pie could be yours (for a low and sensible price, the ad is quick to emphasize).

The unquestionable star of the spread is the pie, of course, accompanied by a ramekin of coconut pudding in the background, because this stuff is nothing if not versatile. There's an illustration of the Jell-O pudding box too—above all the goal is to make money. But there's one other figure tucked into the full-page spread, the only sign of humanity in the frame.

It should come as no surprise that the figure is a woman. More specifically, a housewife. And when I say housewife, I'm talking about the most basic sketch of a mid-century white housewife you could picture: tidy blue dress that falls past her knees, neatly tied stark white apron, hair pinned back, obnoxiously beatific smile, and homemade pie cradled in her outstretched, giving hands. Just in case, you know, it wasn't already obvious who this advertisement was directed toward.

At one point on the page, the Jell-O coconut pie is described as "quicker, easier, more economical—and a beauty besides!" All worthy attributes for a pie, sure, but it's not a stretch to say these qualities were also for women themselves to aspire to. Because we've now entered the 1950s, an era that meant a lot of different things to a lot of different people, but for a certain subset of middle-class white families signaled suburbs and suppertime, stability—and stereotypes.

And amidst a redefining (or recommitment) of domestic American values, pie emerged not just as a symbol, but as a cash cow. With its wholesome comfort, patriotic zeal, and gendered associations, it became something of a Trojan horse for food corporations to sell more products by capitalizing on its mass appeal and the societal expectations of women of the era.

Now, I know what you're thinking. Hasn't this already been happening for a while now? Isn't this how not one, but two pies already got popular: Karo's pecan pie and Ritz's mock apple pie? To which I say, first of all, thank you for paying attention! And secondly, yes, you are absolutely right! The seeds of this story were already planted in prior decades, because pie and capitalism have been around since the very beginning of our country. But as America entered the postwar era, two things happened to these commercial pie promotions. To begin with, they exploded; suddenly, advertisements for pie made with store-bought products were *everywhere*, particularly in the pages of magazines. And secondly, they shifted. The demands of marriage and motherhood have always been embedded in culinary advertising (remember the ludicrous health claims Karo used to make to get women to feel better about serving literal corn syrup to their kids for breakfast?), but starting around the 1950s that connection became overt.

Bolstered by the changing domestic landscape of a large swath of the American population, food corporations began blatantly tailoring their advertising to women laboring at home to sell product, frequently using pie as a vehicle to do so. Why? Because pie was a potent symbol of successful American family life. Remember all the patriotic zeal of the pumpkin pie chapter? Exactly. One quote shared in Sherrie A. Inness's *Dinner Roles* sums it all up: Cookbook author Jessie DeBoth wrote in her 1951 book *It's Easy to Be a Good Cook*, "[Pie] symbolizes so many things: the energy and effort of the woman [a man] married; her wish to give him the utmost in eating enjoyment; her competence in fitting a pie into her never-ending day of homemaking."

For further context, "American as apple pie" had already become a national phrase by this time as well (more on the how and why of that particular story in Chapter Twelve). And some brands even got explicit with this symbolic association: In the 1950 *Betty Crocker's Picture Cook Book*, a chapter header on pie called it "a symbol of good eating in a good land." The fictional Crocker went on to add, "If I were to design a coat of arms for our country, a pie would be the main symbol . . . Every American home has its favorite pie."

As a result, women were burdened by the societal expectation to bake pie for their husbands and children—to prove their worth, to prove their love, and to prove their skill. Not only did products like Jell-O's magical pudding and pie filling mix make successfully achieving that mission guaranteed, but it also offered a much less lofty advantage: a shortcut that made baking easier, more time-efficient, and cheaper. What Jell-O and other corporate food advertisers sold was a better pie, and thus a better housewife. The concepts were inextricably linked.

To really understand why and how such pie promotions played out, we've got to first situate ourselves in this profoundly unique era. In the grand landscape of twentieth-century history, the 1950s tend to be a bit of flyover country. I mean, try comparing it to events like two literal world wars. But just because the drama was more small-scale doesn't mean it wasn't there.

Our previous destination was the Great Depression, and between that deeply traumatic experience and where we find ourselves now was, obviously, yet another traumatic experience: World War II. Like all wars, its reverberations echoed long after the last gunshot, and when men returned home from Europe, it was to a distinctly different country. One in which (gasp!) women were *working*. In fact, 35 percent of women (including 25 percent of married women) were in the labor force by 1944, a record amount. That number quickly plummeted, as women returned to their traditional roles at home now that the boys were back to take over their perceived rightful place in the workforce. Those women who did continue to pursue employment or educational advancement were accused of symbolically castrating American men, while working women were called a "menace" and a "disease" in the pages of magazines like *Esquire* and *Life*. (It would appear many social critics of the day could have used a dictionary to look up the actual meaning of their word choices before putting pen to paper.)

Meanwhile, the housing boom sparked by the GI Bill for returning soldiers accelerated the development of suburbs, which provided an affordable solution for families looking to settle down. *White* families, that is. Because in addition to affordability, suburbs also offered exactly what a lot of white people were looking for: a convenient separation from the rising number of Black residents living in urban centers after moving to work in Northern wartime factories. White flight was in full swing this decade.

Soon, the postwar baby boom erupted, and the American population spiked. And as women toiled away at home with all those squalling babies and hungry mouths, American society both implicitly and explicitly promoted the good old-fashioned ideal of married women as homemakers and mothers. As one 1957 cover story for the *Saturday Evening Post* asserted, "It is the duty of every girl to talk to boys on the telephone, kindle romantic sentiments, round-up potential husbands and thus help perpetuate the race by assuring that by and by she will become a homemaker."

Finally, American domestic life was also shaped by the other major political development of the era: the Cold War. Stalking the

American consciousness was a crippling fear of the communist bogeyman, as the United States fought to ward off any possible encroachment on its sterling and definitely not hypocritical values of freedom and self-determination. Naturally, the antidote to communism was simply more capitalism. America leaned full tilt into the sacred act of buying things, a trend that did nothing but help the continued rise in corporate food products that shaped pie-making of the decade. With per capita income rising—it grew by 35 percent between 1945 and 1960—there were even more disposable dollars for people to spend on their love of country (and pie).

But even beyond just a clear and explicit devotion to capitalism, the Cold War also bolstered the identity of the wholesome suburban family as an answer to communism's threat. As Stephanie Coontz recounts in *The Way We Never Were: American Families and the Nostalgia Trap*, during his 1959 "kitchen debate" opposite Soviet leader Nikita Khrushchev, Richard Nixon proclaimed that the suburban home embodied the essence of capitalism; in particular, he noted that the system was "designed to make things easier for our women."

Now, I want to be very clear that this domestic trend and housewife track wasn't all-encompassing. The postwar years didn't send every woman back home to the kitchen, nor did it mean a comfortable, bland middle-class existence for all Americans. To solely abide by the pervading cultural domestic stereotypes of the decade flattens the perspective into something very simplistic, while the reality for most American women was much more complex than what's often portrayed. During the 1950s and '60s, women participated in trade unions, the Civil Rights Movement, civic reform, and movements for peace; and at the time, many women still sought wage-earning jobs outside the home. Meanwhile, poverty affected 25 percent of Americans—up to fifty million people, many of whom had bigger concerns than how to make a perfect pie or occupy oneself as a stay-at-home mom. Ultimately, the pristine "Leave it to Beaver" version of America so popularized in this period didn't exist for most people in the United States.

But for a certain subset of the American population—you know the one: white, middle class, straight, suburban, Christian—this reality was true and very potent. Suburban "family values" certainly reinforced ideals like conformity and like-mindedness, and those values were perpetuated even more aggressively by brands looking to sell as much of their products as possible. It's these women who food advertisers zeroed in on, and thus it is their experience that this chapter will be examining.

The push toward domestic female conformity came from all directions, many of which were beyond a woman's personal circle. Cultural figures including, of all ladies, Eleanor Roosevelt (!) had promoted the ideal as early as 1933. In her book *It's Up to the Women*, written with a clear focus on financial efficiency for an audience in the Great Depression, she firmly instructed, "Too much emphasis cannot be laid on the importance of the preparation of food and the choice of food where the family is concerned . . . it is fairly important that the mother study all the latest suggestions in the way of inexpensive and yet nourishing meals."

Even education, typically a means of eventually securing lucrative employment, became a training ground for future housewives. With a rising number of women going to college, educators suggested they should be receiving better instruction in domestic arts. That way, they would be fully prepared for their lives after graduation, when they would trade their careers for marriage and motherhood (who needs one of those fancy things like a job, anyway?). I mean, there was literally a film called *Why Study Home Economics* released in 1955. Unsurprisingly, home economics became a prominent, widely taught subject directed only toward female students. (In 1970, it became required for both boys and girls.)

Beyond the classroom, women's magazines were also a particularly pervasive breeding ground for this sort of traditional domestic mindset, both in their editorial pages as well as in their accompanying advertisements. Such ads shilled everything from cleaning products to kitchen appliances—anything associated with home-based labor (not that anyone would ever actually refer to it as *labor* . . . caring for your loved ones was a privilege). And leaping out from those pages, with colorful illustrations and blazing text and so many extraneous exclamation points, were magical food products that would make a woman's life better. Many of which were used to make pie.

Frozen orange juice pie. Fruit basket pie. Fruit cocktail eggnog pie (I don't discriminate against pies, but WTF). Even our good friends at Karo Corn Syrup popped up with a pastry innovation for their products: the Karo Ko-Ko-Nut Pie. (And in case you're wondering, they did decide to stick with the dubious health claims: The tagline at the bottom of the advertisement read, "Karo supplies vital food energy . . . right thru life!")

While pie, of course, wasn't the only dish used to sell corporate food products, it was incredibly prominent. Knox Gelatine, for whom pie was a true favorite, even offered a free "Treasury of Pie Recipes" in the pages of one 1956 magazine. Upon mailing in the coupon attached to the ad, a woman would be granted "a refreshing array of Chiffon and Cream Pies, and special holiday candies, all in the color-illustrated Recipe Bulletin of sweet-tooth treats."

Several things were typically included in these ads, most of which took up a full page in their respective magazines. There was an illustrated photo of the pie itself, almost always with a slice already neatly cut to showcase how it would be served. The pies were eye-catching but never elaborate, boasting simple flourishes like whipped cream or a lattice crust. They were clearly homemade and boasted none of the intimidating finesse of a professionally prepared pie. In other words, they were something you—yes, you!!—could make.

As long as you have Crisco or a packet of Jell-O in your pantry, that is.

Which ties into the next element trumpeted by these ads—the inevitable product callout. Alongside that perky pie illustration was frequently an accompanying image of the actual product responsible for such an irresistible dessert. And who were the main culprits? There was the crust camp: Gold Medal Flour, for instance, and Crisco, who declared their shortening was "the sure way to Perfect Pie Crust." Perhaps even more frequent were ingredients designed for the pie filling itself. Karo Corn Syrup, as mentioned, went beyond pecan to offer other pie innovations. Carnation Evaporated Milk also popped up, in one instance used to make "high and fluffy" Frosty Fruit Pies (and known today as a primary ingredient in custard-style pies like pumpkin or chocolate). Knox Gelatine was another highly prominent brand, a staple in delicate chiffon-style pies (shoutout Monroe Boston Strause!). The gelatin company actively leaned into its role as a housewife's companion, even releasing corporate cookbooks like 1963's *Knox On-Camera Recipes: A Completely New Guide to Gel-Cookery*. (Naturally, there were quite a number of pies included.)

Perhaps the biggest poster boy for this corporate pie takeover was Jell-O. Like most industrial-era foods, Jell-O became a prominent force in American cuisine because it made a difficult and time-consuming culinary process quick and simple. Instant gelatin checked all of the boxes of the time period's domestic needs: efficiency, cleanliness, order, and affordability. But beyond the culinary benefits inherent in Jell-O's original gelatin products, the company took an extra step to cater to women's domestic needs by broadening its offerings to include pudding mixes, pie fillings, and even a low-calorie option for topping pies: Dream Whip. (One ad boasted it could be used both on *and* in pies for "magic lightness.")

As a result of its keen ability to serve women's needs in the kitchen, "Jell-O was all but universal" writes culinary historian Laura Shapiro in *Something from the Oven*. The brand molded itself over the course of the early twentieth century, peaking in sales in the early 1960s. As Laura Schenone explains in *A Thousand Years Over a Hot Stove*, "Pliable in spirit and texture, it could form itself to the trends of any generation—not unlike the stereotypes of women. During the 1920s, it had been dainty. During the 1930s, economical. During the 1940s, quick. Now, during the 1950s, JELL-O was light-hearted and comforting, perfect for a generation struggling with the memories of war, fear of communism, and worry that an atom bomb might fall."

Another key element of these pie-centric advertisements was the recipe itself. Jell-O promoted recipes for classic pies like lemon meringue and tasty inventions like Butterscotch Cream Pie. And they couldn't be simpler. To make that butterscotch one, all a woman had to do was "prepare 1 package Jell-O Butterscotch Pudding and Pie Filling as directed. Turn into a baked 8-inch pie shell. Chill. Top with sweetened whipped cream." No matter your skill in the kitchen, or lack thereof, surely such a simple pie was still within reach. And it was impressive too—the plethora of pie recipes shared in 1963's *Joys of Jell-O* cookbook almost all harp on the dessert's ability to impress a crowd while still fitting into a busy schedule. It's notable, too, that amidst the vast array of dessert recipes shared in that book—everything from Rainbow Cake to the Cherry Cheese Charmer—the only one to explicitly use the term "homemaker" in the headnote is a pie recipe. That specific pie was Grasshopper Pie, which Jell-O proclaimed was "a gourmet's delight that can be a busy homemaker's specialty."

The inclusion of recipes was both practical—*we'll show you just how simple it is to make this pie by giving you all the steps right here*—and also purposeful. Because the reason these brands sold pie ingredients and not, say, frozen pies already prepared, was because women were so burdened by the expectations of being a wife and mother that they couldn't simply defrost a pie to serve to their family. That was too easy. It was too impersonal. It was cheating. It was even, for some women, simply boring.

This balance between baking and buying boils down to one of the chief anxieties for many housewives during this period. If one of the primary caregiving roles of a woman was to cook and bake for her family, was she failing to meet those standards if she didn't actually do much cooking or baking in the kitchen at all? As Laura Shapiro has written on this phenomenon, "The faster the cooking, the less it was going to feel like real cooking and the greater the potential for guilt on the part of the homemaker." Simply adding water and mixing up something like a pudding mix wasn't enough effort for women to feel that they had successfully fulfilled their cooking responsibilities. To solve this problem, products incorporated extra labor to create full dishes like a pie, while still keeping the process and subsequent results simple and uniform.

According to Shapiro, corporations introduced the concept of "glamorizing" to elevate the perception of commercially processed products. By turning a mix or processed ingredient into something greater than the sum of its parts, recipes had a whiff of gourmet to them, rather than merely mundane. And a pie fit that bill quite nicely. The dessert had multiple components, unlike a simple stir-and-serve dish. There was the crust, then the filling, and possibly a topping. And it was easy to dress up without the need for too much skill or effort. Rather than, say, elaborately assembling and decorating a layer cake, a woman could artfully apply some whipped cream and a garnish (not coincidentally, exactly like the pie described in the Jell-O ad at the start of the chapter) and be proud of her pie's ultimate appearance. Pies were meant to be rustic and homemade, after all. Made with an ingredient like Crisco or Knox or Jell-O, they were accessible and achievable, while still being impressive.

This targeted appeal wasn't just some vague projection on the part of companies and copywriters, either. Advertisers acutely understood the burdens and anxieties of the women they were shilling their products to, and they tailored their pie advertisements accordingly. In one section of *The Feminine Mystique*, Betty Friedan shared an extended look at the thought process of one ad man on how to sell a baking mix to housewives. According to him, "Stress should be laid upon the cooking manipulations, the fun that goes with them, permitting you to feel that *X Mix baking is real baking*." (Emphasis mine.)

The concept of "real baking" was utterly fraught, and a point of true concern and consideration for a lot of women. In *Something from the Oven*, Laura Shapiro recounted how one *Boston Globe* article of the decade that praised the beneficial science of modern-day food products was met with vehement backlash by female readers, who decried the loss of classic baking and cooking as a result of these new modern offerings. Elsewhere in *The Feminine Mystique*, Friedan shared one woman's fond recollection of what "real baking" meant to her: "The way my mother made them, you had to sift the flour yourself and add the eggs and the butter and you knew you'd really made something you could be proud of."

If a woman just slapped together something out of a baking mix, could she really be proud of that? And on a much darker note, would she be abandoning her family? After all, how much could she really love her husband and kids if she wouldn't even deign to spend some time baking them a pie?

Such considerations were a point of crushing guilt for many women. Ever ones to exploit the debilitating burden of being a woman in the United States of America, those wily little buggers down at the ad agency seized on that guilt as an opportunity to make even more sales.

The ad man quoted in *The Feminine Mystique* suggested that instead of soothing women's guilt, companies should simply transfer it instead. Tell women that *not* to take advantage of all the different uses a mix offers actually means you're limiting your effort to make your family happy. He explained: "Rather than feel guilty about using X Mix for dessert food, the woman would be made to feel guilty if she doesn't take advantage of this opportunity to give her family 12 different and delicious treats." By upcycling processed ingredients and using them to make baked goods out of actual recipes, like the multitude of pies printed in the pages of domestic magazines, a woman proved "her personal participation and her concern with giving satisfaction to her family," as Friedan explained.

This all feeds into the broader concept of "creativity" that percolated around the role of women in the home, including how it related to pie. Faced with the drudgery of housework, many homebound women found that, unsurprisingly, their lives seemed to be devoid of a ton of meaning. Everybody told these women they should be fulfilled catering to the needs of their families, but what if . . . they actually weren't? Don't worry—advertisers already anticipated that, too. By overlaying their products with a shiny veneer of creative possibility, corporations turned seemingly mundane tasks like pie-making into projects of endless possibility. Wasn't a wife clever and talented, after all, to be able to tear open a small packet of gelatin and use her skill to create a delicious, eye-catching dessert? Friedan's advertising buddy (I don't think they were buddies) summed it all up: "The appeal should emphasize the fact that X Mix aids the woman in expressing her creativity because it takes the drudgery away." As he further explained, "We help her think of the modern home as the artist's studio, the scientist's laboratory." In other words, an equivalent to the workspace of a much more accomplished (and possibly fulfilling) profession.

Advertisers recognized that women yearned for creative expression and personal fulfillment—you know, basically the exact kind of benefits they would receive from careers outside the household. So instead, they just decided to give it to them in a branded recipe like Pumpkin Dream Pie instead. Colorful, shimmering, ethereal products like Jell-O only further emphasized pie's new (very much manufactured) artistic bent. Shapiro hit the nail on the head: "Above all, creativity was the fairy dust that would transform opening boxes into real cooking."

The irony of it all, of course, is that food brands pedaled conformity just as much as creative freedom. Isn't the whole point of these scientifically manufactured products, after all, the fact that they work perfectly every time, for everyone? The same could be said of each pie recipe tucked in the pages of each *Good Housekeeping* magazine read all across the country. Your neighbor Gail made a perfect custard pie during last week's dinner party? *Guess what, ladies, so can you.*

Along similar lines, an emphasis on competition and appearances was threaded throughout pie advertisements, many of which explicitly focused on a woman's hosting ability. Because nothing counted more than showing off and showing up when company came over. And pie, with its communal nature and American wholesomeness, was the perfect dessert for such occasions. Even more so because pie-making was frequently the barometer by which a woman's baking ability (and thus status as a homemaker, and thus status as a human worthy of American society) was measured. (There was literally an old American folk tune that asked a young man intent on marrying his sweetheart: "Can she bake a cherry pie?") So corporate brands offered reassurance; alongside one recipe for Brown Derby Black Bottom Pie (shoutout Monroe Boston Strause . . . again), Knox Gelatine promised, "This scrumptious pie will add stature to your reputation as a hostess."

Accompanying the recipes and the illustrations of the pies themselves, the final piece of these pie advertisements (forgive me for the pun) was the copy. And here's where things went from subtle to super in your face. Corporate pie ads almost always included words and phrases that touched on the superlative benefits that made these dishes better than your average pie. You know, things like "close to magic," "so easy," "perfect," "economical," and more. One Karo ad went full hype person, telling the assumed reader, "Lady, you're *in* . . . as a champion pie-baker." Cue the hair flip. In other words, they explicitly appealed to the expectations of contemporary womanhood, and they told you just how these pies (and the products they were made from) would help you achieve them.

And I guess it's worth noting—though you probably already assumed this based on quotes like the one previous—that the copy explicitly addressed women as their primary demographic. This included claims like "more women cook with Crisco than any other brand of shortening" and images of homemaking women beaming out from the page directly to the reader. Another advertisement bragged "homemakers voted this one of the best Betty Crocker pie recipes of all time." In a world shaped by conformity, the immense pressure to follow what everyone else was doing—even in pie-making!—was inescapable (and profitable).

The claims of exemplary taste and foolproof success were fairly obvious, but interestingly enough, there were also frequent references to the economy of products and pies—emphasis placed on the fact that not only would this dish please the family with its taste and appearance, but it would also be a sensible budget decision as well. Such characteristics appealed to women tasked with making their husbands proud by smartly and efficiently spending the money he worked so hard to earn. One 1950 ad for Gold Medal Flour, adorned with a resplendent slice of orange pie, declared the product and accompanying recipe would help a woman "avoid costly baking failures"—both literally and figuratively. As the ad explained, "The flour you use in a recipe costs but a few cents. Yet if it fails, your baking can fail—and ingredients costing many times as much may be wasted." By relying on not only Gold Medal's trusty flour, but also on the accompanying recipe, a woman could ensure she wouldn't waste ingredients and money on an unsuccessful pie. A great baker *and* smart with money? What a lady!

As industrialized food products embedded themselves more deeply into the culinary arsenal of American housewives, they started showing up beyond the paid-for promotions of magazines: Now, brands popped up in the pages of cookbooks as well.

Some of these were cookbooks proffered by culinary corporations themselves, carrying on a long tradition of products burrowing themselves more deeply into the American kitchen through branded cookbooks. Betty Crocker was a particularly prolific proponent of this tactic. There were tons of Betty Crocker cookbooks published during this time designed specifically to help women bake and cook. And not just simply succeed at that one act . . . Betty Crocker was also there to ensure a reader was the perfect wife and the perfect mother. For beyond just simple directions on how to bake a successful cherry pie, Betty took things a step further, like a page in the Beginner's Luck section of *The Bisquick Cookbook* on Breads a Bride Can Bake. The handful of recommended recipes were accompanied quite helpfully (it wasn't helpful) by an illustration of a blonde woman in full wedding dress and veil baking, sporting the biggest smile you've ever seen, while her perplexed husband (still rocking his nuptials tux) looks on from the background.

Meanwhile Wesson Oil, which sold a type of "pourable shortening," published a 1955 cookbook called *Quicker Ways to Better Eating: The Wesson Oil Cookbook* that, naturally, included a section on pie. One came complete with an illustration of a housewife rolling out pie dough while her young son observes, and noted, "There's warm and happy satisfaction when the pies we bake for our families come out of the oven as perfect and pretty as we hoped." And thanks to Wesson Oil's "famous" stir-n-roll method, women could make a pie crust deemed "fast," "a real time-saver," and "simple and sure." In fact, "nine out of ten women who've tried Stir-N-Roll say even beginners can make successful pastry the first time they try," proclaimed the cookbook. With Wesson, who needs good old-fashioned butter?

And then there were regular, non-branded cookbooks that still took up the mantle of female domesticity and spoke directly to the narrow role women were expected to play in the kitchen. Like 1956's *To the Bride,* a non-subtle directive on how to achieve marital bliss through homemade food. As bad as you might be thinking this book's approach was, trust me, it was worse. It was the kind of book that opened with a note from the editors that read, "Soon you will reach that day for which you have planned and dreamed since you were a little girl . . . Your Wedding Day!! . . . You are about to assume the most important role of your life . . . The composite role of sweetheart, wife and mother." In one whimsical poem, the editors assured the reader that "The talented gal / Who can whip

up a pie, / Rates a well deserved rave / From her favorite guy." Cue
the eye rolls.

In its chapter on pie, *To the Bride* spoke to the importance of
pie in a wife's repertoire, as well as the common anxieties around
the dish: "Pie is a challenge to any bride because it is one of America's favorite desserts." Thankfully, this book would enable women
to summit the pie peak and overcome their pastry fears, with the
help of not only carefully constructed recipes but also . . . wait for
it . . . food brands! That's right, the recipes filling *To the Bride*'s
pages were stuffed with specific recommendations for culinary
convenience products, ranging from Blue Bonnet Margarine to
Kellogg's Corn Flakes to that old standby, Knox Gelatine. Their
presence proved these products had officially leapt from beyond
the pages of mere magazine ads and corporate cookbooks to firmly
embed themselves in the ways in which housewives baked.

IN THE END, not every woman took the bait. I mentioned at
the beginning of this chapter that the bland, monotonous ideal
of a perfect housewife tending to her family in the middle of a
cookie-cutter suburb wasn't the reality for every woman—or even
most women—in the postwar era. And similarly, there were women
cooking and baking at home who simply didn't like to cook and
stubbornly refused to give in to the prevailing domestic stereotype
they were expected to uphold. To them, convenience products didn't
replace personal passions and the freedoms of the world—they
made them easier to achieve for a more fulfilled life.

The spokeswoman for such ladies was Peg Bracken, the hilarious author of the *I Hate to Cook Book* (1960). In her chapter on
desserts, she wrote in a pure voice-of-a-generation monologue:

I understand that the ready-mix people, through exhaustive surveys, learned that most women prefer not to have the entire job done for them. The theory is that if women realize they haven't done a thing besides add water, mix, and set the pan in the oven, they miss the creative kick they would otherwise get from baking that cake or pan of muffins . . . But so far as we are concerned—we ladies who hate to cook—they needn't have bothered. We don't get our creative kicks from adding an egg, we get them from painting pictures or bathrooms, or potting geraniums or babies, or writing stories or amendments, or, possibly, engaging in some interesting type of psycho-neuro-chemical research like seeing if, perhaps, we can replace colloids with sulphates. And we simply love ready-mixes.

In the chapter that followed, Bracken shared numerous easy dessert recipes and a rant on cheese trays. There wasn't a single recipe for pie.

JELL-O COFFEE 'N' CHOCOLATE CREAM PIE

From Jell-O advertisement in
Better Homes and Gardens, June 1956

MAKES ONE 9-INCH (23-CM) PIE

If you're skeptical of Jell-O pies, don't be. This one is genuinely delicious. Creamy, light, and flavorful, it threads the needle of homemade and convenience—exactly what this company was aiming for. And you know what? It's a simple process that results in a no-fail, thoroughly tasty pie. That's something we can all embrace. Also, serving with whipped cream (or Cool Whip, to really double down on the convenience angle) is highly recommended.

1 All-Butter Pie Crust (pages 12–13)*

1 package (3.4 ounces/96 g) Chocolate Jell-O Pudding and Pie Filling

1 package (3.4 ounces/96 g) Vanilla Jell-O Pudding and Pie Filling

1 tablespoon instant coffee

2 tablespoons granulated sugar

PRE-BAKE THE CRUST: Preheat oven to 375°F (190°C). Line a 9-inch (23-cm) pie pan with the prepared crust. Trim excess dough and crimp the edges. Line the crust with parchment paper and fill three-fourths of the way with pie weights or an equivalent, like dried beans or rice. Chill for 30 minutes. Bake for 20 minutes, then remove the parchment

* Feel free to lean in to the spirit of this recipe and go with a store-bought crust (either pastry or graham cracker)—no one's judging here.

paper and weights and continue baking for 15 to 20 minutes. Let cool completely before adding the filling.

MAKE THE FILLING: Prepare the chocolate pudding mix according to the package directions. Pour into the pre-baked crust, and refrigerate 5 to 10 minutes, until softly set.

Prepare the vanilla pudding mix according to the package directions. Mix in the instant coffee and sugar. Pour over the chocolate filling, and refrigerate about 3 hours, until fully set. Top with whipped cream to serve, if desired.

CHAPTER NINE

BEAN PIE

IF YOU DRIVE through the right parts of South Los Angeles, walk certain stretches of Brooklyn, or spend time on particular corners in the South Side of Chicago, you might encounter clusters of men in dark suits on the corner, proffering bean pie to pedestrians and drivers passing by. There's a jovial nature to their business, and pies often come with a newspaper circulated by the Nation of Islam and a good-natured, "Bean pie, my brother?"

It's a practice that stretches back decades, a tradition imprinted on generations of Nation of Islam members. For many, selling bean pie on the street is like a rite of passage. In fact, it's almost secondary that the bean pie is delicious (though it is—creamy, rich, and sweet, like a better, much more complex sweet potato or custard pie. And no . . . just because it's made from beans does not mean it tastes like dinner; consider the many sweet bean desserts in East Asian cuisine). The origins of the pie itself, the money it raises, the people who have made it and eaten it—all make it much more than just a curious dessert.

The bean pie's basic ingredients are simple: navy beans, sugar, eggs, milk, spices, and a whole-wheat crust. The execution is also straightforward, much like that of other custard-style pies. But the deceptively simple pie is one of the most enduring symbols of revolutionary Black Power in the twentieth century. It has been sold on street corners and in high-end restaurants. It has been referenced in television shows and rap music, and Will Smith feasted on it with friends on *The Fresh Prince of Bel-Air.* Boxer Muhammad Ali even blamed one of his most famous losses on it. Today, it continues to be sold in bakeries and outside mosques, an enduring symbol of protest and revolution.

The bean pie first came to prominence through the Nation of Islam, the Black nationalist and social reform movement founded in 1930, and its history is intertwined with the legacy of this influential and controversial organization. To understand the bean pie, we must first dive into the complex, inspiring, frustrating, and sometimes downright weird history of the NOI.

Despite its prominence, the Nation sprung from rather obscure and somewhat curious origins. In 1930 in Detroit, a little-known Black salesman named Wallace D. Fard began preaching a Black-centered mythological origin story that reframed race relations. According to Fard, the Black population originally lived in peace before the white race was created by an evil wizard named Yakub. This devilish, blue-eyed race eventually seized power, which it had held for the last six thousand years, and systematically enforced the widespread oppression of Black people. Fard preached that this reign was drawing to an end, and followers should prepare for an epic struggle between the races in which the Black population would take control, ending white domination and reasserting their rightful dominance. As part of this origin story and supposed natural racial divide, Fard argued that Islam was the true religion of the Black population, and that Christianity was only for whites—a tool through which they enforced their dominance.

Stories of evil wizards and apocalyptic race wars might have seemed farfetched, but Fard's teachings were intertwined with doctrines of Black independence, justice, and equality, and as a result his words quickly caught on. He attracted followers who identified with his messages of Black nationalism, ideas that aligned with the kind of Black separatism advocated by activists like Marcus Garvey earlier in the century.

While the organization he founded continues to this day, Fard himself didn't last long. In a move befitting the mystical bent of his teachings, he disappeared without a trace in 1934, leaving his dedicated disciple Elijah Muhammad in charge of the burgeoning Nation of Islam. It was a position he would occupy for the next four decades. Under Elijah Muhammad's leadership, the Nation continued to advocate for Black independence, and the organization backed up these messages through concrete measures like buying land, establishing temples, and even organizing an elite paramilitary unit, the Fruit of Islam, which doesn't sound all that aggressive but could be downright intimidating. By putting economic and militaristic weight behind its words, the NOI evolved into a group with real influence and power, despite its small size.

Then, in the 1950s, the Nation of Islam experienced a meteoric rise, largely on the back of its most promising young orator, Malcolm Little, later known as Malcolm X. You, uh, might have heard of him.

Having converted and joined the Nation of Islam while serving a prison sentence in Massachusetts for grand larceny and breaking and entering, Malcolm X ascended rapidly in the organization after his release from jail in 1952. He traveled the country on behalf of the NOI from Chicago to Detroit to Philadelphia, recruiting new members in the process. And the hard work and long hours on the road paid off. His charisma, oratorical skills, and unapologetic assertions of Black superiority proved irresistible for many, especially amidst the ongoing turmoil of the Civil Rights Movement, and the Nation's membership skyrocketed. According to historian John Henrik Clarke, "Malcolm X preached black pride, black redemption, black reaffirmation . . . [He] instilled admiration and pride in most black Americans." Though Malcolm X eventually left the Nation in 1964 and was assassinated by one of its members just a year later, he left an indelible mark on the organization and its philosophies, vaulting it into the national spotlight.

Eventually, under the continued leadership of Elijah Muhammad (a big theme of this story is the continued leadership of Elijah Muhammad), the Nation grew to become one of the largest and best-organized Black organizations in the country, and its influence challenged prominent philosophies that had shaped the Civil Rights Movement of the 1950s and into the 1960s. With its emphasis on beliefs like Black supremacy and self-reliance, the NOI represented a profound shift from strategies promoted by groups like Dr. Martin Luther King Jr.'s Southern Christian Leadership Conference. Where King had preached nonviolence and peaceful integration, the NOI vehemently argued for self-defense and Black separatism. But as Malcolm X had written in his memoir, *The Autobiography of Malcolm X*, they were both fighting for the same outcome, however different their methods: "The goal has always been the same, with the approaches to it as different as mine and Dr. Martin Luther King's non-violent marching."

With its more radical approach, the NOI promoted fiery rhetoric that uplifted the Black population but could also be deeply divisive, and as a result the group was steeped in controversy. Coupled with leaders' emphasis on self-defense and militant power, the organization was frequently denigrated as a hate group, and was even the subject of a 1959 television documentary titled *The Hate That*

Hate Produced. And indeed, rhetoric could imply harsh violence, with Malcolm X's famous declaration of achieving equality "by any means necessary" taken to include violence, among other methods. King called it "a hate group arising in our midst that would preach the doctrine of Black supremacy." Despite what Malcolm X wrote in his autobiography, things weren't exactly hunky dory amidst these Black leaders and their followers.

As one of its most distinguishing doctrines, the Nation preached a separatist movement that rejected all enforced elements of white society, from clothing to surnames to religion to food (which extended to pie). Instead, it advocated for a new Black identity free from the legacies of enslavement. Christianity, for example, was abandoned in favor of Islam, and surnames given by slave owners were famously replaced by an X. According to NOI leaders, only through such radical separation from white society could Black people elevate themselves from whites' ongoing oppression.

Across the country, the Nation of Islam's followers took steps to eradicate white influence from their lives. Most prominently, the promising young Black boxer Cassius Clay converted to Islam and adopted a new moniker, Cassius X, and eventually, Muhammad Ali. You, uh, might have heard of him as well. "Cassius Clay is a slave name," said the brash twenty-two-year-old. "I didn't choose it and I don't want it." Nor did he want the white man's religion, either.

The movement away from white society extended to all aspects of life, including music, fine arts, literature, and fashion. Wrapped up in the racial pride of the burgeoning Black Power movement, almost every element of daily culture became a tool of protest and a canvas of racial expression. Including pie.

Pie eventually became so prominent in the Nation of Islam because a follower's diet was promoted as one method to embrace this new identity. In the 1960s, during the peak of the Civil Rights

Movement, soul food had been championed by many middle-class Black Americans, who asserted that this style of traditional cooking was a way to honor their roots. As a result, many Black-authored cookbooks of the decade featured recipes for dishes like collard greens, macaroni and cheese, fried chicken, and, perhaps most famously, sweet potato pie (the importance of which you hopefully recall from our earlier chapter).

With the onset of the 1970s and the continued rise of the Nation of Islam, however, diets—and by extension, pies—changed. As part of their newly constructed Black identity, the Nation's leaders began advocating for a new Black diet; they argued that many dishes and ingredients traditional to Black foodways, particularly soul food, were relics of the "slave diet" and had no part in the lives of contemporary Black Americans.

In fact, leaders connected soul food to the medical woes that disproportionately affected the Black community, blaming classic dishes' higher salt, fat, and sugar content for chronic diseases like high cholesterol, high blood pressure, hypertension, and obesity. Soul food, the Nation's leaders believed, was just another means through which whites sought to control and destroy the Black population. They argued that it killed Black people and made white doctors and undertakers rich. As Elijah Muhammad wrote in his seminal two-book series, *How to Eat to Live*, "You know as well as I that the white race is commercializing people and they do not worry about the lives they jeopardize so long as the dollar is safe. You might find yourself eating death if you follow them." A touch dramatic? You bet. But Elijah Muhammad did have a point, and his words resonated.

Sadly, a dish like sweet potato pie, full of fat and sugar and directly traced back to plantations, embodied these problems almost more than any other. As Elijah Muhammad wrote, ". . . sweet potatoes and white potatoes are very cheaply raised foods. The Southern slave masters used them to feed the slaves, and still advise the consumption of them." But when one (oven) door closes, another one opens: With the rejection of sweet potato pie and soul food came the rise of a new pie that would reshape Black American culinary traditions.

In order to replace the oppressive "slave diet" that he railed against, Elijah Muhammad created his own radical—and perplexing—new diet for his followers to adhere to, one influenced by both health and identity. In *How to Eat to Live*, which was pub-lished in 1967, Muhammad emphasized vegetarianism, consuming whole grains and vegetables, and limiting sugar, processed grains, and traditional soul food ingredients, like sweet potatoes, corn, col-lard greens, and pork—the latter of which was vehemently forbid-den to Nation members in accordance with Muslim law. Alcohol and tobacco were also prohibited. In their stead, Black chefs cooked with ingredients like brown rice, smoked turkey, tahini, and tofu—which, as Black culinary historian Jessica B. Harris writes in *High on the Hog*, "appeared on urban African American tables as signs of gastronomic protest against the traditional diet and its perceived limitations to health and well-being, both real or imagined." These alternate ingredients transcended the table to become symbols of the new Black power movement.

It should be noted that the trend away from soul food to a new Black cuisine was not isolated to the Nation of Islam. In the late 1960s and '70s, other Black food activists such as Dick Gregory and Dr. Alvenia M. Fulton began distancing themselves from tra-ditional soul food and its complicated history in favor of healthier diets more in line with traditional African cuisine. Because most people could not trace their ancestry directly to a single country, however, this new African diet was broad and flexible, often cen-tered on ingredients more than specific techniques or dishes. Like the Nation's Islam-inspired diet, vegetarianism was a central tenet, as well as overall healthier foods like whole grains and fresh vegetables. *Ebony* even published a 1974 report on the subject titled, "A Farewell to Chitterlings: Vegetarianism is on the Rise Among Diet-Conscious Blacks."

The Nation of Islam, however, took things a step further by folding diet into its core philosophy, using food as a powerful tool of the new Black identity it championed. The NOI's training program for new converts, for instance, included a significant focus on nutrition. Fasting became a prominent practice as well, taught as a way to train both the body and the mind; in this way, dietary enlightenment became linked to spiritual enlightenment. NOI leaders, meanwhile, incorporated the message into their teachings. At one point, Muhammad Ali gave a speech at Howard University in which he decried eating pork and made fun of fellow Black Americans for eating pig feet. Much like his race-inflected taunts toward Joe Frazier in the boxing ring, Ali's comments were harsh, mocking, and rooted in his own superiority. There's a reason he was The Greatest, not The Kindest.

The NOI even linked meat consumption in general to white brutality and barbarism. While meat wasn't technically outlawed for followers—only pork—Elijah Muhammad scorned it, declaring it un-nutritious. Whites, he argued, were the original carnivores. Malcolm X also associated killing and hunting for meat with whites' violent and animalistic nature: "They're blood-thirsty, they love blood . . . I've watched them; when I was a little boy, I lived on a farm with white folks. When they shoot something, they just go crazy, you know, like they were really getting their kicks." No wonder he was so persuasive, when he was throwing around imagery like that.

Beyond just dietary habits, the Nation of Islam also used food to fight for social and economic equality, targeting all aspects of the food system, from production to purchase. They opened restaurants that became economic centers in urban Black neighborhoods, and the Nation's newspaper, *Muhammad Speaks*, included calls for followers to pursue self-sufficiency by cultivating their own food. The initiative was referred to as "Muhammad's Program" (after Elijah Muhammad, not the prophet).

Recognizing that food insecurity contributed to economic oppression and the devastating health consequences that afflicted the Black community, the Nation also took to the fields, buying farms across the South whose yields were used to feed the Black population. Part of a broad program of economic nationalism, the Nation's farms encouraged land ownership and self-sufficiency, which historian Jennifer Jensen Wallach recounts in her analysis of this movement, "How to Eat to Live: Black Nationalism and the Post-1964 Culinary Turn." In addition, the NOI founded Black-owned grocery stores and even a fish-importing business. With each farm, venture, and dish, they were taking charge of another level of a vertically integrated system to create a separatist food system isolated from white influence, a core tenet of Black power.

The Nation's emphasis on nutrition and the switch to healthier foods had a tangible effect on its members, and many testified to the profound change they experienced after embracing the new diet. Their experiences were published throughout *Muhammad Speaks* as a way to encourage other followers and support the effectiveness of the NOI's teachings (and probably boost Elijah Muhammad's ego in the process). In an article titled "Islam Has Started Life Anew for Me," NOI member Sister Josephine X wrote that Elijah Muhammad had changed her life because he "teaches us the way to prolong our lives while we are steadily killing ourselves by taking into our system the wrong food and liquids."

In another piece, titled "How Messenger Muhammad's Dietary Laws Saved My Life," Brother Allen 3X listed the litany of poor health problems he had suffered—including headaches, heart-burn, and hemorrhoids, a pretty terrible-sounding combination—and how following Elijah Muhammad's prescribed diet had largely eradicated them. In particular, he noted, "I stay off pastries." He concluded, "I write this article because I know that many Black people suffer needlessly from many symptoms that could be eliminated by putting into practice what the Honorable Elijah Muhammad teaches." As a result, "they would bear witness that the Honorable Elijah Muhammad, the last and greatest Messenger of Allah, is fulfilling that prophecy, attributed to Jesus, wherein it reads, 'I am come that ye may have life and life [sic] more abundantly.'"

One can imagine Elijah Muhammad was quite pleased with this particular editorial.

Amidst this broad, impactful shift in diet, the navy bean some-what inexplicably emerged as one of the Nation's most important new ingredients, laying the foundation for the groundbreaking pie that eventually followed. According to Elijah Muhammad, all other beans were divinely prohibited, though he gave no reason for this oddly specific ban. "Do not eat any bean but the small navy bean—the little brown pink ones, and the white ones," he wrote in *How to Eat to Live*. "Allah (God) says that the little navy bean will make you live, just eat them. . . . He said that a diet of navy beans would give us a life span of one hundred and forty years. Yet we cannot live [half] that length of time eating everything that the Christian table has set for us."

Just why, exactly, the navy bean was deemed so sacred remains unclear. Sure, it was a useful source of protein in a diet largely absent of meat, but there's a whole lot of other vegetarian protein options out there. And this particular ingredient isn't mentioned in the Quran or referenced elsewhere in the Muslim faith. In fact, prior to Elijah Muhammad's proclamation in *How to Eat to Live*, the navy bean hadn't played a significant role in the Nation of Islam in any capacity.

Nevertheless, Elijah Muhammad was a revered, totalitarian figure in the organization (four decades in charge, remember?), and his influence over the Nation was total; in all, his declarations could shift the course of the movement. It didn't matter why he said the navy bean was sacred, only that he had said it in the first place. Imagine having that power! Truthfully, the navy bean also demonstrated the complete control Muhammad exerted over the Nation of Islam, and the way he shaped generations of culture simply with his (sometimes, seemingly random) opinions.

As a result of *How to Eat to Live* and the Nation of Islam's emphasis on creating new Black foodways, the navy bean was suddenly used in a number of new Muslim recipes published in cookbooks and pamphlets, including soups, salads, and side dishes. One creative recipe even used the beans to make cake frosting (!). But in the end, it was via the bean pie—a new take on a classic American dish—that the navy bean truly rose to prominence.

The pie's origins are unclear. Lance Shabazz, an archivist and historian of the Nation of Islam, told the *Chicago Reader* that the pie allegedly came from the Nation's original founder, our old mysterious friend Wallace D. Fard, who supposedly bestowed the recipe upon Elijah Muhammad and his wife, Clara, way back in the 1930s. This claim, however, has no concrete proof to back it up. Meanwhile, in one newspaper interview, Lana Shabazz, Muhammad Ali's personal chef, also claims to have invented the dish (more on her baking in a second).*

---

* Some of Ali's confident boasting must have rubbed off on Shabazz—she claimed that "a story about Lana Shabazz will sell more newspapers in New York than a story about Muhammad Ali."

Elijah Muhammad never explicitly mentioned the bean pie in *How to Eat to Live*, but the dish reflected many of the elements of the NOI's diet that he wrote about in his seminal work, particularly its emphasis on health. For instance, it was typically made with healthier ingredients like a whole-wheat crust made with oil instead of butter. In addition, the pie frequently called for brown sugar or natural sugar, which was deemed less harmful than processed white sugar. These details were reflected in Elijah Muhammad's own teachings; he wrote in *How to Eat to Live*, "Pastries and cakes—the kind made with crusts of white flour and sweetened with white sugar, so sweet you can taste them the next day—are not good for our stomachs. . . . Use brown sugar and whole wheat flour for your pie and cobbler crusts."

Paradoxically, however, the bean pie itself was laden with sugar (even if it was technically unprocessed), often including more than a cup in the filling. No matter what kind of sugar you're using, that's never going to be healthy. Curiously enough, Elijah Muhammad had made sugar an important tenet of his dietary teachings, identifying the ingredient as one of the biggest threats to Black health. "You eat too much sugar," he advised in 1970. "That is why we are troubled with diabetes. We eat too much starchy foods, [so] lay off all those sugar and starchy foods." Not only did the bean pie's sugar count directly contradict the health teachings of the Nation's diet, but the legacies of slavery that shaped the sugar industry ran counter to Elijah Muhammad's determination to free Black people from the shackles of enslavement that lurked in what they ate.

I've asked plenty of food historians and bakers about the irony of the bean pie's sugar count, and, to be honest, no one really has much of an answer about how to reconcile this key trait of the dish. The closest I've gotten to any sort of concession is that, in the end, it *is* supposed to be a dessert. Which, to be honest, is exactly the kind of healthy eating philosophy I can get behind!

In fact, the bean pie was one of the only desserts in the Nation of Islam diet, and it quickly rose to prominence in the Black Muslim community. With a rich, custard-like filling from starchy mashed navy beans, the pie was generously spiced and pleasantly sweet. The beans' nuttiness, combined with the warming kick of nutmeg and cinnamon, proved an irresistible dish, and soon, as Jessica B. Harris wrote, it could be found "hawked by the dark-suited, bow-tie-wearing followers of the religion along with copies of the Nation's newspaper, *Muhammad Speaks.*" Muslim bakeries in cities from New York to Chicago offered it to customers; as Black food historian Thérèse Nelson told me when I reported on the pie for *TASTE* a few years ago, "that's where you would go to buy it, like going to get bread."

The bean pie also became a staple on the menus of restaurants owned by Nation members. At the iconic Temple No. 7 Restaurant in Harlem, for instance, customers could indulge in the restaurant's "original bean pies" or other health-minded fare, such as whole-wheat muffins. In Cleveland, Shabazz Restaurant & Bakery advertised it was the "home of original bean pies," which it served alongside "Asiatic style and American cooked foods." Later, when the *New York Times* covered the splashy 1995 opening of a $5 million Nation of Islam–backed restaurant in Chicago, the article's headline declared "Bean Pies Have Grand New Home." When asked about the opening, one neighbor summed up the lavish opulence by saying, "It makes you want to get dressed up to eat bean pie."

At these restaurants, the bean pie and the Nation's new diet became not only a tool of Black identity, but also an economic force that revitalized Black neighborhoods and funded the ongoing work of the movement. Just years earlier, the central fight for

Black Americans had centered on their right to dine in white-owned establishments. With the sit-in movement, restaurants became battlegrounds, and war was waged over requests to eat traditional American cuisine—and pie—prepared by white chefs. But now, instead, Black Americans were creating their own establishments and their owns dishes, built from a fully formed Black identity. And unlike the diners and restaurants of the South, these were not intended as settings for interracial cohesion.

Muhammad Ali's chef, Lana Shabazz—the same one who claimed to have invented bean pie in that newspaper interview—was renowned for her version of the dish, and she included a recipe for it in her cookbook, *Cooking for the Champ*. As Shabazz wrote, the pie was a personal favorite of the boxer's, and when he would come to the restaurant where she worked in New York City, more often than not his meal ended with a bean pie. A 1964 *New York Times* profile of Ali, published not long after he publicly announced his conversion to Islam (so recent, in fact, that the title reads "Day with Clay"—willful ignorance of his Islamic conversion or just an admirable journalistic commitment to a catchy headline?), captured the boxer at Temple No. 7 Restaurant eating not one, but two bean pies. In fact, according to Shabazz, he so loved the pie that he even blamed it for his loss to Joe Frazier in the 1971 heavyweight title fight:

> After Ali lost the championship boxing title to Joe Frazier in 1971, he blamed it all on me and my bean pie. I knew he was not supposed to have sweets during training, but he would always ask me to fix it. Sometimes I felt sorry for him and would make a pie, leaving a small slice for him in his cabin. It never failed. The following day he'd announce to everyone within earshot of the camp that I had left bean pie under his pillow.

Eventually, perhaps because it was so distinct or just that delicious, the bean pie became emblematic of the Black Muslim diet—a "juggernaut," to use Nelson's term. Not only could it be found at temples and in bakeries, but it was also a fundraising tool to support the broader mission of the Nation across the United States.

One theory behind the bean pie's potent symbolism is that it not only employs Elijah Muhammad's beloved navy beans but is also believed to use them as a replacement for sweet potatoes, one of the most prominent symbols of traditional Black cooking and a direct relic of the "slave diet." In some ways, swapping sweet potatoes for navy beans in a pie was akin to replacing one's slave name with an X, as Muslim American historian Zaheer Ali has proposed. By baking the pie, Black Muslim Americans rejected the social bonds imposed by white society and instead created a new identity, in the process establishing their own foothold in American culinary traditions.

Despite the powerful symbolism of the dish, the strict standards NOI leaders had set for the pie—namely, that it be wholesome and healthful, and made with all-natural ingredients—were frequently brushed aside. In his book *Black Muslim Religion in the Nation of Islam*, Edward E. Curtis recounts how one former NOI minister came across a version of the pie in Baltimore that was the best he'd ever had. Determined to find out what made it so great, he traveled to the local NOI bakery in Baltimore to unearth the secret . . . only to find that the bakers were using artificial flavoring! He was, needless to say, bummed. According to the same minister, these kinds of variations in ingredients weren't uncommon; often bakeries didn't use brown sugar or a whole-wheat crust, whether because of taste, expense, or both.

In addition to evolving beyond the strict ingredient guidelines of Elijah Muhammad, the bean pie also became so popular that it transcended the narrow confines of the Nation of Islam itself to be served and eaten elsewhere. Bean pie, for example, was served at Tamu-Sweet East, a food and dessert shop operated by The East, a community-oriented Black nationalist space founded in 1969 in Brooklyn. Though the organization had similar principles, it was not affiliated with Nation of Islam, or even Islam itself. Rather, The East served bean pie because it was a familiar dish and culinary touchstone for many customers invested in a new, modern Black identity. Interestingly, this culinary radicalism didn't reach quite as far as the Nation of Islam's; Tamu-Sweet East also offered sweet potato pie, that powerful symbol of traditional Black soul food and a dish firmly denounced by Elijah Muhammad.

Since the 1970s, the bean pie has continued to endure and become a fixture in Black American culture, referenced in rap, comedy, television, and movies. In her song "Just Another Day . . . ," Queen Latifah raps, "Stomach ache, head to Steak-N-Take for a bean pie / Get a Final Call from the brother in the bow tie." (When she performed at NOI leader Louis Farrakhan's alma mater, Winston-Salem State, Queen Latifah was presented with a copy of the Nation's newspaper, *The Final Call*, and—what else?—a bean pie.) Ice Cube proclaimed that "I might start slangin' bean pies" in a "Steady Mobbin'" verse. Meanwhile, in one sketch from *In Living Color* featuring a Star Trek/Nation of Islam mashup titled "The Wrath of Farrakhan," an NOI member dressed in the organization's iconic red hat and bowtie offers bean pie to Star Trek proxies with a classic "Bean pie, my brother?"

Most prominently, the bean pie continues to be served after mosque services and sold on street corners, typically with a copy of *The Final Call*. Today, recipes can still be closely guarded secrets; often a certain level of trust must be earned before you might be gifted a recipe from another Nation of Islam member. Over the years, online outlets and lifestyle gurus have published their own takes on the bean pie, but those are, essentially, irrelevant. When Martha Stewart publishes a recipe for bean pie—described on her website as a "fall-friendly pie" and with no mention of the Nation of Islam—you know it's not the real thing. I mean, I love Martha as much as the next baker, but this is not a culinary matter in which I trust her expertise.

Not just relegated to mosques and street corners, the bean pie is also sold at many landmark Muslim bakeries, such as the iconic and sadly closed Your Black Muslim Bakery in Oakland and Abu's Homestyle Bakery in Brooklyn. Abu's Homestyle Bakery, curiously enough, didn't even sell bean pies when it first opened in the late 1990s. The community's imam, however, told the owners they couldn't have a Muslim bakery without selling bean pie, and so they sought a recipe from one of the community's elders, who had been a member of the Nation and thus privy to the recipe. After some cajoling, they were granted the traditional recipe, and once introduced to the menu, the pie quickly became a hit.

Idris Braithwaite, who now runs Abu's after taking over from his father, says that the bean pie is, in fact, more American than apple pie. Apple pie, he points out, has origins in England (see Chapter One), whereas bean pie originated in America. And, as Braithwaite told me when I first wrote about bean pie for *TASTE*, it's all about "being creative, being innovative, taking sort of what you've been presented with and making something unique and awesome."

And on top of all that powerful symbolism, he said that the bean pie also "happens to be a great dessert. It tastes wonderful, it looks nice, it smells wonderful. And so, it's all that and then some."

BEAN PIE

Adapted from *Cooking for the Champ: Muhammad Ali's Favorite Recipes* by Lana Shabazz

MAKES ONE 9-INCH (23-CM) PIE

This pie is smooth, sweet, and rich—extremely comforting, which may not be the first thing you think of when it comes to a pie made from beans. When you blend the mixture, make sure it's totally smooth, as you don't want any chunky bits of bean to ruin the texture. Oh, and if you're training for a heavyweight title fight, maybe wait to make this until after you win.

For the crust
¾ cup (95 g) all-purpose flour
½ cup (65 g) whole-wheat flour
1 tablespoon granulated sugar
½ teaspoon salt
8 tablespoons (1 stick/115 g) unsalted butter, cold, cut into
    ½-inch (12-mm) chunks
4 to 8 tablespoons (60 to 120 ml) cold water

For the filling
8 tablespoons (1 stick/115 g) unsalted butter, room
    temperature
1½ cups (300 g) granulated sugar
2 tablespoons ground cinnamon
¼ teaspoon ground nutmeg
1 tablespoon cornstarch
¼ teaspoon salt

3 large eggs

1½ cups (275 g) canned navy beans

1 cup (240 ml) evaporated milk

1 teaspoon vanilla extract

Zest of 1 lemon

MAKE THE CRUST: In a large bowl, combine the flours, sugar, and salt. Add the butter to the flour mixture and lightly toss until all the butter is coated in flour, then use your fingers to work the butter into the flour, smashing the butter into flat pieces as you do so.* Do this until you have a crumbly mixture that's still full of large, visible butter chunks, about the size of dimes or lima beans.

Drizzle in the cold water 1 tablespoon at a time, lightly stirring the mixture until you have a shaggy, mostly cohesive dough. It's okay of there are still dry patches—in fact, that's ideal. Gently form the dough into a disc, then wrap tightly in plastic or a reusable alternative and chill in the refrigerator for at least 30 minutes before using. You can store the chilled crust in the fridge for a few days before using and a few months in the freezer.

Preheat the oven to 425°F (220°C). Roll out the pie crust on a lightly floured surface until around 12 inches (30.5 cm) in diameter, then use it to line a 9-inch (23-cm) pie pan. Trim excess dough and crimp the edges. Place in the refrigerator while you make your filling.

MAKE THE FILLING: In a food processor, blend the butter and sugar. Add the cinnamon, nutmeg, cornstarch, and salt, blending until combined. Add the eggs, one at a time, and blend, waiting until each egg

---

* Working the butter in with your fingers can be physically difficult for some people, so you can easily do this part with a pastry cutter, food processor, or even in the bowl of your stand mixer.

is thoroughly combined before adding the next one. Once all the eggs have been added, use a spatula to scrape down the food processor and blend again until smooth.

Add the beans, and process until the mixture is completely smooth. Add the evaporated milk, vanilla, and lemon zest, and blend until completely smooth.

Pour the filling into the prepared crust. Bake for 5 minutes. Lower the oven temperature to 325°F (165°C) and bake for 45 minutes more. Let cool completely before serving.

CHAPTER TEN

QUICHE

IN OUR PATRIARCHAL society, Americans often assume pie is made by women. But they also assume the dish is enjoyed by everyone. Men and women, city dwellers and rural recluses, families both rich and poor. Sure, certain pies have been geared toward certain populations, like the bean pie we just talked about. But for the most part, they're not bound by rules of consumption.

Until a young humorist by the name of Bruce Feirstein* dropped a satirical book in 1982, and an unprepared American public suddenly had very strong opinions about who could, and more importantly, couldn't, eat pie. Specifically a rustic, egg-based, savory French version: quiche.†

---

* Feirstein went on to have quite the prolific career, including writing three James Bond movies and consulting on national security for the US government.
† I know what you're thinking: Is quiche technically a pie? Some people are adamant that it's a tart, while others feel it belongs in its own special category. But pie is a fluid thing, and since quiche is a circular dish with a filling baked in a crust, I'm considering it a pie. And as you'll see throughout this chapter, Americans throughout the years have called it a pie as well, which is good enough for me.

The book in question was literally titled *Real Men Don't Eat Quiche*.* And that title was, essentially, everything readers needed to know about how to be a man in one handy, easy-to-internalize five-word phrase. In addition to banning the consumption of a perfectly innocent savory custard, Feirstein's book—subtitled *A Guidebook to All That Is Truly Masculine*—laid out everything a "real" man did and did not do, such as support feminist movements, "play games with wine in restaurants," or have meaningful dialogues. Other items banned from a truly manly menu, according to Feirstein, included bean curd, tofu, pâté, yogurt, and light beer. And all the way through his book, he lambasted quiche and those who ate it, for instance, declaring that a real man would be an airline pilot while a quiche-eater would be a travel agent.

In case you haven't picked up by now, Feirstein wrote *Real Men Don't Eat Quiche* as a wry joke of a book shrewdly poking fun at masculine stereotypes.† Except that's not entirely how it was received. The book proved immensely popular at the time of its publication: It sold 2.1 million copies and was translated into sixteen languages. It even appeared as assigned reading in a Rutgers University men's studies class. On the back of that success, the saying "real men don't eat quiche" embedded itself into the public consciousness

---

* According to Feirstein, he first wrote the phrase as a line of dialogue in a film script. A studio executive circled the line and wrote, "This is what's wrong with the script. It's not funny." From there, he turned it into an article for *Playboy*, and then into a book.

† It's unclear if Feirstein himself eats quiche. When I asked him, he said via email: "The head of publicity at Simon & Schuster took me out to lunch and issued an edict: 'No matter what anyone asks, and no matter what you eat in private, you say you don't eat quiche, you've never eaten quiche, and you never will eat quiche.' Seems to have worked out pretty well for me, so far."

and became a popular phrase—sometimes entirely unironically. The majority of people who read the book picked up on the satire (it was pretty heavy-handed), but as the title outgrew the confines of the book, many associated the dish with gender performance, particularly in the pages of magazines and newspapers. Feirstein himself doesn't think the book's success actually impacted quiche consumption; he wrote me via email, "I don't believe a single piece of it wasn't eaten, or served, because of the book. But the phrase resonated, and became a shorthand to describe things masculine."

And thus, with that one highly specific dictum, quiche became a shorthand for gender identity and social norms in 1980s America.

TO UNDERSTAND WHY men got so worked up about quiche, you have to look at the environment in which Feirstein wrote his book in the first place. It was a response to the anxiety bubbling up around America over the recent rise of Second-Wave Feminism; across the nation, empowered women were ramping up public initiatives to achieve gender quality in the '60s and '70s by increasing women's possession of economic resources, achieving more access to higher education, paid jobs, and political office, and attaining power and independence. The country was engulfed in a public reckoning over gender roles, tradition, and expectations, and many men, as a result, began questioning just what it meant to be an American man in the first place.

This gender analysis occurred in nearly every facet of life (as Feirstein covered throughout his book), but one key battleground was the kitchen. Amidst broad aims to shift their status in both the public and private spheres, women had begun reexamining and reframing cooking and their relationship to it.

Unsurprisingly, they started rejecting that old housewife role. As one of their methods to achieve personal liberation, feminists sought to share domestic cooking duties with the men in their lives. Basically, the idea was for men to cook half the time, which would change the gendered associations of this culinary work and divorce it from its restrictive feminine associations. This attempted domestic movement saw the rise of terms like "househusbands" and images such as men wearing aprons in *Ms.* magazine. Liberal feminists even published cookbooks that were meant for men to cook from as much as women, which even—hold your hats here— included recipes that had been contributed *by men*. Radical stuff (but seriously, for a lot of people it was).

Needless to say, the movement to get men in the kitchen didn't exactly catch fire. In part because—shocker—men enjoyed being shackled to the home about as much as women had. Said one man who switched places with his wife to start working at home: "My biggest emotional letdown was when I realized I had completely supplanted my own career goals with my wife's. When she put on her white coat, it was great for her, but there was not a whole lot there for me. I felt empty."

With all these new rules about what men should and shouldn't be doing to promote a more equal society, there soon arose a specter of the "new man," one who was sensitive, emotionally aware, and gender egalitarian. "In the 1970s," wrote Barbara Ehrenreich, "it had become an article of liberal faith that a new man would eventually rise up to match the new feminist woman, that he would be more androgynous than any 'old' variety of man, and that the change, which was routinely expressed as an evolutionary leap from John Wayne to Alan Alda, would be an unambiguous improvement." (Alan Alda, for what it's worth, was frequently dissed in *Real Men Don't Eat Quiche.*)

This "new man" identity coincided with a rising focus on health and fitness in men, which came about during an increase in national conversations on nutrition and weight. Suddenly confronted with these new expectations for how they were meant to exist in American society—not to mention all the new ways women were asserting *they* should get to exist in American society—men launched a public questioning of their masculine identity. And from this questioning and anxiety there sprung a reactionary movement of "men's liberation."

Instead of bending to the will of these bra-burning feminists and their sissy male allies, many American men dug their heels into the traditional identities they had always embodied. Real men weren't weak or emotional; they were strong, mighty, virile, and definitely in control.

Ultimately, Feirstein's *Real Men Don't Eat Quiche* was published as a satirization of this mindset amidst changing national trends. And quiche became one of the primary symbols through which to engage in this dialogue, thanks to the negative connotations it bore with everything from France to vegetarians.

THE MARRIAGE OF food and gender was a part of American cuisine long before Feirstein started satirically defining which foods could and couldn't be considered manly. In the first half of the twentieth century, American culture began assigning gender associations to food and food preparation, organizing them neatly along the lines with which most of us are familiar. The main message, of course, was that cooking was for women, not men. But this period of time also saw the organization of foods themselves into narrow definitions of gender, a message spread through a combination of cookbooks, advertisements, and women's magazines.

Specifically, the press started emphasizing that women should consume foods that were delicate, fanciful, and ornamental. Meanwhile, the husbands, boyfriends, and other men in a woman's life needed heartier, more substantial food for their rough-and-tumble manly activities. As an example, some of the female-oriented dishes that popped up as early as the 1910s included tomato and cucumber jelly salad, lemon honey tarts, crystallized strawberries, and pink frosted cakes; far on the other end of the spectrum, masculinity was associated with (what else?) steak.

So men and women had been bound by arbitrary definitions of what was and was not socially acceptable for them to eat for decades, and both genders already operated within these constructed culinary lines by the time Feirstein's book rolled around. Perhaps none of these rules, however, struck such a strangely specific, not to mention resonant, chord. And of course, all that history still begs the question: Why quiche? It's heartier and more wholesome than delicate and dainty. Wasn't there a more feminine dish (or pie) Feirstein could have picked on?

Ultimately, there were four primary reasons why quiche was cast in the titular role of an anti-masculine villain in the early 1980s: It was a tired fad, a staple of counterculture cuisine, frequently vegetarian, and, perhaps most damning of all, it was French.

First, the meteoric rise and tragic fall of a shining culinary star. Emerging from the bland cookie-cutter food of the 1950s, American cooks entered the '60s with a new interest in gourmet cooking, one that employed foreign ingredients and lots of time and was actually, you know, creative. To spark their interest and rev their appetites, cooks began looking beyond America's borders for inspiration, and one of the first places they did so was France. This decade saw the rise of Julia Child, the beloved evangelist of French cuisine and staunch proponent of scratch-cooking with whole ingredients. In 1961, volume one of her landmark work, *Mastering the Art of French Cooking*, was published, with volume two following in 1970. Between her books and her television show, *The French Chef* (which ran from 1963 to 1973), Child helped shift the American culinary consciousness away from pre-boxed mixes to a more creative, internationally inspired cuisine.

It wasn't just Julia who did so, either; Pierre Franey's "60-Minute Gourmet" column began running in the *New York Times* in 1975, for instance. In addition to the passionate advice doled out by such professional cooks and their cookbooks, Americans also expanded their palates a little wider while traveling, as the rise of postwar tourism in Europe had helped them broaden their horizons before bringing home a new appetite for foreign foods.

Bolstered by this new interest in creative, gourmet international cuisine, quiche arrived in the United States. The dish had been popular in Europe for centuries, of course, particularly in France, Germany, and Switzerland, but it hadn't hit America until the twentieth century. Even still, it really didn't gain a strong foothold until the '50s and '60s. When it did, however, it was with a huge splash. Quiche started trending across the country in the '60s and '70s, popping up on restaurant menus and home dinner tables alike. As a 1995 *Los Angeles Times* article put it, "Back in the disco days, quiche was the white three-piece suit of the food world. It was every home cook's solution for what to serve for brunch and every cafe's solution for what to pair with a salad for the daily lunch special. It was omnipresent." The article also called it the "quintessential '70s cliché." (Shots fired at ABBA.)

During this heyday, quiche morphed from a traditional European dish with standard variations (like Lorraine and Alsatian) to little more than a blank canvas into which chefs and home cooks could stuff every filling ingredient and flavor combination imaginable. Soon, you could hardly throw a rock without hitting some form of quiche on a cafe menu, and by the time the early '80s arrived, "Americans had been served too many quiches," wrote Sylvia Lovegren in her book *Fashionable Food: Seven Decades of Food Fads*.

When Feirstein wrote *Real Men Don't Eat Quiche* in 1982, quiche wasn't just a versatile dinner or a random savory pie. It was an aging and tired trend, a fad that was dying an unglamorous death. And as Feirstein noted, "today's Real Man is unaffected by fads or fashion."

Beyond its status as a '70s culinary cliché, quiche was also burdened by other undesirable and unmanly associations. Specifically, its relationship to another emerging phenomenon of the era: the counterculture movement. (We couldn't talk about the '60s without mentioning hippies!)

As young people started protesting war and promoting love, they also began considering the type of foods they were eating. Food was such a focus of their movement, in fact, that author Warren Belasco has used a separate label specific to their culinary revolution: countercuisine. As he explains in his book *Appetite for Change: How the Counterculture Took on the Food Industry*, the countercuisine started in the 1960s and was marked by three hallmarks: avoiding processed foods; making food more fun through improvisation and ethnic or regional cooking; and decentralizing the food system through systems like co-ops, organic farms, and more. There was also a significant focus on vegetarianism, for both health and environmental reasons. As Belasco wrote, "the implicit agenda of the countercuisine [was that] food was a medium for broader change."

Countercultural youth sought to effect this change through a wide variety of methods primarily focused on the foods they ate and how they sourced them. For the sourcing: They grew organic vegetable plots in their backyards and shopped for grains in the bulk-bin section of their local co-op. For the foods themselves: a lot of fruits and vegetables, whole grains, nuts, lentils and beans, and soy milk. Basically, what we would think of as the stereotypical diet of a thirty-something Los Angeles yoga instructor. And there was one additional element: how those foods were prepared. The countercuisine movement delighted in traditional peasant fare and regional country cooking, the kind that featured simple preparation methods and hearty, wholesome ingredients. And, ironically, they also loved French cuisine, reveling in repurposing traditionally "high class" foods for their own purposes. There was an additional practical element to integrating French dishes into the countercultural diet—it was a lot easier to convert people to vegetarianism when the foods they ate were full of rich ingredients like cheese, cream, and eggs (basically the Holy Trinity of the French diet).

So take a movement that values vegetarianism, whole foods, French cuisine, and rustic country cooking, and what do you have? Basically a focus group designed specifically to love quiche. While Julia Child was extolling the virtues of quiche Lorraine to middle-class housewives, hippies were adapting the dish for their own underground use. Soon, quiche popped up on the menus at faddish communal restaurants, like one in Massachusetts that served a "quiche and curry menu" (an almost too-perfect example of the broad international inspiration from which the countercuisine drew). Eventually, quiche became "the symbol of an emerging socioeconomic class, a class of college graduates and young professionals whose eclectic tastes and non-traditional values gave birth to the term 'quiche culture,'" wrote a reporter for the *Burlington Free Press* in a 1983 article titled, "A Question of Quiche." These freewheeling youths—who shirked responsibility and meat in equal measure—were the antithesis to good old-fashioned American values, and their diet represented that un-American (and by extension, unmanly) spirit.

Though counterculturists seized on quiche for a variety of reasons, perhaps the most significant part of its appeal was its suitability to a vegetarian diet. Chock-full of protein-rich eggs and cheese and stuffed with a whole lot of vegetables, it was perfectly suited to those who didn't partake in meat. (Although it must be said that this status as a vegetarian star is somewhat ironic, since the original versions of quiche found in Europe were typically full of rich meats like bacon.) Regardless of this backstory, the American version of quiche—though often served with meat fillings like its European cousins—became linked to vegetarianism, even beyond the narrow confines of the countercultural movement. And vegetarianism, meanwhile, was linked to femininity.

Many scholars have explained the associations of meat with masculinity and vegetarianism with femininity, including the 1980 feminist cookbook, *The Political Palate*, but perhaps none have done so as well as Carol J. Adams in her book *The Sexual Politics of Meat*. In her landmark work, Adams unpacked "the assumption that *men need meat*, have the right to meat, and that meat eating is a male activity associated with virility." (Emphasis hers.) Adams illustrated how the consumption of meat is inherent to maleness, while vegetables are a food for women. Such dietary choices go beyond just what's consumed on the plate to have a tangible impact on the way men and women interact in the world beyond the dinner table. As Adams wrote in the preface to the twenty-fifth-anniversary edition of her work, "Being a man in our culture is tied to identities that they either claim or disown—what 'real' mean do and don't do. 'Real' men don't eat quiche. It's not only an issue of privilege, it's an issue of symbolism. Manhood is constructed in our culture, in part, by access to meat eating and control of other bodies."

The performance of masculinity and the way it played out in what a man ate may seem trivial, but the reality of men's relationships to their diet and its symbolism could be all too real. One American wife recounted the dangerous effects of her failure to provide an adequately "masculine" meal for her husband: "A month ago he threw scalding water over me, leaving a scar on my right arm, all because I gave him a pie with potatoes and vegetables for his dinner, instead of fresh meat." In a less horrifying example of the way such stereotypes perpetuated, Burger King once ran ads railing against "chick foods," as embodied by asparagus quiche. In a completely reasonable display of their maleness, men were also depicted throwing a truck off an overpass. The message was once again clear: If you ate (vegetarian) quiche, you weren't truly a man. Moreover, it's no surprise that bean curd and tofu—two classic meat alternatives—were listed as unmanly foods right alongside quiche in Feirstein's book.

In addition to black marks on its reputation from the likes of hippies and veggie-eaters, quiche had one final fatal flaw, an association so perverse there was no possible way it could ever be accepted by American males: It was French.

This rejection wasn't just some fealty to patriotic duties. Historically, Americans have perpetuated gender-coded stereotypes of France and French culture as overwhelmingly feminine. According to Polly Platt, author of *French or Foe?: Getting the Most Out of Visiting, Living and Working in France*, in an Anglo-Saxon's view, France is the country of four *F*s: food, fashion, fragrance, and frivolity. Plus, a bonus fifth *F*: femininity. Such ideals (regardless of how absurd they are) run counter to the narrow definition of manhood that so many Americans like to perpetuate. Unlike French men, American men (supposedly) don't concern themselves with culture, romance, fine food, or aesthetic details. (In other words, they hate anything pleasurable.) They stand in opposition to the archetype of the French man, who is considered undisciplined, out of touch, impractical, and frivolous—coincidentally the same sort of silly characteristics that plague women. Such stereotypes sound ridiculously childish, but they go all the way back to the days of the American Revolution, when Patrick Henry launched a zinger at Thomas Jefferson by claiming he had an "effete taste for French cookery."

It's no coincidence that Patrick Henry specifically zeroed in on food with that biting insult. Perhaps because of the international culinary reputation France bears for its cuisine, Americans frequently criticize and reject French femininity through its food. The renowned travel writer Rick Steves has, in the past, referred to the classic French dish as "sissy quiches." One man who self-identified as a "mainstream American" wrote a letter to the editor criticizing media coverage of the Persian Gulf War in 1991, in which he proudly asserted, "Most of us would feel much more comfortable sharing a hot dog and a beer with Norman Schwarzkopf than quiche and Perrier with Dan Rather."*

Feirstein, too, brought that stereotype into *Real Men Don't Eat Quiche*, repeatedly dissing the "French maître d'" throughout the book's pages. According to him, the term was "a satiric trope for someone who was snooty and pretentious, who ran a snooty and pretentious restaurant . . . if you're doing a satire about 'Real Men' who eat steak, and drive nuclear waste for a living, a French maître d' is pretty much on the other side of the 'compare and contrast' spectrum."

---

* In addition to quiche and Perrier (the French water has gotten A LOT of heat from "mainstream Americans" throughout the years), another French food considered too fancy for a proper American has been Grey Poupon, which was lambasted by one Texan who didn't realize that the fancy mustard was actually an American product.

While quiche was widely embraced in the United States in the 1960s and '70s, it could never fully ditch its French (and thus feminine) associations. This is perhaps due to the fact that early American quiche recipes were often published in French-inflected books, or at the very least with nods to the savory pie's European ancestry. Examples include a recipe in 1946's *Home Cookbook: French Cooking for Americans* by Louis Diat, and the 1931 edition of *Joy of Cooking*, in which a quiche recipe was accompanied by headnotes detailing the story of the Swiss cook from which the recipe came. And when Craig Claiborne wrote about the dish in the pages of *The New York Times Cookbook* in 1961, he mused, "It seems odd that this very special pie, traditional in France, was so long in gaining popularity in America."

So all in all, quiche pretty much had the deck stacked against it by the time Feirstein set out to write his book. As one 1983 newspaper article summed up in an impressively comprehensive roundup of all these stereotypes, quiche was "a spineless and custard-like substance made of various dairy products and other stuff that leads people to drinking bottled water from France, hanging out in health food stores, jogging and using the word "infrastructure" to distraction." (No idea why the banal term "infrastructure" caught a stray bullet here.)

And yet. Even with all of that—the silly macho American pride and the overly sensitive opinions and the mounting backlash to Second-Wave Feminism—it's still unbelievably remarkable just how much the American public ran with the idea that quiche was the antithesis of manliness after Feirstein's book hit the mainstream.

IN 1983, THE food section of the *Fort Lauderdale News* ran an article titled "Let 'em Eat Quiche," which described how "the epithet of 'quiche-eater' was transformed from compliment to slur." The same article referenced an incident in which daytime talk-show host Phil Donahue was met with an audience's roars when he admitted, "I eat quiche, too," and also cited a joke in *10 to Midnight* in which a tough Los Angeles policeman is mocked by his colleague for eating quiche at the cafeteria; in quick defense of his actions he protests, "I thought it was pie." Ray Hudson, a member of the Fort Lauderdale Strikers soccer team, was quoted in the article saying, "I absolutely don't eat quiche. The most exotic food I eat comes from Burger King or McDonald's. I have a hearty English appetite and I don't go for anything exotic." And one Miami Dolphins defensive player secretly confided, "Yes, I do enjoy quiche but I have never eaten it in public."

Another article, published in 1982, mused, "It's difficult to imagine Clint Eastwood, say, tucking into a slice of zucchini quiche when he could be eating raw sirloin." Indeed, the hallowed image of famous manly men was a key touchstone in many people's opinions about quiche. The owner of a restaurant in Burlington, Vermont, told a local reporter, "Some of the heroes of [my restaurant] the Last Chance have been John Wayne, Johnny Cash, Clint Eastwood—and for the life of us we couldn't picture any of them eating quiche." Needless to say, the dish wasn't on his menu. He even sold a bumper sticker that said, "Ten years in business and proudly not serving quiche."

According to one newspaper, there was supposedly an organization formed in Austin, Texas, called Men Against Quiche, Hairdressers and Other Such, a "consumer organization of sorts" made up of eight or so geologists from the University of Texas. (Evidently, they also hated houseplants; one member declared, "We really have a united front against ferns." This statement may have been in reference to the concept of "fern bars," a pejorative term used to describe preppy or "yuppie" establishments in the '70s and '80s that potentially had homophobic undertones.) Instead of quiche, they enjoyed local staples like "The Hole in the Wall's Reality Sandwich, a chicken-fried steak with cheese and jalapeños served on a bun, and Dirty's O.T. Special, a greasy cheeseburger with two pieces of meat, bacon, lettuce, tomato and mayo." Greasy, spicy, and loaded with meat—that's a real man's kind of meal.

Even those articles that defended the consumption of quiche did so in recognition of the prevailing stereotypes against it. One article that appeared in the *Calgary Herald* asserted "Real Men Do Eat Quiche"; it went on to cite the "real men" who ate the dish and included such characters as "hockey players, construction workers, cowboys, cops, and football players." Indeed, almost all of these quiche defenses tried to make the dish acceptable by leaning into the public perception of what constituted a real man, desperately proclaiming that it was consumed by the kinds of masculine professions a ten-year-old boy might dress up as for Halloween: cops, firemen, athletes, cowboys, and more. A separate article, advocating for the dish ahead of Father's Day, rather dramatically asserted that "rugged, energetic, adventurous and loving fathers—REAL fathers!—do eat quiche." Even when they were arguing in favor of quiche, such authors still did so within the strict gender rules of American manhood, rather than trying to challenge such clearly meaningless conventions.

Others tried to reframe the dish into more masculine terms, like one lighthearted newspaper article that chided men, "You like eggs, don't you? You like bacon? You like pie crust? You put 'em together, you got your quiche." So did another reporter, who tried to convince men to come over to the quiche side of life by imploring,

"Instead of calling it quiche, think of it as a savory pie." To them, the publicly pillaged pastry just needed a little rebranding, demonstrating that the problem never had anything to do with the actual dish to begin with.

In addition to trying to frame quiche as just another savory pie, many defenders harped on its "meat-like" characteristics, quick to point out that although everyone assumed quiche was low-fat and low-calorie, it was actually a heavy, protein-rich food. According to one body builder, quiche was initially described as a "sissy food," but actually it was "good for building muscles." Another newspaper article proclaimed, "Never let it be said quiche is not for real men, especially when it can be made with a He-Man ingredient, spinach. Didn't our mothers tell their sons to eat lots of spinach to build muscles?" In doing so, such articles translated quiche into acceptable manly foods in order to make them more palatable to their audience.

Even women were affected. A newspaper food editor, haunted by the associations tied to a perfectly tasty dish, expressed anguish over developing a quiche recipe: "I thought for a long time before I would confess that I eat these things. I had planned to title this recipe something like egg 'n' pepper surprise or pepper dinner pie, anything to avoid using a name now long-associated with hanging ferns and bentwood chairs." (Again with the potential nod to "fern bars" . . . or just some anti-fern bias!)

If food writers wrung their hands over whether or not to indulge in an egg-based pie, or bent over backward to convince themselves (and everyone around them) that it was actually okay to consume, other Americans latched onto the symbolic power it bore to achieve their own nefarious gains. I'm speaking specifically here of the United States' very own horror movie villain: Phyllis Schlafly.

***

AS SCHLAFLY PLOTTED and schemed her way to blocking the Equal Rights Amendment from passing, she once turned to quiche for a bizarre PR stunt. Putting her Eagle Forum army to work, she delivered fifty quiches to members of the US Senate who supported the reintroduction of the ERA. Affixed to each quiche was a note: "Real Men Do Not Draft Women." According to Noreen Barr, national legislative director of the Eagle Forum, the group wanted to make all the quiches homemade, had time allowed for it. The varieties they ended up delivering ranged from spinach to mushroom.

In response to the delivery, senator Bob Packwood from Oregon declared, "Of course I'm a Real Man . . . and I like quiche. Should women go into combat? That's not even an issue we have to face right now. I'm going to take my quiche home and eat it. . . . It only makes me more determined to support ERA." Senator Dennis DeConcini of Arizona supported the ERA but was unexpectedly snubbed; his lack of quiche led his spokesperson to announce: "We're very upset. Mr. DeConcini always has been and always will be a supporter of ERA. We think we should have our choice of what kind [of quiche]."

As the reporter of an article covering the whole debacle pointed out, Schlafly could have studied her source material a little more closely; Feirstein's later book *Real Men Don't Cook Quiche* asserted, "ERA: Real Men are not frightened to deal with anyone as equal."

Like the myth of Thanksgiving, the debate over whether or not "real men" eat quiche has endured through the decades. The famed James Beard Award–winning chef Gabrielle Hamilton wrote about the dish for the *New York Times* in 2018, and the subsequent article was boldly headlined, "Real People Eat Quiche." While advocating for quiche, Hamilton acknowledged, "I was writing the menu for our lunch service at [my restaurant] Prune a few weeks ago and kept crossing out then penciling back in a classic: quiche Lorraine. I just wasn't quite sure where we stood, as a nation, on the subject these days." She went on to add, "You don't want to go through the considerable work of putting together a warm, trembling, fragrant quiche Lorraine—with a perfect flaky crust and a silken custard streaked with Gruyère and salt pork—to discover that while you were downstairs in the prep kitchen, quiche had been conscripted into some new culture war."

"Culture war," however tiresome or nausea-inducing the term may be, isn't a terribly off-base way to describe this whole dustup. It stems from the conflict between a set of ideologies supposedly rooted in "traditional" American values and forward-looking social progress toward a more egalitarian society. Also, it features a lot of ridiculous chest-puffing and hot takes completely divorced from fact. But in reality, quiche is just an unlucky little pie that became a blank slate onto which angsty men (and women) could project all their fear and anger over gender identity. The dish may have its origins in France, but in the end, there's really nothing more American than that.

QUICHE LORRAINE

Adapted from Charlyne Varkonyi and her article
"Quiche Still Unbeatable Egg Dish"

MAKES ONE 9-INCH (23-CM) QUICHE

In a 1983 edition of the *Fort Lauderdale News*, food editor Charlyne Varkonyi shared a variety of quiche recipes, with the note: "Whether it is safe for 'Real Men' to eat quiche or not, food authorities, such as Julia Child, consider quiche fundamental to French cooking." This one is hearty and nourishing yet light enough that you can tuck away a few slices without feeling like you immediately need a post-brunch nap.

1 All-Butter Pie Crust (pages 12–13)
1½ cups (170 g) shredded Swiss cheese
8 bacon slices, crisply cooked and crumbled
¼ cup (15 g) green onion, thinly sliced
4 large eggs
1½ cups (360 g) half-and-half
Pinch of ground nutmeg

Preheat the oven to 425°F (220°C). Line a 9-inch (23-cm) pie pan with the prepared crust. Trim excess dough and crimp the edges.

Scatter the cheese across the bottom of the crust. Sprinkle the bacon and green onion on top of the cheese.

In a medium bowl, whisk the eggs, half-and-half, and nutmeg until thoroughly combined. Pour into the crust, covering the cheese, bacon, and onion.

Bake for 15 minutes. Reduce the oven temperature to 325°F (165°C), then bake 25 to 30 minutes more, until the filling is mostly set but still jiggles a bit in the middle. Serve warm or at room temperature.

CHAPTER ELEVEN

TOFU CREAM PIE

ONE FEBRUARY DAY in 1998, Bill Gates was in Brussels, Belgium. He was there to meet with Belgian computer industry and government leaders, a pretty reasonable activity when you're the richest man in the world. As the sun shone down, Gates emerged from the kind of nondescript black car that all rich and famous people get carted around in, smiling and nodding pleasantly at the people gathered to greet him on the sidewalk. He began walking up the handful of steps that led to the grand building's entrance, when suddenly two figures sprung from behind an ornate pillar to his right, bearing something white and fluffy.

That something was pie, and they proceeded to smash it directly into Bill Gates's face.

Stunned, Gates fell back against the pillar, hands immediately going to a face now completely invisible behind a thick layer of gloopy whipped cream. It covered the shoulders of his undoubtedly expensive suit and was splattered across his chest. Frozen in shock, Gates remained immobile for a moment; everyone surrounding him, in fact, was slow to take action, stunned into a delayed response. They quickly kicked themselves into gear and huddled around the dripping billionaire, urgently ushering him away. As they steered him toward the safety of the building, the sneak attack continued, with assailants swiftly launching two more pies at Gates before security finally managed to tackle one person to the ground.

Gates continued his way inside, wiped his pie-covered face (not very successfully—a large glob of whipped cream remained lodged in his right ear), then proceeded with his scheduled meeting. Business stopped for nothing and no one, not even pie.

THE TRUTH IS, I could have opened this chapter with any number of stories, because people getting pied in the face was downright common in the late twentieth century and early aughts. And it's not like this anecdote was notable because Bill Gates was the only famous person to get a face full of custard. Practically everyone who was anyone got pied at one point or another: from Sylvester Stallone (reportedly a good sport about it) to San Francisco mayor Willie Brown (reportedly not). Basically, if you were middle-aged anytime between the years 1970 and 2008 and you were actively destroying the world through capitalism, power, or greed, you were in danger of having a pie launched at your head.

Made up of "revolutionary bakers and pie-slingers," the political pie protest movement recognized that "the technocrats who dominate industrial society may call us radical and unrealistic, but the dream of a biodiverse and socially just future is one that we will fight for until the day we pie," as one group solemnly vowed. It was a surprisingly long phenomenon, one that ebbed and flowed over the course of several decades, with a sort of mini-resurgence as recently as 2011.

Technically, it all started in 1970 (more on that in a second) but its roots trace back even further, to the days of silent film stars and the Three Stooges, when comedians ran around in a frenzy, hitting people with pie. More than three thousand pies were reportedly thrown in the 1927 Laurel and Hardy film *Battle of the Century*. And Moe Howard of the Three Stooges supposedly had his own secret pie recipe: "A vat of whipped cream, marshmallow sauce and pumpkin filling," the executive director of the International Clown Hall of Fame and Research Center claimed in an article on pieing for the *Washington Post*. "That made it very gooey. It really stuck to the target's face." Some pie activists reached back to beyond the twentieth century, referencing the sly mayhem of the Boston Tea Party or claiming their protest was descended from the days of medieval courts, where jesters made fun of kings to keep them grounded and humble. (I assume there was no pie involved in such courtly antics, but the same spirit was there.)

Such historical inspiration was cited by individual pie-throwers and prominent pie groups as justification for their pastry pranks, but it's entirely possible this whole sticky movement would never have gotten off the ground (or soared through the air) without the actions of one legendary pothead: Thomas King Forçade.

Forçade was the kind of man with wild anecdotes that sound like something from a not-very-realistic myth: A prominent drug smuggler, he once spent two nights hiding out from police in a mosquito-infested Florida swamp before escaping by crawling past a herd of cop cars parked in a sheriff's substation lot. He was most prominently known as the founder of *High Times* magazine, a drug-culture magazine read by four million people at its height, and his work with the publication made him one of the most famous drug advocates in the country. Described as a "counterculture guru and drug culture mastermind," he was also involved with the Youth International Party, whose members were known as "Yippies." In the spirit of the wild and wacky protest antics that the Yippies were known for, Forçade inspired legions of radicals and activists through the mischievous performances he called "guerrilla theater."

One of Forçade's most publicized stunts came in May 1970, when he spoke before the President's Commission on Obscenity and Pornography on behalf of the Underground Press Syndicate, a network of countercultural media outlets that he ran. True to his ridiculously provoking form, he showed up outfitted in a clerical costume, complete with hat, black suit, and a reversed collar, a nice bit of theatricality. Taking the stand, Forçade denounced the commission, decrying it as nothing more than "McCarthyesque witch hunts and inquisitional hearings." His rant mostly concluded, he then proceeded to launch a custard pie (some accounts have described it as a "cottage cheese pie" instead) into the face of Otto N. Larsen, a professor at the University of Washington who was part of the commission. He capped things off by shouting, "Pie power!"

His explanation for the stunt? He claimed it was to demonstrate how ludicrous the idea of the whole commission was in the first place.

Forçade's pie protest came on the heels of violent and tragic protests like the infamous Vietnam War demonstration at Kent State, which had occurred only a week earlier. It made front-page news around the US; the caption of a photo that ran in the *New York Times* recapped with an admirable attempt at stoicism: "Cottage cheese dribbling from the side of his face, Prof. Otto N. Larsen holds pie plate emptied on his head by Thomas K. Forcade."

The event wasn't just a short-lived media flare-up, either; later, Forçade was denied a press pass for the White House, which culminated in a lawsuit, *Forçade v. Knight* (officially known as *Sherrill v. Knight*, a long story), which affected how press passes were issued. The legal decision continues to have ramifications to this day; in what should likely come as no surprise, it was cited by the media in multiple instances during the Trump administration's assault on freedom of the press.

Forçade's actions inspired others to raise their pie plates in protest. One such activist was Pat Small, a man referred to in a 1972 newspaper article as "the world's most celebrated pie-thrower." Small was a member of Forçade's Underground Press Syndicate and the leader of the Zippie faction of the Youth International Party, a breakaway group in Miami. His most prominent hit was throwing a pie at Miami Beach councilman Harold Rosen (the weapon itself was alternately identified as a pumpkin tart and a cream pie) in protest of a decision to deny protestors a campsite during the Democratic National Convention—an action that was later described by the press as "the splat heard 'round the world." Small was subsequently sentenced to ninety days in jail for creating a disturbance, and as a result of his sentencing, a group of local Zippies organized a "pie-in" at Miami Beach municipal court that featured an assortment of peach, cherry, and banana pies to communicate their outrage.

It wasn't just Small who took up the pie plate from Forçade— radical activists around the United States seized on pieing as their newest form of protest, and it particularly caught on in the Yippie movement, inspired by the ridiculous, humorous stunts of leaders like Abbie Hoffman and other modes of guerrilla theater. Rex Weiner, a buddy of Thomas Forçade's who was also involved with *High Times*, decided to put his own spin on the pie-in-the-face genre. "Goaded by the political zeitgeist," as he wrote in *The Paris Review*, Weiner started a group called Agents of Pie-Kill. As he wrote:

> Taking a businesslike approach, we created a brochure offering a menu of attacks: Squirt Gun Ambush, Seltzer Bottle Blitz, and the classic Pie-in-the-Face, with a choice of flavors (chocolate cream, lemon meringue, etc.). Fees

began at a basic $150, with upward adjustments depending upon the difficulty involved. Their anonymity guaranteed, customers signed a contract authorizing the hit. Payment was 50 percent up front, with the remainder, plus expenses, due on the successful conclusion of the mission. For an extra fee we provided photographic evidence.

Riding the pastry-pranking trend, Weiner's operation took off, steadily growing beyond the founding duo of Weiner and his girlfriend. At the company's height, the members of Agents of Pie-Kill numbered up to six, but without a doubt, the most significant recruit was its first: Aron Kay. Or, as he later became known, Aron "Pieman" Kay.

Pat Small may have been known as the most celebrated pie-thrower in the world in 1972, but it wasn't long before Kay overtook that title. A pieing prodigy in the making, he got his feet wet doing hits for Weiner's Agents of Pie-Kill, launching custards at everyone from bosses to landlords to a nun who was referred to by the students she taught as "The Bitch." (Guess who paid for the pieing.) These were standard hires that came through as part of the job, for which Kay was paid by the company. But soon, on something of pastry power trip, Kay started to go off script. "It wasn't long before we noticed Agent Kay had switched to autopilot," wrote Weiner. "He couldn't stop throwing pies at people: Watergate operative Gordon Liddy, New York City mayor Abe Beame, Senator Daniel Moynihan, and even rock poet Patti Smith.* The list goes on." He added solemnly: "Agents of Pie-Kill had created a monster."

---

* Patti might have been more inspired than angered by the stunt—in 1976, she smashed a pie in the face of the Velvet Underground's John Cale while performing onstage in Cleveland.

With Nixon out of office and the end of the Vietnam War, plus one rogue agent on its hands, Agents of Pie-Kill soon closed up shop. But by that time, Aron Kay had internalized the ability of pie to speak truth to power (or, at the very least, humiliate some people), and he soldiered on. As Weiner described, he'd easily graduated from regular everyday folks to set his sights on loftier targets.

Like many pie-throwers, Kay had started with the Youth International Party (a.k.a. the Yippies) and came up with the likes of Tom Forçade, Abbie Hoffman, and Jerry Rubin. "I was always a follower of the Marx Brothers and the Three Stooges. Then, in 1971, Thomas Forcade of *High Times* magazine pied a commissioner," Kay told an interviewer in 2018. (He was a little off with his dates, but the sentiment was there.) "Then a year or so later, Pat Small pied a councilman in Miami Beach. I took up the idea from all of them." The first pie he ever threw was a cherry pie (as he later said, "Get it? It was my pie virginity"). As he broadened his repertoire to more politically minded targets, he zeroed in on members of the conservative establishment, crooked politicians, corrupt public figures, and other scumbags. Some of the many (many!) people he pied included Andy Warhol (simply because he had met the Shah of Iran), Senator Daniel Moynihan (because he was "a fascist pig," as Kay yelled when he threw his pie), and Phyllis Schlafly (because she was literally the worst).

True to form, Schlafly sniffed a conspiracy behind her gloopy spectacles, claiming years later that "he was out for hire. Obviously he was backed by the feminists."

Many of his pies were specially tailored to their victims. When Kay hit New York mayor Abraham Beame, it was with "an apple crumb pie because he was a crummy politician in the Big Apple," said Kay. As for former CIA director William Colby, "he got a Bavarian chocolate and blueberry cream cheese pie because he was the big cheese of the CIA," Kay recalled. And lastly, there was Edward Teller, the "Father of the A-Bomb." In 1983, his pastry "was a mushroom and tofu pie—mushroom for all the mushroom clouds."

Kay's prolific pieing (he kept it up until 1992) earned him what he claimed was a 120-page file at the FBI and a slew of colorful nicknames, including the "Pied Sniper of New York" and "Chef of America's Pieromaniacs." He was, as such titles indicate, the avatar for pie-tossing in New York and all of America. But not necessarily in the rest of the world. You may be thinking that's because pieing was isolated to the United States, but in fact, it's quite the opposite. In reality, it's because Kay's Belgian counterpart, Noël Godin, was the poster boy of pie in Europe.

That's right, I said Europe . . . we're going to take a quick international detour.

THOUGH THE POLITICAL pie-tossing movement technically started in the US with Forçade and the Yippies, it eventually spread across the globe, mostly due to the admirable (and messy) efforts of Noël Godin. He founded the International Patisserie Brigade, and he was the devious mastermind behind the 1998 pieing of Bill Gates, an event that made international headlines and launched Godin's name into the global spotlight. (You can find a clip of it online—I highly recommend it.) In a *Wall Street Journal* report on the Gates hit, the unidentified Godin was referred to only as a prankster who was "well-known in Belgium as an 'entarteur'— someone who throws pies in famous peoples' faces as a form of harmless disrespect." Describing the motives behind the Gates pieing, Godin said, "He is the master of the world. He's offering his intelligence, his sharpened imagination, and his power to the governments and the world as is today—that is to say gloomy, unjust, and nauseating. . . . So Bill Gates was at the top of our lists of victims. The attack against him was symbolic; it was against hierarchal power itself." Ultimately, Godin's tireless efforts to pie problematic people in power—Gates and beyond—was cited as inspiration for many a subsequent pie-tosser.

Pie-throwing also caught on in England: Toward the end of the century, People Insurgent Everywhere (PIE) popped up in London, hitting victims that included scientist Keith Campbell (otherwise known as the guy who co-created Dolly the sheep) and Renato Ruggiero, director-general of the World Trade Organization. Indeed, pie throwing reached such a fever pitch in Britain that the grocery chain Tesco started testing their pies for throwing after they received customer requests for tossing pies. The grocery chain organized a whole excursion to a school gym outside of London, where employees launched pies at each other to see which varieties were the best for throwing. Criteria for evaluation included how well they flew through the air and the mess they left upon impact. The ultimate goal, according to a Tesco spokesperson, was to "not make an absolute mess, but a nice, polite mess." (Classic England.) Their final recommendations after such extensive scientific research? Egg custard, lemon meringue, and fruit pies.

Pieing even infiltrated the British music scene: In 2004, English rock band Chumbawamba released their eleventh studio album, *Un*, which included the pie power–inspired song, "Just Desserts." An homage to the pieing movement, the song fit neatly alongside the album's themes of individualism and anti-consumerism and included lyrics like, "We talk without words, and everybody understands / Just desserts, delivered by hand / Nobody move or the CEO / Gets it in the face with cream and dough."

Elsewhere, in Canada, the political pastry movement was boldly carried forth by Les Entartistes, a group that took to throwing pies in people's faces—including the Canadian prime minister's—after being inspired by Godin's hit on Bill Gates. Their operations were highly organized and efficient; they could involve anywhere from four to sixteen operatives, and they liked to hide their pies in pizza boxes until the very last minute. After the pie had been launched and the target was covered in a sticky sweet mess, the attackers would chant "Gloup, gloup" (imitating the sound of the filling dripping from face to floor—an almost outstanding level of coldhearted disrespect) before running off.

Entartistes member Evan Brown, who hit the prime minister, explained the impetus behind their movement in a statement he made to the court after being arrested for his pie antics (unsurprising given that he hit *the prime minister*): "There are issues that need to be addressed but they're sometimes ignored and that leads people to desperate protest." (In staunch defense of his client, Brown's lawyer proclaimed to the court, "This is a story of cream and punishment.") One prominent Entartistes member, who went by the codename Pope-Tart, summed up the activists' attitude even further: "The pie gives power back to the people because so many feel powerless in the face of big politicians and industrialists." He added: "The pie delivers a human political message. What we're trying to say is, 'You work for us. You can't be too big for your britches or you'll get a pie in the face.'" This explanation makes sense for most of the people they targeted, but perhaps less so for one particular victim: Sylvester Stallone, who they nailed at the opening of a Planet Hollywood restaurant. Their reasoning? Just for being Sylvester Stallone.*

It's no surprise that political pie-throwing turned into a global movement that expanded beyond America's borders. That's

---

*The one person Les Entartistes refused to pie was Celine Dion. Said Pope-Tart, "She is lovely."

because so many of the social, political, and economic problems that sparked protestors' discontent were rooted in globalization, particularly in the '80s and '90s, when the pie-in-the-face phenomenon continued to gain steam. As American history professor Alexander Bloom told the *New York Times* in a 2000 report on the uptick in pieing, "There is this basic undercurrent of people who are feeling that all these forces beyond their control—from the I.M.F. to the W.T.O. to Y2K to H.M.O.'s—are in charge of their lives and are operating outside of the political process." He added, "I think people feel frustrated."

"Frustrated" was one way to put it. As one pie-throwing group asserted, "This uprising has its roots in the belief that our planet is not dying, it is being killed; and the ones doing the killing have names and faces." It wasn't just frustration that motivated protestors—it was fury. With globalization accelerating the rates of environmental destruction, poverty, and social decline, targets frequently included leaders directly involved in international decision-making. For instance, Frank E. Loy, undersecretary of state for global affairs during the Clinton administration, was hit in the face with cream pie by a protestor while delivering a briefing at the United Nations climate conference at The Hague in November 2000. That same year, International Monetary Fund managing director Michel Camdessus got a pastry plastered all over himself.

These pie protests came at the same time that the broader anti-globalization movement was developing internationally. Worried and angered by the rise of corporate power, global trade, and an accelerating wealth gap, members of the movement asserted their opposition to neoliberalism in an activist crusade perhaps best embodied by the "Battle for Seattle" protest in 1999. During the protest, an estimated fifty thousand to seventy thousand people descended on Seattle during the World Trade Organization negotiations looking ahead to the new millennium, which many feared would implicate the entire world in a massive global trade deal with far-reaching (and pretty much all harmful) ramifications.

The protestors in Seattle included Indigenous groups, environmentalists, students, anti-capitalists, labor unionists, and more. Unlike similar protests in the '80s and '90s, which could be serious and dour, this gathering was a party. There was rave music, dancing, and sea turtle costumes—pretty much everything you could ask for to have a good time. In some ways, the lighthearted spirit in Seattle echoed that of fellow pastry activists making their point by running around smashing pie in people's faces. All that revelry, however, came to an end when law enforcement assaulted the nonviolent protestors with tear gas and rubber bullets, leading to violent chaos in the city. The meeting was subsequently canceled and trade talks shut down, a major victory for the activists.

This willingness to stand up in opposition to the "new world order" being proclaimed by international leaders—one that would make rich people richer and poor people poorer—was found in countries all over, such as in Italy in 2001, when two hundred thousand anti-globalization activists arrived to demonstrate at the G8 summit for a protest that ended up turning violent and bloody.

Many such protesters also turned to food to get their message across, though not necessarily always pies—instead, they transformed other culinary delights into resistance weapons. Once, a protestor slapped a minister in the Portuguese government back and forth in the face with a cod, yelling, "That'll teach you how to govern!" as they did so. Another time, a British musician dumped a bucket of ice water over the head of the deputy prime minister while attending an awards dinner, an act the victim complained was "a contemptible publicity stunt." But though culinary protests like these occurred, the most prominent (and organized) such method was still very clearly pie. Which begs the question: Why, exactly, was pie the edible vehicle of choice?

As Bloom explained to the *New York Times* in that report on pieing, "Pies defuse the anger and identify the target as a clown. If someone dumped feces or blood or mock toxic waste on you, that would be a lot more threatening." This idea of a clown echoes the term once used to describe pieing: "carnival humor." But even beyond just being not human waste, there's a deeper element to the whole joke that pie, by its very nature, gets at. "Pie is goopy, a treat, and meant to be served in moderation," wrote Ben Paynter in his deep dive on the history of pieing for *Fast Company*, "How Pie Became a Powerful Punchline in Political Provocation." As Paynter pointed out, "When weaponized, it becomes a comedic way to exert power over someone—you just gave them too much of a good thing, in a way they can't control—making it clear that not everyone takes that person or their agenda so seriously." In addition, some pie-tossers cited the activist handbook *Rules for Radicals* to explain the reasoning behind pie, particularly author Saul Alinsky's assertion that "ridicule is [hu]man's most potent weapon. It is almost impossible to counter-attack ridicule. It also infuriates the opposition, who then react to your advantage." Nothing, it turns out, is more ridiculous—and humiliating—than a custard-covered face.

ONE GROUP THAT truly embraced the international nature of the whole pie-throwing movement—which they called a "Global Pastry Uprising"—was the San Francisco–based Biotic Baking Brigade (BBB), who described themselves as "flan-archists." The BBB was one of the most prominent and prolific pastry protest groups to come out of this whole period. Like many of their brethren across the globe, they targeted politicians, capitalists, executives, and government officials whose greed and corruption ran unchecked, protected by their own power. Such victims, for instance, included the chief executive of Monsanto at the time, Robert Shapiro, and Nobel Prize–winning economist Milton Friedman. The BBB wrote of their mission, "As multinational corporations accelerate the plunder of our world, a militant resistance has formed in response. Diverse in philosophy and targets, diffuse in geography and structure, the movement comprises freedom-loving folks with a sense of aplomb and gastronomics. Fighting a guerrilla media and ground war with the titans of industry, these revolutionary bakers and pie-slingers have achieved in short order what can truly be called a Global Pastry Uprising (GPU)."

One of the group's most famous operations occurred in 1998, when they tossed a pie at San Francisco mayor Willie Brown in opposition to his policies against the unhoused population. Brown proceeded to throw a huge stink about it, ranting about how unacceptable such behavior was. As he said at the time, "You can't punch me in the nose and then claim it's a political statement" (perhaps missing the whole point of the protestors having done something *other* than punch him in the nose). Brown went on to press charges against the pie-tossers, who were sentenced to six months in jail after being convicted of conspiracy and battery and went on to be known as the infamous "Cherry Pie Three."

What happens when a group of pie-throwing activists become martyrs for their cause? They produce a new wave of pie protestors, of course, like the mythic Greek Hydra sprouting many cream-filled heads. The arrests of BBB agents resulted in the sudden appearance of a mysterious group known as the National Pies Association (NPA), who participated in a practice referred to as "ritual public pieicide" (which appears to involve smashing pies into their own faces) and operated under the motto, "They can have my pie when they pry my bloated, overweight fingers from it." They popped up in San Francisco when they protested the justice system's harsh treatment of BBB agents, and their arrival on the scene was, in true pie protest fashion, chaotic: They interrupted a chamber of commerce seminar by yelling "death to all tyrants" in both English and Latin (echoing John Wilkes Booth and other figures throughout history), then hit themselves in the face with pie.

The Biotic Baking Brigade engaged in a sort of mythmaking and culture-building that stood out even in an era full of cleverly named groups and larger-than-life figures. The group had their own song, which warned transgressors that they risked being treated with a visit from "the vegan vigilantes of the biotic baking brigade." Like the previous Agents of Pie-Kill, the group's members went by code names such as Agent Lemon Custard and Agent Apple, one of the most prominent of their members, who stalked the nightmares of guilty capitalists. The Biotic Baking Brigade even released a cookbook in 2004 called *Pie Any Means Necessary*, which captured decades of pie protest philosophy and technique in a comprehensive volume that included everything from the history of pieing to philosophical arguments promoting the practice, "as well as recipes, songs, verses, and frontline accounts of the most outstanding deliveries," as the book promised in its introduction.

In order to spread the movement and empower even more pie-tossers, *Pie Any Means Necessary* was chock-full of tips and advice on pie-throwing. For example, the group cautioned against using cherry pies because the effect could look like blood, which might cause unnecessary alarm among spectators. (Although such a result could sometimes be desired, and was specifically recommended as a "great choice for a homophobic preacher or neo-Nazi Klansman.") More seriously, they included a section about how to remain active in the movement while serving jail time for a pie hit.

And beyond simple action items for smuggling pies into crowded locations (briefcases and the aforementioned pizza boxes were commonly used) or debates about whether it was better to toss the pie through the air or smush it directly onto the victim (a hotly contested topic among agents), the book also included more strategic recommendations for achieving its high-minded goals of speaking truth to power. In one section, the group explained, "If we hold a rally in demonstration-jaded San Francisco, the media usually will not cover it. If we write letters to the editor, they don't get printed. However, the visual of a pie in the face makes a sizable chink in the media armor through which we can then put forth the reasons why a figure deserved to be pied in the first place. It allows us to communicate our message beyond what traditional means allow." As a result, the Biotic Baking Brigade prepared ready-to-send press releases for their pieings, which were distributed as soon as the deed occurred to maximize media coverage.

This perspective zooms in on just why such an absurd comedy routine became a dearly beloved activist tool that lasted decades. "Opponents of the current system are disillusioned with traditional channels of dissent—writing letters, voting, complaining, and being ignored," the group wrote. The usual means of raising one's voice and being heard by people in power had become ineffective, and if it took a pastry crust and some whipped cream to garner attention instead, then so be it.

The pies themselves weren't only valued for their messy spectacle. They also represented the counterculture-inspired ideals of the people throwing them, a membership that was mostly made up of "experienced activists involved in ecology, social justice, animal rights, anti-racist, and feminist movements, who participate in groups such as Earth First!, Food Not Bombs, and ACT UP." The BBB emphasized homemade pies whenever possible, and preferred them to be vegan and organic. In fact, they even developed a recipe for tofu cream pie—entirely vegan, of course—that was specifically meant for throwing.* Made with ingredients like tofu, sucanat, almond butter, and maple syrup in place of the commonly used whipped cream (which agents described as "that late-twentieth-century, nutritionally void, environmentally wasteful decorative product"), the pie's natural, health food bent aligned with broader counterculture protest ideals of the '80s and '90s. The accompanying headnotes to the recipe printed in *Pie Any Means Necessary* shared, "Using some variation of a cream pie is your best bet. Leaving the pie-ee with a face full of light-colored goop not only accomplishes your goal more effectively, it also communicates what's going on better. This can also help avoid situations where you get your ass kicked."

Such a recipe—and in fact, such an approach to pie in general—is a first in this book and a unique anomaly in the history of American pie more broadly: a pie whose purpose and value had absolutely nothing to do with being eaten. Not to get all existential on you, but what is a pie if not something to be consumed? Am I overthinking this one?

It doesn't matter, of course. Really, the moral of this story comes down to the simple fact that pie, as a symbol in the American consciousness, is infinity malleable and, frankly, powerful. It brought titans of industry and world leaders to their knees! (Mostly metaphorically, but still.) If ever there was an example to prove that pie is more than just a tasty food, this is it: the use of pie to achieve goals completely unrelated to bodily hunger. In fact, pie might be even more effective when it's *not* being eaten. Just ask Bill Gates.

---

* They weren't the only ones to turn to tofu. When pie-tossing duo Al-Pieda hit Ann Coulter in 2004, it was reportedly with a tofu lemon pie.

TOFU CREAM PIE

Adapted from *Pie Any Means Necessary*

MAKES ONE 9-INCH (23-CM) PIE

Though it was originally developed for tossing in people's faces, this pie is surprisingly tasty. Those revolutionaries evidently knew their way around a kitchen. Be sure to get silken tofu in a shelf-stable package, not from the refrigerated section, for a smoother texture and less noticeable tofu taste.

For the crust
2 cups (240 g) graham cracker crumbs
3 tablespoons neutral oil
2 tablespoons pure maple syrup
¼ teaspoon almond extract

For the filling
1 pound (455 g) silken tofu, firm or extra-firm
⅓ cup (50 g) sucanat
1 tablespoon tahini or almond butter
½ teaspoon salt
½ teaspoon lemon zest
2 tablespoons lemon juice
½ teaspoon almond extract

For the topping
1 pound (455 g) extra-firm silken tofu
¼ cup (60 ml) pure maple syrup
1 tablespoon vanilla extract
2 tablespoons nondairy milk
Pinch of salt

MAKE THE CRUST: Preheat the oven to 350°F (175°C). Grease a 9-inch (23-cm) pie pan.

In a medium bowl, combine the graham cracker crumbs, oil, maple syrup, and almond extract until evenly moistened. Press into the prepared pan, packing tightly and evenly. Bake for 5 minutes.

MAKE THE FILLING: In a blender or food processor, combine the tofu, sucanat, tahini, salt, lemon zest and juice, and almond extract and process until completely smooth. Pour into the baked pie shell. Refrigerate for an hour or two to chill completely.

MAKE THE TOPPING: In a blender or food processor, combine the tofu, maple syrup, vanilla, milk, and salt and process until completely smooth. Apply to the top of your pie with a spatula, or transfer to a pastry bag and pipe it on.

CHOCOLATE HAUPIA PIE

APPLE PIE MIGHT be a quintessential American dish in part because of its universality, but there are other types of pies that capture nostalgia and devotion for the opposite reason: because of their narrow specificity. They embody a place so clearly and distinctly that locals put them on a pedestal, claiming ownership for the simple reason that this pie embodies their history and their way of life.

Hawai'i's chocolate haupia pie is one such dessert. A rich, custardy pie, it's made up of a crust (often made from macadamia nuts), a layer of haupia, a chocolate layer, and a topping of whipped cream. If you're not from Hawai'i, you may be wondering what haupia actually is. Which is exactly the point.

Haupia is a classic dessert on the islands: a rich coconut milk pudding thickened with arrowroot or cornstarch, which sets into a firm, sliceable consistency. The sweet, gelatinous dessert can often be found cut into cubes and served at a traditional luau or on a Hawaiian mixed-plate lunch, at home alongside the other tropical flavors and ingredients that make up much of Hawaiian cuisine. It's only natural, then, that it should be turned into a pie. Particularly one that incorporates chocolate as well, drawing on cacao's centuries-long history in the islands: It first arrived in the 1830s and has been cultivated since King David Kalakaua grew the crop in his gardens. Today, Hawai'i is the only state to grow cacao (and it's barely able to—the islands sit at the very top of the tree's cultivation range).

Easily the most famous purveyor of chocolate haupia pie is Ted's Bakery on Oahu's North Shore, the self-proclaimed "Home of Chocolate Haupia Cream Pie." Tourists and locals alike flock for a creamy slice. Like the pie that made it famous, Ted's Bakery also bears a quintessentially Hawaiian backstory. It all started in 1906, when Torojiro Nakamura emigrated from Kumamoto, Japan, to Maui to work on sugar plantations. He eventually saved up just enough meager earnings to lease three acres of poor land, then proceeded to cultivate that small swath into a flourishing farm. He ultimately bought more land in Sunset Beach with his son Takemitsu, who went on to open the Sunset Beach Store in 1956. Then *his* son, Ted, opened his own spot, Ted's Bakery, which was integrated into the store, and started selling his chocolate haupia pies alongside donuts, corn bread, and other pastries.

Though chocolate is the most classic iteration, haupia pie is prevalent in many forms across the state. Another popular version is sweet potato haupia pie. Ever ones to latch onto local food customs to try to ingratiate themselves into a market, McDonald's also seized onto the pie's popularity, offering its own version of haupia pie at locations across Hawai'i—a spotlight that's usually reserved for America's apple pie. But in a country woven from a fabric of distinct cultures, histories, and customs, the haupia pie is just as unmistakably emblematic of this land.

CHAPTER TWELVE

REVISITING APPLE PIE

WHEN WE LAST left apple pie, its recipe was printed for the first time on American shores in Amelia Simmons's *American Cookery*, a representation of the new cuisine developing in the infant United States. Fast-forward a couple hundreds of years, and the pie is now one of the most potent (and cliché) symbols of American identity, with everything from suits to movie stars dubbed "as American as apple pie." So how, exactly, did this dessert turn into such a patriotic behemoth, eclipsing not just every other pie but also every other *food* to get here?

And a less obvious but arguably more important question: Despite Amelia Simmons's best intentions, is apple pie even really that American after all?

As we all (hopefully) remember, apple pie as we know it first originated in England, rather than the good old US-of-A, and it developed from culinary influences from France, the Netherlands, and even the Arab world, which likely introduced the concept of small, sweet pastries to Europe, according to food historian Janet Clarkson. And if you recall, apples weren't even grown in North America until the Europeans arrived.

Indeed, many of the other ingredients necessary for apple pie also come from beyond America's borders. Wheat originated in the Middle East, while pastry fats like lard and butter arrived with Christopher Columbus. The same goes for sugar, a non-native crop that only solidified its place in the American diet through global trade and the enslavement of West Africans. Crucial spices like cinnamon and nutmeg, meanwhile, came from far-flung countries like Sri Lanka and Indonesia. And of course, the art of pastry stemmed from a melting pot of culinary traditions abroad, particularly French, Italian, and Arabic.

As for the dish itself, we know the British and Dutch made their own versions of apple pie long before they set foot on the New World's shores. So how did apple pie, a dish eaten centuries before America's first president was even born, become an enduring patriotic symbol and nativist myth?

IT WAS A long, winding road full of petty patriotism, sentimental soldiers, and plenty of pastry. Though the pie became a staple in American cuisine throughout the eighteenth and nineteenth centuries because it was an easy, affordable, and adaptable dish, merely being tasty and convenient is a far cry from being an American symbol that's been compared to the Constitution itself.

Apple pie started to become specifically associated with the United States around the latter half of the nineteenth century, when some of the earliest references to its status as an explicitly American dish cropped up. Such mentions included one 1881 satirical hotel writeup that referred to "a patriotic love for the American dried apple pie," and a made-up story printed that same year about the late Russian czar that cited "American apple pie" as a weapon employed by his foes against him. Meanwhile, as far away as Australia, the grand opening of Kaiser's Model American Restaurant included "American Apple Pie" on the menu (alongside Washington Pudding, Philadelphia Custard, American Custard Tart, and more). And when 1887 promised a spectacular apple crop, that only meant one thing to Americans: pie. As one newspaper explained, "The devotees of that great American institution Apple Pie will rejoice at the news which comes from the orchards of down East. There is a glorious apple crop." The reporter sharing the good news expounded on the virtues of the humble (non-native) apple, writing "All history shows that no people ever lost heart or went about asking the pessimistic question 'Is life worth living?' so long as apples were plenty in their cellars."

Similarly, there was a controversy in Rochester, New York, a few years later when a local group of capitalists cornered the market on dried apples. Their misdeeds were filtered through a distinctly nationalist lens, with the nefarious scheme viewed as not just dishonest, but unpatriotic, because it would deprive Americans of their favorite dish: "A rumor which spread through the city yesterday was sufficiently startling to catch the attention of every patriotic American. . . . The far-reaching consequences of this combine were at once seen. Pie is the favorite dish of all the Americans, and apple pie is the prince of pies."

But it wasn't until 1889 that one of the first explicit mentions of apple pie as a national symbol occurred. That year, the *Sacramento Daily Record-Union* reprinted an article from the *Milwaukee Sentinel* that proclaimed, "The National Emblem: What is the Matter with the American Apple Pie?" The author went on to lay out a compelling argument for why the country should anoint this humble dessert as its national emblem. Their reasoning referred to many of the same virtues suggested in the decades to come when people discussed apple pie's status as an American institution: its universality ("The apple pie grows in every section of our beloved country. . . . Every true American eats apple pie"); its hardiness ("It is substantial, it is satisfying, it is hard to digest, and therefore it is no light and trifling symbol of the solid, satisfying and tenacious life of America"); and its lack of acceptance in other countries ("It is hated, reviled, and feared by foreigners, just as our great Republic has been. Like our free institutions, the apple pie has held its own against all the world"). Not only did the author want to crown the pie as our national emblem, but they advocated to make it a requirement of American life, declaring, "We should embody in the Constitution of the United States a requirement that no foreign immigrant should receive his final papers of naturalization until he should eat an apple pie in the presence of the Court."

Only a few years later, by 1891, apple pie seemed to have secured its place as a purely American construct: There was a widely circled report around this time that "Queen Victoria recently ordered her baker to make her an American apple pie." The pie's English origins had been discarded, and the dish was now solidly entrenched as American, even in the land one could technically consider its birthplace.

IF THE HUMBLE apple pie had now become "*American* apple pie" by the end of the nineteenth century, it was during the twentieth century that it emerged as part of the cultural lexicon, when such influential factors as advertising, news, and war created a new narrative that officially transformed the dish into a grand nationalist symbol.

One of the earliest examples of this shift can be traced back to 1902, when a *New York Times* editorial argued for the dish's national importance by asserting that pie had become "the American synonym for prosperity." "Pie is the food of the heroic," it declared. "No pie-eating people can be permanently vanquished."

Perhaps that kind of thinking was what propelled soldiers in World War I, which was instrumental in providing a big boom for apple pie's prominence as an American symbol, representing all that was good and comforting about home. A 1918 report described how women traveling to the front lines served apple pie and other delicacies from home to weary soldiers. "Back from the front line trenches in France, where for hours they have given battle to the Boches, the American soldiers first want what? A cigarette, as has been stated time and again? Not at all. A piece of homemade pie, brown crusted and spiced—the kind mother used to make in the yester years."

Indeed, apple pie proved a key strategy in boosting soldiers' morale. One said that "one of the biggest problems was that of overcoming the longing for home which attacked almost every soldier at some time. . . . To Colonel Barker came the thought of furnishing the boys with old-fashioned American apple-pie made by American women," reported one newspaper. These women's efforts didn't go unnoticed, either; soldiers wrote poems about apple pie, including one ode to the female Salvation Army volunteers abroad that included the line, "What better reminder of home? / What brings mother's love touch so nigh / To American soldiers in France / As American apple pie?"

The lack of apple pie abroad remained a constant source of frustration for Americans after the war. The *New York Times* published a 1926 article with the headline "The Tourist Apple Pie Hunt Is Ended: American Army Abroad Has Failed Again to Find in Europe 'the Kind They Make at Home.'" (Confusingly, "army" referred to tourists, rather than the actual military.) It recounted the desperate search tourists underwent trying to find their favorite food in Paris (evidently forgetting the whole point of traveling is to experience other cultures) and the lengths to which they went trying to track down a decent slice when all they could find were desserts like an apple cake with a crust that "would make excellent paving material." (We've come full circle from Dr. Acrelius's wagon-wheel-resistant pies of the colonial era.)

This quick dismissal of foreign foods—especially those that claimed to hold a candle to American apple pie—was constant. Indeed, part of apple pie's patriotic power came from how frequently Americans used the dish to assert their country's superiority over other nations, either by directly comparing the American version to inferior attempts elsewhere or by asserting that it was better than another country's national dishes. As early as 1891, one woman claimed in a Montana newspaper that "Nothing in European dinners can compare with the American custards, puddings and pies." She acknowledged that cakes in Paris are "pretty to look at, but oh! how they break their promise when you eat them. . . . After years of foreign travel I have never met a dish so perfect as the American apple pie can be, with cream."

The French, in particular, caught a lot of flak for their lack of apple pie, perhaps because the country was considered the international master of pastry. One reporter took a cold-hearted appraisal of the desperate measures the French were forced to take during World War I, writing, "The French have banned pastry as a food conservation measure. If they had American apple pie in France they'd never have done it." This opinion doesn't just seem rooted in apple pie tasting better than French pastry; it also linked the dish (and the people who ate it) to being tough and tenacious. The same year, one headline took a shot at the French's culinary abilities: "French Cannot Bake Apple Pie." Writing from France to his brother, an American stationed in France named Myrick Sublette (great name) called his French apple pie "a tragic disappointment," recounting that "The color was brown and it had the consistency of hardtack. . . . It tasted somewhat like a stale salmon sandwich."

When soldiers like Sublette returned home, some Americans were seized by a desperate fear not that they would suffer from "shell shock," but that they would succumb to foreign influence and no longer prefer apple pie. Civilians worried their boys abroad might favor *lemon* pie, an incomprehensible horror. "Such a pastry propaganda, however, entails a very real menace to the nation's legends and digestion," fretted a writer in the *New-York Tribune*. "Lemon pie at best is no food for the strong men of a great world power." To save the nation, he directed that women get to work in the kitchen, and "out with the real apple pies, crisp and spicy."

The Germans, too, were mocked for their pitiful pie: "German inventive genius, seeking to attract American dollars, tried its hand today at American apple pie. It was a partial success, but German inventive genius didn't understand the intricacies of the great American national dish." Neither, of course, did the English: "The American pie is totally different from the sweet, sickly, unappetizing, undersized English tart," sniffed an American reporter.

And in an article that worried, "What Has Become of American Cookery?," it wasn't just a particular nation that was lambasted for its lack of pie prowess. Instead, the piece took a much more nativist approach, implying that anyone born outside the borders of the United States should be forced to master this most beloved of dishes. When it came to hiring foreign cooks, "We shouldn't therefore lose track of the dishes that have proved suitable for Americans for generations. . . . Just because your Hungarian cook can make a delicious egg noodle, don't fail to teach her how to make plain, old-fashioned American apple pie." In circumstances like these, apple pie was deemed a requirement to be a true American.

Unsurprisingly, not every nation took this kind of apple pie antagonism lying down. In 1927, the British went *after* apple pie. The *London Evening News* wrote, "American pie breeds dyspepsia, dyspepsia breeds restlessness, and restlessness begets a feverish but none the less formidable material progress. . . . The American apple pie is the sheer gastronomic equivalent of an incendiary bomb." The French, too, eventually had enough. One Frenchman wrote about American workers living in his home country: "Why, they even believe that their good apple-pie was first made in America. In spite of the fact that I explained that practically the same dish, our tarte aux pommes, had been seen since time immemorial in little French villages." He added, "I found them to have a most exaggerated national pride, pride in everything to be found in America and believing always that every good thing had its origin with them." Almost a hundred years later, and that observation is still pretty darn accurate.

Sometimes, Americans used apple pie as a way of "winning over" foreign adversaries, proving the might and power of the dish (and, of course, of its home country). There are many anecdotes of people from other counties being seduced by this distinctive dessert, from the Belgian violinist Eugène Ysaÿe (who reportedly ate two pies a day while traveling through the US in 1904) to Poland's chief of state. Even King Peter II of Yugoslavia became enamored with the dish. The Washington correspondent of the *London Times* once admitted, "I like American apple pie so much that I want to stay here," and in response, an American reporter crowed, "This conversion is proof of the patriotism of the elder statesmen of the United States senate in providing for the senate restaurant a cook who brings apple pie and apple dumplings and baked apples to the very pinnacle of culinary perfection—dishes that the gods envy."

***

OF COURSE, WE can't talk about apple pie's status as a national symbol without discussing the iconic phrase "as American as apple pie."* It began to crop up around this same time, in the early part of the twentieth century, though its exact origin is unclear. One early example appeared in 1924, when an advertisement that ran across the country promoted suits "that are as American as apple pie." Meanwhile, a 1928 *New York Times* article quoted the phrase to describe the homemaking abilities of First Lady Lou Henry Hoover: "as American as apple pie or corn pone." The reference to corn pone or any other similarly American dish was eventually dropped, and "as American as apple pie" flourished. By 1940, it was referred to as a "familiar phrase" in an Oregon newspaper. Sometimes the phrase was extended to "as American as apple pie for breakfast," such as one instance in which it was used to refer to a particular breed of dog. Other times, it was accompanied by additional "American" symbols, like baseball or chewing tobacco.

A newspaper once printed that "advertising is just as American as apple pie. It shows up most of our national faults, just as it sets forth our national virtues." This proved to be an ironic declaration, since the phrase "American as apple pie" was constantly used in

---

* "As American as apple pie" wasn't the only saying to embed itself into the national lingo, either, even if it was far and away the most popular. There was also the phrase "in apple pie order," meant to describe neatness and tidiness. According to one 1901 newspaper, there's a legend that the saying dates back to the Puritans (well before the United States of America), when a woman named Hepzibah Merton (another great name) baked dozens of apple pies each Saturday for her family. She placed the pies on her pantry shelves with careful labeling for each day of the coming week, an orderliness that came to be known throughout the settlement and referred to as "apple pie order."

advertising to sell products, movie tickets, books, and more by literally capitalizing on the dish's patriotism. Promotions for a 1930 play *The Patsy*, 1934 novel *The Folks*, 1935 movie *Steamboat Round the Bend*, and 1940 film *Young Tom Edison* all included the phrase. The saying was also, quite inevitably, used by politicians in their campaigns to construct the image of an authentically American representative.

Eventually apple pie became explicitly associated with the US government, another powerful force in its mythmaking. In 1935, Congress turned to apple pie to settle a squabble between New York and Oregon, which got into a heated debate over who produced the best apples. After Oregon sent free apples to Congress to prove their superiority, New York retaliated by sending seventy-five apple pies to the Capitol. Representatives on both sides of the divide sampled slices and offered their take, while the Oregon representative sniffed, "The crust was excellent, but there was not enough filling to really find out what New York apples taste like." Peeved to be left out of the debate, Connecticut later chimed in to assert that "apple pie made by a Connecticut cook from Connecticut apples cannot be surpassed by New York, Oregon, or any other state!" This claim was met with swift backlash by a Rochester newspaper, which felt compelled to point out that "the foundation of good apple pie is good apples, and that no good apples grown in Connecticut equal in quality those grown in Western New York."

Similarly, apple pie became directly linked to other explicit American symbols and institutions. While writing of American soldiers' preference for the dish, a reporter claimed, "The Statue of Liberty is not the only thing that is distinctly American." Another writer said that "to banish pie from the American dining table would be like banishing the American constitution." In fact, it was even deemed *more* authentically American than the literal founding document of our country, at one point called "an ancient and

honored American institution, older than the Constitution itself."
People really got worked up over this dish; that same writer went on
to rant, "Let those in whose arteries pulses the red blood of Revolutionary sires rouse themselves, deport these alien kitchen knaves,
dig up grandmother's cook book and set their wives and daughters
to conning it, and boycott every hotel, restaurant and bake shop
that refuses to serve, three times a day as in the Pie Belt's golden
age, real, honest-to-goodness American apple pie." Someone also
dramatically called it "the lone remaining bulwark of American
liberty," which doesn't make a lick of sense.

Disliking apple pie was even linked to treason! During a journalistic tiff that played out on the pages of Missouri newspapers,
an editorial raged, "It's a sad state of affairs when fellows like [local
newspaper editor] Don Wright—and he lives in the apple country, too—refuse to indorse [*sic*] an American institution like apple
pie. . . . Don's views are down-right treason, that's what they are."
Anyone who disliked apple pie, it seemed, couldn't be trusted. Wrote
another writer in a whole separate diatribe on the pie: "Kidnapers,
jail breakers and gangsters are eyed with some toleration—apple
pie critics are frowned upon."

Later, the dessert became even more patriotic when the president got involved. In 1951, Franklin Roosevelt's White House head
housekeeper Henrietta Nesbitt wrote in her *Presidential Cookbook:
Feeding the Roosevelts and Their Guests* that "apple pie was the President's preference among pies" and added that it was "generally
conceded to be the All-American favorite." Roosevelt wasn't the
only president who reportedly took a liking. Calvin Coolidge and
William Taft were both big fans, though Taft was forbidden by his
physician from eating apple pie at one point. (Once, when a banned
slice was served to the president, several of his companions confis-
cated it and ran off to devour it themselves.)

And of course, there was a boost from war, yet again. During World War II, the dish was the most popular dessert in the American army. Most notably, American soldiers began to proclaim they were fighting for "mom and apple pie," an assertion that firmly established the dessert as a metaphor for the United States. So much so that the *Akron Beacon Journal* suggested the war should be referred to as the "Pie War." "How much pie do you think we might get if Germany and Japan win this war?" the writer fretted. "Pie is worth fighting for."

One newspaper ad describing the brief bliss of soldiers' leave wrote: "The smell of Mom's hot apple pie. . . . That's what he's fighting for . . . that's what he's dreaming of . . . that's what he's coming back to." Many American soldiers, in fact, believed in "the homely American tradition that 'Home' means 'Mom' and apple pie." And once they returned to it, they savored it with deep-rooted happiness. When a solider named Lloyd R. Bridgford returned to civilian life after four years in the navy, he told a reporter that he was just glad to be home eating his mother's apple pie.

IN 1943, THE *New York Times* dubbed an actor the perfect choice to depict American ambassador Joseph E. Davies in a film because, in part, "his manners are as indigenously American as apple pie." The inclusion of "indigenous" is particularly notable because, of course, it wasn't remotely true. Using a word like that to describe the dish was hardly surprising, though. This particular idea of "American" apple pie was a constructed one built through mythology, rather than reality. And it was a practice that spanned years.

A 1907 article titled "The Apple, King of the Fruits" taught readers that "the apple is the descendent of the wild crabs of Europe and was brought to America with the Caucasian race of man and, like the race, has found a congenial home in most of the United States and in large acres of adjacent British America." This story isn't technically wrong—apples did, in fact, come to North America with the Europeans—but it took a decidedly colonizing slant that ignored any history of the continent before a white person stepped foot on it. Similarly, a later newspaper referenced that "pie followed the western expansion of the country. Every covered wagon had pie cans and the makings for apple pie," thus linking the dish to ongoing colonization of North America and its Indigenous people. This mythological messaging echoes the legend of Johnny Appleseed, known for spreading apples throughout the Midwest in a method that mimicked western expansion.

References to colonists and Pilgrims, the nation's heartwarming origin story, were common with this pie, from mentions around Thanksgiving to a *Los Angeles Times* article that informed readers: "The meat pie is British and from it our Pilgrim fathers (Pilgrim mothers, rather) evolved the apple pie." Another paper in Iowa told the story of how a Pilgrim woman invented apple pie when she started baking with "the fruits of the New World" (which, as we know, was pretty much impossible to do when the British first stepped off the *Mayflower,* as the writer claims).

Sometimes apple pie language went a step further with decidedly nativist rhetoric, such as when the US was referred to as the dish's "native land." At times, this nationalist origin story was used as a way for later generations to question their American identity through pie. Worried one writer about apple pie: "Are we unworthy of our forebears? Are we too dull of apprehension to realize the merit of our own, our native pie?" In an echo of the nationalist and inflammatory rhetoric used by a few notable American politicians, they added, "Let us turn back to the foods that made our parents great."

Apple pie has also been used to illuminate the darker aspects of American identity. "Lynching is as American as apple pie and does not exist in Canada or Mexico, but only in our nation," wrote Wisconsin's Ernest L. Myer in 1938. Others have echoed this refrain: While writing about the KKK in the Heartland, James H. Madison stated unequivocally, "The Ku Klux Klan of the 1920s was as dark as the night and as American as apple pie." The same goes for an article published in the *Journal of Race & Policy* with the accurately straightforward title "The Killing of Black People by the U.S. State is as American as Apple Pie." Audre Lorde, too, knew that "oppression is as American as apple pie" for Black women, and her comments inspired an analysis of "'Apple Pie' Ideology and the Politics of Appetite in the Novels of Toni Morrison" by Emma Parker in *Contemporary Literature*, in which that "apple pie ideology" referred specifically to "the effects of dominant (white, male) American cultural values."

Apple pie hasn't just been an avatar for America's racism; it's also been used to draw a stark line between who can be considered "truly" American and who is destined to be labeled "other." After being confined for two years in the Heart Mountain Relocation center amidst the anti-Japanese racism that engulfed the US after Pearl Harbor, Japanese American boys and girls were described as "still as American as apple pie." Another newspaper echoed this same language:

> One of the most difficult tasks faced by this country after Pearl harbor [*sic*] was to adopt an immediate policy and take quick action with respect to the Japanese living on the west coast. . . . Some were actively subversive, some were actively loyal, and some were on the fence. Some were foreign-born, the majority were native-born, some

had been exposed to the indoctrination of the Japanese government and even the Black Dragon society, *some were as American as apple pie in spite of their skin color and eye shape.*" (Emphasis mine.)

I wish I could say that such blatant anti-Asian racism was limited to this dark period of national history, but of course it wasn't. In 1937, the actress Anna May Wong, frequently cited as the first Chinese American movie star, was described in a profile in which the author wrote: "Born and raised in Los Angeles, she was as American as apple pie, but not so her portly papa." The implied message being that with the proper amount of assimilation, an accomplished actress *born in the United States* is generously granted "apple pie status" by those Americans who are naturally entitled to it, but her father hasn't become "American" enough to qualify. Despite the fact that he was *also* born in the US!

Apple pie was so effective as a marker between "American" and "other" in part because its association with mothers and home during and after the two World Wars conjured a wholesome, hearty image for the dessert that hammered home idealistic (white) American purity. This can be seen, in particular, with the emergence of the phrase "as American as motherhood and apple pie" (a phrase once used to describe actor Jimmy Stewart in 1983), which led the dish to become a shorthand for feminine love.

And beyond just motherly love, the dish represented a rustic, agrarian past that evoked nostalgia for the mythic America of a simpler time, before the widespread urbanization of the country. As one domestic writer reminded her readers, "A glance into some of the much used cook books of old times may give amusing proof of the fact that the page on which there were apple pie recipes got the hardest wear of any."

The dish even became a patriotic avatar for the middle class and Western values amid the ideological struggles of the Cold War. An American named Virginia McCleary sent an apple pie from her Texas home to Soviet Premier Nikita Khrushchev during his visit to New York City in 1960. According to McCleary, "The Communist pie is nothing but crust. In America we have an upper crust and a lower crust but it's what's between—the middle class—that gives the real flavor."

With these kinds of associations, apple pie became emblematic of a very specific American ideal: wholesome, hearty, pure, noble, and free. (And mostly white.) Because of its association with powerful factors like the US government and military, it was rewritten as a symbolic dish that (somewhat absurdly) represented classic American ideals like liberty and democracy, and, by extension, traditional American families and their homes. This symbolism also carried the implication that the dish itself was native to the United States, a mindset that echoes a history of willful ignorance of white colonialism.

Of course, this framing ignores the actual history of apple pie and its origins overseas, and it represents a falsely constructed narrative of our culture and past. But should all of this mean, ultimately, that apple pie can't be a symbol for our nation?

DESPITE ITS MANUFACTURED symbolism, apple pie actually does embody American values—just not for the reasons we may automatically think. Apple pie is not American because it is wholesome and hearty, and certainly not because it is indigenous. It's American because it embodies the way cultures and traditions from all over the world have blended, reshaped, and ingrained themselves into the fabric of this country to define the reality of our national narrative.

As John Lehndorff of the American Pie Council has commented, "When you say that something is 'as American as apple pie,' what you're really saying is that the item came to this country from elsewhere and was transformed into a distinctly American experience." Indeed, Libby O'Connell wrote in *The American Plate*, "The phrase 'as American as apple pie' is only misleading to those who forget that, except for American Indians, we are all transplants on this continent, just like apple trees."

While writing about her identity as a Muslim American, Ranya Tabari Idliby titled her 2014 book *Burqas, Baseball, and Apple Pie.* It's "the story of one American Muslim family. The story of how through our lives, our schools, our friends and neighbors, we end up living the challenges, myths, fears, hopes, and dreams of all Americans." And in its pages, Idliby wrote eloquently of the flaws and hopes of the American promise, what she says makes up the country's heart and soul. The defining identity of this country is "its superpower ability to welcome, assimilate, and empower those who continue to flock to its shores. That is truly America's unrivaled, unmatched power, pride, and legacy. It is our own."

In many ways, apple pie embodies this immigrant experience— which, in the end, is perhaps the most distinctly American experience of all. A fruit that originated in Kazakhstan starring in a British pastry and beloved by people across the United States transcends national and cultural boundaries in much the same way my Greek great-grandparents did when they opened an American-style diner as immigrants. This dessert has been embraced by Americans from every background and heritage; indeed, there's a reason that one author used the dish to capture the diverse cuisines of the

North Shore in Massachusetts she documented in a book titled *From Apple Pie to Pad Thai: Neighborhood Cooking North of Boston.*

In *American Like Me: Reflections on Life Between Cultures,* actor America Ferrera recounted her experience growing up with apple pie and the way it intersected with all aspects of her identity: "Speaking Spanish at home, my mom's Saturday-morning-salsa-dance party in the kitchen, and eating tamales alongside apple pie at Christmas do not in any way seem at odds with my American identity. In fact, having parents with deep ties to another country and culture feels part and parcel of being an American." Such experiences can be found across the nation, from the recollections in Edmund S. Wong's *Growing Up in San Francisco's Chinatown: Boomer Memories from Noodle Rolls to Apple Pie* to the recipe swapping in "Apple Pie and *Makizushi*: Japanese American Women Sustaining Family and Community" by Valerie J. Matsumoto in *Eating Asian American.* Indeed, at their core "apples are a part of Americans' national identity in a way no other fruit is," wrote Anne Dimock in *Humble Pie: Musings on What Lies Beneath the Crust.* "Maybe we embrace its immigrant heritage and hybrid vigor as a reflection of ourselves."

The United States was woven from the cultural influences, histories, and traditions of countless populations who have made this country their home, creating a richly vibrant culture that is distinct all on its own. So too was apple pie.

AKIM'S APPLE PIE

My entire life, I've made this apple pie every October in celebration of my dad's birthday. Once, I flew all the way across the country to do it. (My mother, despite her many, *many* skills, is not much of a baker, and I couldn't trust this important duty to her.) There are two non-negotiable elements to this recipe: The first is that you use Granny Smith apples, which bring a welcome tartness and retain a slight crunch even after a long bake in the oven. The second is that you carve the name of your loved one in the crust—it's the best way to show how much you truly care.

2 All-Butter Pie Crusts (pages 12–13)
6 to 7 medium-to-large Granny Smith apples, peeled, cored, and cut into ¼-inch (6-mm) slices
Juice of ½ lemon
⅓ to ½ cup (65 to 100 g) sugar (depending on your preferred sweetness)
⅓ cup (40 g) all-purpose flour
1½ teaspoons ground cinnamon
½ teaspoon ground nutmeg
½ teaspoon salt
1 large egg, lightly beaten, for brushing the crust

Preheat the oven to 425°F (220°C). Line a 9-inch (23-cm) pie pan with one of the prepared crusts. Place in the refrigerator while you make your filling.

In a large bowl, toss the apples with the lemon juice.

In a medium bowl, combine the sugar, flour, cinnamon, nutmeg, and salt. Add the sugar mixture to the apples and toss until the apples are completely coated. Place the apples in the prepared crust by laying them in a circle, moving from the outside of the crust and working toward the inside until you've used them all. Pour any juices over the filling.

Place the second pie crust over the filling, sealing the sides by pressing the edges of the two crusts together. Cut the name of your loved one in the crust with a sharp knife (or just cut some vents if you want to be boring). Brush the crust with egg.

Bake for 40 to 50 minutes, until the crust is golden brown and the filling is bubbling though the name. Let cool slightly before serving, so that the filling can set and be cut neatly.

ACKNOWLEDGMENTS

THE FIRST PERSON I can ever remember officially calling me a writer was my yiayia Rosie, who was proudly reciting her grandchildren's professions and dropped "writer" alongside more conventional careers like lawyer, dentist, and engineer. "Huh," I thought. I guess, technically, I was a writer. Given that I was in my early twenties at the time and had absolutely no idea about what I wanted in a career, or even believed was possible, it felt powerful to have a concrete name to return to. I was, and am, a writer. And now an author.

So thank you to her (even though she has no recollection of this moment) and to the rest of my family for their love and support. Thank you to my sister, Hali, for always keeping me humble. Thank you to my parents, Akim and Constance, whose unwavering faith in me has taught me that I am capable of anything, even when most of the time I don't really believe that. I am so so lucky to have parents as loving and supportive as you two. It's a cliché to say something wouldn't have been possible without someone, but this book really and truly wouldn't have been possible without y'all.

To my friends, thank you for listening to me give the exact same life update for the past year and a half: "I'm doing well, mostly been working on the book." So boring. Now I can be fun again! In particular, 406 (Lindsay, Nikki, and Caroline) and 301B (Laura, Emily, Leah, Lauren, and once again Caroline) have been the best cheerleaders in the world. I owe you all a Blue Cup.

More thank-yous for important people: my incredibly supportive King Arthur family—I love geeking out over baking with you! Every editor who ever let me write for them. Nikki Hardin, whose writing made me want to be a writer. Generations of bakers, both celebrated and unacknowledged, who shaped this pie story. Whoever decided to let me into UNC-Chapel Hill, you changed my life.

Part of the reason UNC changed my life is because it connected me to Chris Combemale, who in turn connected me to Robert Guinsler, who have both been the best agents any author, let alone a first-time one, could ever hope for. Thank you both for understanding this book from the very beginning. It's pretty, shall we say, unconventional, and having agents who knew what I was trying to do and championed that from the beginning was huge.

On that note, thank you to the whole team at Abrams, particularly to my editor, Chelsea Cutchens. Your warmth, understanding, and diligence have made this experience a joy, and this book infinitely better.

Thank you to Theo Anastopoulo, the most thorough and enthusiastic research assistant around, whose assistance bringing some of these chapters to life was crucial.

And my deepest, most heartfelt thank-you to you, dear reader, for picking up this book and diving into these stories and pies along with me. During one of my lower moments of writing, I told a friend that I wished I could write this book and ensure that no one would ever read it. But that's not true. I'm so glad, if still slightly terrified, that you've read these words and hopefully had a laugh and a deep think as a result. Happy baking (and eating)!

NOTES

INTRODUCTION

2 Inspired by nonviolent . . . : "A Passive Insister Ezell Blair Jr." *The New York Times*, March 25, 1960.

2 The tactic—which . . . : Harvey Harris, "First Sit-In Participant Finally Gets Cherry Pie," *Greensboro Daily News*, February 4, 1973.

2 First, the group . . . : Jim Schlosser, "Jan. 27, 1985: Four men summon courage to alter course of history," *Greensboro News & Record*, January 26, 1985, greensboro.com/townnews/commerce/jan-27 -1985-four-men-summon-courage-to-alter-course-of-history/article _c60882e6-7a13-11e3-bdc3-001a4bcf6878.html.

2 Finally, they took . . . : Harris, "First Sit-In Participant Finally Gets Cherry Pie."

3 The next day . . . : "Greensboro Lunch Counter Sit-In," *The African American Odyssey*, Library of Congress, December 9, 1998, www.loc.gov/exhibits/odyssey/educate/lunch.html.

3 "We bowed our . . .": Quoted in Marcie Cohen Ferris, *The Edible South: The Power of Food and the Making of an American Region* (Chapel Hill: University of North Carolina Press, 2014), 255.

4 And when, over . . . : Harris, "First Sit-In Participant Finally Gets Cherry Pie."

4 Joseph McNeil also . . . : Matt Cherry and Emanuella Grinberg, "Sit-in vet: 'Never request permission to start a revolution,'" CNN, February 1, 2010, www.cnn.com/2010/US/02/01/greensboro.four.sitins/index .html.

CHAPTER ONE

16 Pie, for instance . . . : John Ayto, *An A–Z of Food and Drink* (Oxford, England: Oxford University Press, 2002), 254.

17 Colonial expansion was . . . : Lizabeth Cohen and David M. Kennedy, *The American Pageant*, 15th ed. (Boston: Cengage Learning, 2012), 26–27.

17 The establishment of . . . : Karen Ordahl Kupperman, *The Jamestown Project* (Cambridge, MA: Harvard University Press, 2009), 191.

18 Apple pie emerged . . . : Andrew F. Smith, ed., *The Oxford Encyclopedia of Food and Drink in America, Volume 1* (Oxford, England: Oxford University Press, 2004), 43.

18 This dish, however . . . : Janet Clarkson, *Pie: A Global History* (London: Reaktion Books Ltd., 2009), 19.

18 Pastry cooks began . . . : "Pie and Pastry," The Food Timeline, accessed April 6, 2016, www.foodtimeline.org/foodpies.html.

18 By the time . . . : Robert May, *The Accomplisht Cook, Or, The Art & Mystery of Cookery: Wherein the Whole Art is Revealed in a More Easie and Perfect Method, Than Hath Been Publisht in Any Language. Expert and Ready Ways for the Dressing of All Sorts of Flesh, Fowl, and Fish, with Variety of Sauces Proper for Each of Them; and how to Raise All Manner of Pastes; the Best Directions for All Sorts of Kickshaws, Also the Terms of Carving and Sewing. An Exact Account of All Dishes for All Seasons of the Year, with Other À-la-mode Curiosities* (London: O. Blagrave, 1685).

18 In England, bakers . . . : Clarkson, *Pie*, 25.

19 "Tak gode Applys . . .": Samuel Pegge, *The Forme of Cury: A Roll of Ancient English Cookery, Compiled, about A.D. 1390, by the Master-cooks of King Richard II, Presented Afterwards to Queen Elizabeth, by Edward, Lord Stafford, and Now in the Possession of Gustavus Brander, Esq.* (London: J. Nichols, 1780), xxiv.

19 "Take your apples . . .": *A Proper Newe Booke of Cokerye*, ed. Catherine Frances Frere (London: W. Heffer & Sons Ltd., 1913), 29.

20 "Thy breath is . . .": Robert Greene, *Menaphon* (London: T. Orwin for S. Clarke, 1589), 87.

20 "Of all the . . .": *The Northern Atalantis: Or, York Spy* (United Kingdom: A. Baldwin, 1713), 13.

20 "Good apple pies . . .": Quoted in Josephine Ross, *Jane Austen: A Companion* (New Brunswick, NJ: Rutgers University Press, 2003), 50.

20 The Netherlands, in . . . : Thomas VanderNoot, *Een notabel boecxken van cokeryen* (Brussels: Thomas VanderNoot, 1514), www.kookhistorie.nl/index.htm.

21 Not to mention . . . : Sally Smith Booth, *Hung, Strung & Potted: A History of Eating in Colonial America* (New York: Clarkson N. Potter, Inc., 1971), 1.

21 That's right—the . . . : Thomas Burford, "Apples," in *The Oxford Encyclopedia of Food and Drink in America*, 2nd ed., ed. Andrew Smith (Oxford, England: Oxford University Press, 2013), 78.

21 What did grow . . . : Ibid.

21 They were also . . . : Andrew F. Smith, *Food and Drink in American History: A "Full Course" Encyclopedia* (Santa Barbara, CA: ABC-CLIO, 2013), 39–40.

21 Plus, they were . . . : Booth, *Hung, Strung & Potted*, 155.

22 Originally, settlers attempted . . . : "Winter Banana, Northern Spy & King Luscious: Apples in America," Cornell University Albert R. Mann Library, accessed November 29, 2020, exhibits.mannlib.cornell.edu/apples/home.htm.

22 A cider apple . . . : "Hewes Crab Apple," Thomas Jefferson Foundation, Inc., accessed September 13, 2021, www.monticello.org/site/house-and-gardens/in-bloom/hewes-crab-apple.

22 And that crop . . . : Burford, "Apples," 78.

23 One such book . . . : Mary Tolford Wilson, "Amelia Simmons Fills a Need: American Cookery, 1796," *The William and Mary Quarterly* 14, no. 1 (1957): 16–17.

24 In fact, the . . . : Gervase Markham, *The English Housewife facsimile ed.*, ed. Michael R. Best (Kingston: McGill–Queen's University Press, 1986), 105.

24 Susannah Carter, for . . . : Susannah Carter, *The Frugal Housewife Or, Complete Woman Cook* (London: F. Newbery; reprinted in Boston: Edes and Gill, 1772), 119.

24 Her apple pie . . . : Rebecca Claire Bunschoten, "As American as Apple Pie: The History of American Apple Pie and Its Development into a National Symbol," Bard Senior Projects Spring 2014, 13.

25 "Make a good . . .": Ibid.

25 These published recipes . . . : Mary Tolford Wilson, "The First American Cookbook," in *The First American Cookbook: A Facsimile of "American Cookery," 1796* (New York: Dover Publications, Inc., 1958), vii–xi.

25 They reflected the . . . : Pat Willard, "Pies and Tarts," in *The Oxford Encyclopedia of Food and Drink in America*, *Volume 2*, ed. Andrew Smith (Oxford, England: Oxford University Press, 2004), 272.

26 "Aple" pie, for . . . : John Page, *Diary of John Page, 1757–1781*, Harvard University Archives, accessed October 27, 2021, iiif.lib.harvard.edu/manifests/view/drs:46645632$55i.

26　"Apple pie is . . .": Israel Acrelius, *A History of New Sweden: Or, The Settlements on the River Delaware* (Philadelphia: Historical Society of Pennsylvania, 1874), 159.

26　By drying the . . . : Willard, "Pies and Tarts," 272.

26　In the Massachusetts . . . : "Massachusetts: Government and Society," Britannica, accessed November 29, 2020, www.britannica.com/place /Massachusetts/Government-and-society.

27　In Rhode Island . . . : Alan Taylor, *American Colonies* (New York: Penguin Books, 2002), 182.

27　And he wasn't . . . : "Thomas Hooker," Britannica, accessed November 29, 2020, www.britannica.com/biography/Thomas-Hooker.

27　As colonies continued . . . : William Roger Louis, *The Oxford History of the British Empire: Volume I: The Origins of Empire* (Oxford: OUP Oxford, 2001), 351.

27　Isolated in the . . . : Cohen and Kennedy, *The American Pageant*, 87–88.

28　Meanwhile, the Enlightenment . . . : D. H. Meyer, "The Uniqueness of the American Enlightenment," *American Quarterly* 28, no. 2 (1976): 171.

29　As culinary historian . . . : Karen Hess, "Historical Notes on the Work and Its Author, Amelia Simmons, An American Orphan," in *American Cookery* (Carlisle, MA: Applewood Books, 1996), x.

29　"So, again, what . . .": Ibid., xv.

30　For instance, Simmons . . . : Amelia Simmons, *American Cookery* (Hartford: Hudson & Goodwin, 1796), www.gutenberg.org/cache /epub/12815/pg12815.html.

30　Catering to a . . . : Mary Tolford Wilson, "Amelia Simmons Fills a Need: American Cookery, 1796," 29.

30　"Amelia Simmons's work . . .": Ibid., 19.

30　*American Cookery* knowingly . . . : Ibid., 28.

30　"Apples, are still . . .": Simmons, *American Cookery*, www.gutenberg .org/cache/epub/12815/pg12815.html.

31　"A Buttered Apple . . .": Ibid.

31　In particular, it . . . : Wilson, "Amelia Simmons Fills a Need: American Cookery, 1796," 20.

32　"The pie is . . .": Harriet Beecher Stowe, *Oldtown Folks* (Boston: Fields, Osgood, & Company, 1869), 340.

CHEDDAR APPLE PIE

35 Its roots, like . . . : Michael Waters, "The Long, Storied Controversy Over Cheese on Apple Pie," Gastro Obscura, July 13, 2017,
www.atlasobscura.com/articles/cheese-apple-pie.

35 Cheese, too, was . . . : Bruno Battistotti, Vittorio Bottazzi, Antonio Pic-
cinardi, and Giancarlo Volpato, Cheese: A Guide to the World of Cheese and
Cheesemaking (New York: Facts on File Publications, 1983), 14–15, quoted
in The Food Timeline, "Apple Pie," www.foodtimeline.org/foodpies
.html#applepie.

36 "You have a . . .": Walter Gore Marshall, Through America: Or, Nine
Months in the United States (London: S. Low, Marston, Searle & Riving-
ton, 1882), 99.

36 This pairing was . . . : Phillip Stephen Schulz, As American as Apple Pie
(New York: Simon & Schuster, 1990), 19.

36 One woman used . . . : "A Young Housekeeper's Trials in Serving Japanese Fowl," Quad-City Times (Davenport, IA), November 23, 1891.

36 "But I, when . . .": The World of Eugene Field Vol. 1 (New York: Charles
Scribner's Sons, 1896), 43–46.

36 Southern Living once . . . : Lisa Cericola, "Why Southerners Wouldn't
Put a Slice of Cheese on Apple Pie," Southern Living, accessed October 1, 2021, www.southernliving.com/desserts/pies/apple-pie-with
-cheese.

36 Meanwhile, up North . . . : Sec. 1. 1 V.S.A. § 512 (1999), www.leg.state
.vt.us/docs/2000/acts/ACT015.HTM.

CHAPTER TWO

39 In fact, squash . . . : Cindy Ott, Pumpkin: The Curious History of an American Icon (Seattle: University of Washington Press, 2012), 10.

39 Early pumpkins were . . . : Ibid., 11.

40 Regardless, a large . . . : Sandra L. Oliver, Food in Colonial and Federal
America (Westport, CT: Greenwood Press: 2005), 128–29.

40 "With this corn . . .": Quoted in M. K. Bennett, "The Food Economy of
the New England Indians, 1605–75," Journal of Political Economy 63, no. 5
(1955): 388.

40 Pumpkin, in particular . . . : Ott, Pumpkin, 11, 18.

40 The plant was . . . : Ibid., 12.

41 One Iroquois creation . . . : Ibid., 19.

41 The plant occasionally . . . : F. W. Waugh, *Iroquois Foods and Food Preparation, facsimile 1916 edition* (Honolulu: University Press of the Pacific, 2003), 16.

41 When it came . . . : Ibid., 114–15.

42 And since there . . . : Oliver, *Food in Colonial and Federal America*, 128–29; Waugh, *Iroquois Foods and Food Preparation*, 87–93.

42 Not to mention . . . : Bennett, "The Food Economy of the New England Indians, 1605–75," 384.

42 "They will not . . .": Quoted in ibid.

42 Thanks to Canada's . . . : Waugh, *Iroquois Foods and Food Preparation*, 140–42.

42 Interestingly enough, honeybees . . . : Ibid., 140–43.

42 Columbus's landfall resulted . . . : Nathan Nunn and Nancy Qian, "The Columbian Exchange: A History of Disease, Food, and Ideas," *Journal of Economic Perspectives* 24, no. 2 (2010): 165.

43 These effects are . . . : Alejandro Colás, Jason Edwards, Jane Levi, and Sami Zubaida, "Exchange: The Columbian Exchange and Mercantile Empires," in *Food, Politics, and Society: Social Theory and the Modern Food System* (Oakland, CA: University of California Press, 2018), 43.

43 More than a hundred . . . : Andrew F. Smith, "The First Thanksgiving," *Gastronomica* 3, no. 4 (2003): 79.

44 After a series . . . : Gregory D. Smithers, "Rethinking Genocide in North America," in *The Oxford Handbook of Genocide Studies*, ed. Donald Bloxham and A. Dirk Moses (Oxford: OUP Oxford, 2010), 330–31.

44 With few supplies . . . : Paula Neely, "Jamestown Colonists Resorted to Cannibalism," National Geographic, May 3, 2013, www.national geographic.com/science/article/130501-jamestown-cannibalism -archeology-science.

44 "There was also . . .": Edward Winslow, *Mourt's Relation: A Journal of the Pilgrims in Plymouth* (Carlisle, MA: Applewood Books, 1986), 22.

45 "It is not . . .": Rod Gragg, *The Pilgrim Chronicles: An Eyewitness History of the Pilgrims and the Founding of Plymouth Colony* (Washington, DC: Regnery History, 2014), 103.

45 Years earlier in . . . : David J. Silverman, *This Land Is Their Land: The Wampanoag Indians, Plymouth Colony, and the Troubled History of Thanksgiving* (New York: Bloomsbury Publishing, 2019), 61–68.

45 In the end . . . : David J. Silverman, "In 1621, the Wampanoag Tribe Had Its Own Agenda," *The Atlantic*, November 27, 2019, www.theatlantic .com/ideas/archive/2019/11/thanksgiving-belongs-wampanoag -tribe/602422/.

45 Ousamequin signed a . . . : Silverman, *This Land Is Their Land*, 143–67.

46 As a result . . . : Emory Dean Keoke and Kay Marie Porterfield, "Thanksgiving," in *Encyclopedia of American Indian Contributions to the World: 15,000 Years of Inventions and Innovations* (New York: Facts on File, Incorporated, 2009), 262.

46 It's true that . . . : Smith, "The First Thanksgiving," 81.

46 Supposedly, Governor William . . . : Keoke and Porterfield, "Thanksgiving," 262.

46 A celebration of . . . : Ibid.

47 Besides the deer . . . : Ibid.

47 Indeed, even the . . . : "Fun with Words," Wôpanâak Language Reclamation Project, accessed October 29, 2021, www.wlrp.org/fun-with -words.

48 What's much harder . . . : Silverman, *This Land Is Their Land*, 352.

48 In 1637, following . . . : Delilah Friedler, "This Thanksgiving Marks 50 Years Since Natives Occupied Alcatraz. They Want You to Remember Why," Mother Jones, The Foundation for National Progress, November 28, 2019, www.motherjones.com/politics/2019/11 /unthanksgiving-day-50-anniversary-native-occupation-alcatraz -island-scene.

48 The squash was . . . : Ott, *Pumpkin*, 33.

48 Edward Ward, an . . . : Edward Ward, *Boston in 1682 and 1699: A Trip to New-England* (Providence, RI: Club for Colonial Reprints, 1905), 50 & 58.

49 "This Countrey aboundeth . . .": Francis Higginson, *New-Englands Plantation: With the Sea Journal and Other Writings* (Salem, MA: Essex Book and Print Club, 1908), 93–94.

49 "Instead of pottage . . .": Quoted in Ott, *Pumpkin*, 36–37.

49 At the time . . . : Ibid.

49 One Maine farmer's . . . : Ibid., 36–38.

49 One 1671 cookbook . . . : John Josselyn, *New-England's rarities discovered in birds, beasts, fishes, serpents, and plants of that country* (Boston: W. Veazie, 1865), 148.

50 "boil them whole . . .": Pehr Kalm, *Travels Into North America: Containing*

Its Natural History, and a Circumstantial Account of Its Plantations and Agriculture in General, with the Civil, Ecclesiastical and Commercial State of the Country, the Manners of the Inhabitants, and Several Curious and Important Remarks on Various Subjects (London: The Editor, 1771), 266–67.

50 "the French and . . .": Ibid.

50 "some [Europeans] make . . .": Ibid.

50 Indeed, according to . . . : Ott, *Pumpkin*, 50.

50 So it's no . . . : Amelia Simmons, *American Cookery* (Hartford: Hudson & Goodwin, 1796), www.gutenberg.org/cache/epub/12815/pg12815.html.

51 Throughout the eighteenth . . . : Ott, *Pumpkin*, 39–40.

52 Those values often . . . : Ibid., 104.

52 "I would rather . . .": Henry David Thoreau, *Walden* (New York: Thomas Y. Crowell & Company, 1910), 47.

52 Leaning heavily on . . . : Ott, *Pumpkin*, 68.

52 "one or two . . .": John Palmer, *Journal of Travels in the United States . . . in the Year 1817* (London: Sherwood, Nealy and Jones, 1818), 241.

52 "Having recently traveled . . .": A.B.C., "Pumpkin Pies," *American Farmer* (Baltimore, MD), January 11, 1833.

53 "Yesterday, the first . . .": Susan Fenimore Cooper, *Rural Hours* (New York: G.P. Putnam, 1850), 297.

53 Though it supposedly. . . : "Congress Establishes Thanksgiving," The Center for Legislature Archives, The U.S. National Archives and Records Administration, accessed December 5, 2020, www.archives .gov/legislative/features/thanksgiving.

53 Though it wasn't . . . : Ott, *Pumpkin*, 100.

54 "If Thanksgiving in . . .": "All the Squashes," *American Farmer* (Baltimore, MD), November 18, 1834.

54 "on Thanksgiving day . . .": John Greenleaf Whittier, "The Pumpkin," Poetry Foundation, accessed December 3, 2020, www.poetryfoundation .org/poems/53105/the-pumpkin.

54 "around the same time . . .": Lydia Maria Child, "A New-England Boy's Song about Thanksgiving Day," Poetry Foundation, accessed December 5, 2020, www.poetryfoundation.org/poems/43942/the-new-england -boys-song-about-thanksgiving-day.

54 Perhaps most important . . . : Sarah Josepha Buell Hale, *Northwood; A Tale of New England* (Boston: Bowles & Dearborn, 1827), 109–10.

54 This book wasn't . . . : Smith, "The First Thanksgiving," 82.

55 Hale was convinced . . . : Ibid.

55 "OUR THANKSGIVING UNION . . .": Sarah Josepha Hale, "Editor's Table," *Godey's Lady's Book*, November 1859, 466.

55 "We must advert . . .": Hale, "Editor's Table," 271.

55 A true ringleader . . . : Smith, "The First Thanksgiving," 82.

55 By the late . . . : Ibid., 84.

56 The narrative was . . . : Ibid., 84–85.

56 In one particularly . . . : Hampton Institute, "Hampton School Record," *Southern Workman*, December 1892, 184.

56 "is known to . . .": "The American Pumpkin," *St. Louis Globe-Democrat*, November 7, 1884.

56 One writer for . . . : "He Longs for Pie: Away with Foreign Cooks Who Won't Serve Mince and Pumpkin," *Emporia (Kansas) Daily Gazette*, May 1, 1895.

57 "When properly made . . .": "Genuine Pumpkin Pie," *Kansas City Journal*, reprinted in the *Macon (Georgia) Telegraph*, October 23, 1897.

57 "Surely a Thanksgiving . . .": John L. Cowan, "The Golden Pumpkin Pie," *Pacific Monthly*, November 1906, 570.

57 Pumpkin pie appeared . . . : Emma Paddock Telford, *New York Evening Telegram Cook Book* (New York: Cupples & Leon, 1908), 218; "Inmates of Institutions to Get Holiday Meals," *Daily Record* (New Jersey), November 23, 1932; Ott, *Pumpkin*, 124.

57 "For many, without . . .": Jonathan Hayes, "Pumpkin Pie 101," *Martha Stewart Living*, November 2000, 98.

57 And perhaps most . . . : *Time*, November 19, 2001.

58 Instead, some gather . . . : "Homepage," United American Indians of New England, accessed December 6, 2020, www.uaine.org.

58 Others make their . . . : Friedler, "This Thanksgiving Marks 50 Years Since Natives Occupied Alcatraz. They Want You to Remember Why."

59 Looking at the . . . : Durwood Vanderhoop (Wampanoag language instructor, singer, and artist) in discussion with the author, October 2021.

CHAPTER THREE

64 "Molasses is generally . . .": Quoted in Frederick Douglass Opie, "Molasses-Colored Glasses: WPA and Sundry Sources on Molasses and Southern Foodways," *Southern Cultures* 14, no. 1 (2008): 82.

64 Later, in the . . . : John F. Mariani, *The Encyclopedia of American Food and Drink* (New York: Lebhar-Friedman, 1999), 207–8.

64 By 1820, for . . . : Manuel Moreno Fraginals, "The Crisis of the Plantation: Part One: The years before emancipation," in *General History of the Caribbean Volume IV: The Long Nineteenth Century: Nineteenth-Century Transformations*, ed. K.O. Lawrence and Jorge Ibarra Cuesta (Paris: UNESCO and London: Macmillan Education, 1997), 78.

64 What's more, the . . . : Sidney Mintz, *Sweetness and Power: The Place of Sugar in Modern History* (New York: Penguin Books, 1985) 146.

64 "molasses has been . . . : Opie, "Molasses-Colored Glasses: WPA and Sundry Sources on Molasses and Southern Foodways," 82.

64 One Civil War . . . : William A. Hunter, "The Civil War Diaries of Leonard C. Ferguson," *Pennsylvania History: A Journal of Mid-Atlantic Studies* 14, no. 3 (1947): 219.

64 Indeed, molasses became . . . : Opie, "Molasses-Colored Glasses: WPA and Sundry Sources on Molasses and Southern Foodways," 87.

65 These include 1838's . . . : Helen Duprey Bullock, *The Williamsburg Art of Cookery, Or, Accomplish'd Gentlewoman's Companion: Being a Collection of Upwards of Five Hundred of the Most Ancient & Approv'd Recipes in Virginia Cookery . . . and Also a Table of Favorite Williamsburg Garden Herbs* (Williamsburg, VA: Colonial Williamsburg, 1983), 127.

65 "This is decidedly . . .": "Domestic Receipts," *The Southern Planter* 18, no. 11 (1858): 703.

66 "The molasses pie . . .": Emma Cassandra Riely Macon, *Reminiscences of the Civil War* (Cedar Rapids, IA: The Torch Press, 1911), 118–19.

66 In his extensive . . . : Lafcadio Hearn, *La Cuisine Creole: A Collection of Culinary Recipes from Leading Chefs and Noted Creole Housewives* (Carlisle, MA: Applewood Books, 2007), 193.

66 "wholesome and palatable . . .": Eliza Leslie, *Miss Leslie's New Cookery Book* (Philadelphia: T. B. Peterson, 1857), xxvi.

66 True to its titular . . . : Ibid., 446.

67 Molasses pie was . . . : Fanny Lemira Gillette, *White House Cook Book: A Selection of Choice Recipes, Original and Selected, During a Period of Forty Years' Practical Housekeeping* (Chicago: L.P. Miller, 1889), 296.

67 Interestingly enough, Abraham . . . : "The Best Belt Speed," *The Cracker Baker* 6, no. 1 (1917): 36.

67 Following a drop . . . : Mariani, *The Encyclopedia of American Food and Drink*, 207–8.

68 The sugarcane ultimately . . . : Mintz, *Sweetness and Power*, 37.

69 Bearing sugarcane seedlings . . . : Opie, "Molasses-Colored Glasses: WPA and Sundry Sources on Molasses and Southern Foodways," 82.

69 The sugarcane took . . . : Mintz, *Sweetness and Power*, 34–35.

69 At that point . . . : Khalil Gibran Muhammad, "The Barbaric History of Sugar in America," *The New York Times*, August 14, 2019, www.nytimes.com/interactive/2019/08/14/magazine/sugar-slave-trade-slavery.html.

69 The British, in . . . : "The Caribbean and the Trade," Black Presence: Asian and Black History in Britain, The National Archives, accessed September 25, 2021, www.nationalarchives.gov.uk/pathways/black history/africa_caribbean/caribbean_trade.htm.

70 "It is well . . .": Quoted in Frank Wesley Pitman, *The Development of the British West Indies, 1700–1763* (New Haven: Yale University Press, 1917), 415.

70 But the commodity . . . : "The Caribbean and the Trade."

70 In order to . . . : Ibid.

70 In Barbados, another . . . : John J. McCusker and Russell R. Menard, *The Economy of British America, 1607–1789* (Chapel Hill: University of North Carolina Press, 1991), 151.

70 Meanwhile, 662,400 enslaved . . . : Marc Aronson and Marina Tamar Budhos, *Sugar Changed the World: A Story of Magic, Spice, Slavery, Freedom, and Science* (Boston: Clarion Books, 2010), 32.

70 By 1753, the . . . : Ibid., 35.

70 Across the New . . . : Muhammad, "The Barbaric History of Sugar in America."

71 "They have a . . .": Quoted in Daniel Meaders, *Dead or Alive: Fugitive Slaves and White Indentured Servants Before 1830* (New York: Garland Pub., 1993), 121.

71 Working the sugar . . . : Aronson and Budhos, *Sugar Changed the World*, 36.

71 In the sugar . . . : "Slavery in Louisiana," Whitney Plantation, accessed December 9 2020, www.whitneyplantation.org/history/slavery-in-louisiana.

71 Viewed as nothing . . . : Manuel Moreno Fraginals, "The Crisis of the Plantation: Part One: The years before emancipation," in *General History of the Caribbean: The Long Nineteenth Century: Nineteenth-Century Transformations*, ed. K.O. Lawrence and Jorge Ibarra Cuesta (United Kingdom: Macmillan, 1997), 72.

71 One sugar plantation . . . : Aronson and Budhos, *Sugar Changed the World*, 59.

72 By the late . . . : Andrew F. Smith, *Food and Drink in American History*, 122–23.

72 This successful system . . . : Mariani, *The Encyclopedia of American Food and Drink*, 207–8.

72 In the New . . . : Smith, *Food and Drink in American History*, 122–23.

72 Despite colonists' ample . . . : Waverly Root & Richard de Rochemont, *Eating in America: A History* (New York: William Morrow, 1976), 83.

73 The whole molasses . . . : Smith, *Food and Drink in American History*, 122–23.

73 As early as . . . : "Early Carolina Settlement: Barbados Influence," African Passages, Lowcountry Adaptations, Lowcountry Digital History Initiative, College of Charleston, accessed September 25, 2021, ldhi.library.cofc.edu/exhibits/show/africanpassageslowcountryadapt /sectionii_introduction/barbados_influence.

73 Though the crop . . . : Opie, "Molasses-Colored Glasses: WPA and Sundry Sources on Molasses and Southern Foodways," 82.

73 Sugarcane was first . . . : Muhammad, "The Barbaric History of Sugar in America."

73 The raw sugar . . . : "Slavery in Louisiana."

73 So brutal was . . . : Ibid.

74 "Every body worked . . .": Quoted in Aronson and Budhos, *Sugar Changed the World*, 92.

74 Slave revolts erupted . . . : Muhammad, "The Barbaric History of Sugar in America."

74 And beyond the . . . : Jenifer Frank, Joel Lang, Anne Farrow, *Complicity: How the North Promoted, Prolonged, and Profited from Slavery* (United States: Ballantine Books, 2006), xxv–xxviii.

74 Since molasses was . . . : Opie, "Molasses-Colored Glasses: WPA and Sundry Sources on Molasses and Southern Foodways," 85.

74 "They only had . . .": Betty Cofer, "Negro Folk Lore of the Piedmont,"

interview by Esther S. Pinnix, *Federal Writers' Project: Slave Narrative Project, Vol. 11, North Carolina, Part 1* (Washington, DC: The Library of Congress Project, 1941), 168.

74 Meanwhile, the weekly . . . : Opie, "Molasses-Colored Glasses: WPA and Sundry Sources on Molasses and Southern Foodways," 84–85.

74 "And sugar—we . . .": Fannie Clemons, interview by Pernella Anderson, *Federal Writers' Project: Slave Narrative Project, Vol. 2, Arkansas, Part 2* (Washington, DC: The Library of Congress Project, 1941), 28.

74 Even as far . . . : Jessica B. Harris, *High on the Hog: A Culinary Journey from Africa to America* (New York: Bloomsbury Publishing, 2011), 33.

75 There, enslaved cooks . . . : Opie, "Molasses-Colored Glasses: WPA and Sundry Sources on Molasses and Southern Foodways," 86.

75 It also retained . . . : M. E. Porter, *Mrs. Porter's New Southern Cookery Book, and Companion for Frugal and Economical Housekeepers* (Philadelphia: John E. Potter and Company, 1871), 26.

75 "to the mothers . . .": *The New Dixie Cook-Book and Practical Housekeeper, Carefully Compiled from the Treasured Family Collections of Many Generations of Noted Housekeepers* (Atlanta: L.A. Clarkson & Company, 1889), iii.

75 In addition, the . . . : Reah Jeannette Lynch, *"Win the War" Cook Book* (Missouri: St. Louis County Unit Woman's Committee Council of National Defense, 1918), 106–7.

76 Around the same . . . : Ben I. Isaacs, *The New Orleans Federation of Clubs Cook Book* (United States: n.p., 1917), 23.

76 Quite tellingly, too . . . : The Southern Ruralist, *Favorite Southern Recipes* (Atlanta: Southern Ruralist, 1912), 90.

76 And of course . . . : Advertisement for Brer Rabbit Molasses, *Ladies' Home Journal*, January 1921, 82.

76 "Recipes were passed . . .": Ibid.

77 "The South has . . .": Quoted in Marcie Cohen Ferris, *The Edible South* (Chapel Hill: University of North Carolina Press, 2009), 189.

77 But while an . . . : Robert W. Brower, "Molasses," in *The Oxford Encyclopedia of Food and Drink in America*, ed. Andrew F. Smith (Oxford, England: Oxford University Press, 2004), 122–23.

CHAPTER FOUR

79 When the National . . . : Tracie McMillan, "Don't Mess with the Sweet Potato Pie: A Museum Wrestles with 'Authentic' Black Menu," The

Salt, National Public Radio, April 11, 2018, www.npr.org/sections/the-salt/2018/04/11/599888119/dont-mess-with-the-sweet-potato-pie-a-museum-wrestles-with-authentic-black-menu.

80 *Real* yams are . . . : Lynne Olver, "Sweet potato pie," The Food Time-line, accessed December 17, 2020, www.foodtimeline.org/foodpies.html#sweetpotatopie.

81 Sweet potatoes are . . . : Alan Davidson, *The Oxford Companion to Food* (Oxford, England: Oxford University Press, 1999), 775.

81 Yams, on the . . . : Ibid., 856.

81 Enslaved Africans called . . . : John F. Mariani, *The Encyclopedia of American Food and Drink* (New York: Lebhar-Friedman, 1999), 318.

81 Grown prolifically across . . . : Andrew F. Smith, "Sweet Potatoes," in *The Oxford Encyclopedia of Food and Drink in America*, ed. Andrew F. Smith (Oxford, England: Oxford University Press, 2004), 520; Adrian Miller, "How Sweet Potato Pie Became African Americans' Thanksgiving Dessert," *Washington Post*, November 24, 2015, www.washingtonpost.com/lifestyle/food/how-sweet-potato-pie-became-african-americans-favorite-dessert/2015/11/23/11da4216-9201-11e5-b5e4-279b4501e8a6_story.html.

81 As a result . . . : Miller, "How Sweet Potato Pie Became African Americans' Thanksgiving Dessert."

82 Frederick Douglass Opie . . . : Frederick Douglass Opie, *Hog & Hominy: Soul Food from Africa to America* (New York: Columbia University Press, 2008), 32.

82 Enslaved people used . . . : Harris, *High on the Hog*, 95.

82 The most above-board . . . : Ibid., 84.

82 Not-so-fun fact: Thomas . . . : Ibid.

82 Harris writes in . . . : Ibid., 95.

83 Enslaved cooks transformed . . . : Opie, *Hog & Hominy*, 31–32.

83 "I must confess . . .": Fredrika Bremer, *America of the Fifties: Letters of Frederika Bremer* (New York: American-Scandinavian Foundation, 1924), 107–8.

83 Common hallmarks of . . . : Opie, *Hog & Hominy*, 31–32.

83 Opie writes that . . . : Ibid.

83 "But one vegetable . . .": Frederick Olmsted, *The Cotton Kingdom: A Traveller's Observations on Cotton and Slavery* (Carlisle, MA: Applewood Books, 2008), 90.

83 "Each one receives . . .": Solomon Northup, *Twelve Years a Slave* (Carlisle, MA: Applewood Books, 2008), 168.

83 One enslaved woman . . . : Wilma A. Dunaway, *The African-American Family in Slavery and Emancipation* (Cambridge: Cambridge University Press, 2003), 147.

84 And Booker T. . . . : Ibid.

84 According to Solomon . . . : Northup, *Twelve Years a Slave*, 215.

84 "Only the slave . . .": Ibid., 168.

84 In addition to . . . : Opie, *Hog & Hominy*, 33.

84 Enslaved cooks made . . . : Ibid., 32.

84 One woman, Caroline . . . : Caroline Farrow, "Stories From Ex-Slaves," interview by G. L. Summer, *Federal Writers' Project: Slave Narrative Project, Vol. 14, South Carolina, Part 2* (Washington, DC: The Library of Congress Project, 1941), 40.

84 Another man, Gus . . . : Gus Feaster, "Slave Time Customs on the Plantation of Thomas Anderson Carlisle," interview by Caldwell Sims, *Federal Writers' Project: Slave Narrative Project, Vol. 14, South Carolina, Part 2* (Washington, DC: The Library of Congress Project, 1941), 59.

85 "Jus' thinking 'bout . . .": Emma Virgel, "Plantation Life as Viewed by Ex-Slaves," interview by Grace McCune, *Federal Writers' Project: Slave Narrative Project, Vol. 4, Georgia, Part 4* (Washington, DC: The Library of Congress Project, 1941), 120.

85 These unique iterations . . . : Harris, *High on the Hog*, 95.

85 Interestingly enough, pies . . . : Larry Zuckerman, *The Potato: How the Humble Spud Rescued the Western World* (New York: North Point Press, 1998), 9.

86 In the American . . . : Smith, "Sweet Potatoes," 520.

86 American versions of . . . : Mary Randolph, *The Virginia Housewife: Or, Methodical Cook* (Baltimore: Plaskitt, Fite, 1838), 120; Lettice Bryan, *The Kentucky Housewife* (Carlisle, MA: Applewood Books, 2001), 268; Anna Wells Rutledge and Sarah Rutledge, *The Carolina Housewife* (Columbia: University of South Carolina Press, 1979), 131.

86 "discharge each devolving . . .": Bryan, *The Kentucky Housewife*, vii.

86 "Have established rules . . .": Ibid.

86 Mrs. Mary Randolph . . . : Randolph, *The Virginia Housewife*, vii.

87 In *The Kentucky* . . . : Bryan, *The Kentucky Housewife*, 268.

87 Pie was so . . . : Anne Yentsch, "Excavating the South's African

American Food History," *African Diaspora Archaeology Newsletter* 12, no. 2 (2009): 28.

87   In fact, pastry . . . : Betty Fussell, *I Hear America Cooking* (New York: Penguin Books, 1997), 222.

87   "In the Carolinas . . .": Ibid.

87   Despite such extensive . . . : Harris, *High on the Hog*, 104–5.

88   "The Negro is . . .": Quoted in ibid.

88   White mistresses still . . . : Ibid., 104.

88   Harris shares the . . . : Ibid., 103.

88   Unlike enslaved quarters . . . : Ibid., 69.

89   "Ignoring [enslaved chefs'] . . .": Marcie Cohen Ferris, *The Edible South* (Chapel Hill: University of North Carolina Press, 2009), 89.

89   Additionally, Black chefs . . . : Toni Tipton-Martin, *The Jemima Code: Two Centuries of African American Cookbooks* (Austin: University of Texas Press, 2015), 2.

90   She was born . . . : Malinda Russell, *A Domestic Cook Book: Containing a Careful Selection of Useful Receipts for the Kitchen* (Michigan: The Author, 1866), 3.

90   It was in . . . : Ibid., 5.

90   Russell became a . . . : Ibid., 4.

90   In this way . . . : Yentsch, "Excavating the South's African American Food History," 73.

91   Despite her success . . . : Russell, *A Domestic Cook Book*, 4.

91   "followed a flag . . .": Ibid.

91   It's directed to . . . : Ibid., 23.

92   Similar to Malinda . . . : Abby Fisher, *What Mrs. Fisher Knows about Old Southern Cooking, Soups, Pickles, Preserves, Etc.* (San Francisco: Women's Co-operative Printing Office, 1881).

92   Fisher was actually . . . : Karen Hess, "What We Know About Mrs. Abby Fisher and Her Cooking," in *What Mrs. Fisher Knows about Old Southern Cooking: Soups, Pickles, Preserves, Etc.: By Abby Fisher, with Historical Notes by Karen Hess* (Carlisle, MA: Applewood Books, 1995), 76–78.

92   As she reveals . . . : Fisher, *What Mrs. Fisher Knows*, 3.

92   "Boil the potatoes . . .": Fisher, *What Mrs. Fisher Knows*, 26.

93   "was free from . . .": Frederick Douglass, *Life and Times of Frederick Douglass* (Hartford, CT: Park Publishing Company, 1882), 458.

93   Nevertheless, Reconstruction ushered . . . : "Changing Names,"

The Reconstruction Era and the Fragility of Democracy, Facing History and Ourselves, accessed March 30, 2021, www.facinghistory.org /reconstruction-era/changing-names.

94 After the Civil . . . : Opie, *Hog & Hominy*, 43.

94 For those Black . . . : Yentsch, "Excavating the South's African American Food History," 20.

94 In the sharecropping . . . : Ibid., 20–21.

94 There are even . . . : Emily Mays, interview by Alberta Minor, *Federal Writers' Project: Slave Narrative Project, Vol. 4, Georgia, Part 3* (Washington, DC: The Library of Congress Project, 1941), 119.

94 Other holdovers from . . . : Opie, *Hog & Hominy*, 46.

94 "being poor and . . .": Yentsch, "Excavating the South's African American Food History," 21.

95 In this case . . . : Ibid.

95 As more Black . . . : Ibid., 25.

95 Iconic chef Edna . . . : Francis Lam, "Edna Lewis and the Black Roots of American Cooking," *The New York Times Magazine*, October 28, 2015, www.nytimes.com/2015/11/01/magazine/edna-lewis-and-the-black -roots-of-american-cooking.html.

95 This was a . . . : DeNeen L. Brown, "Black Towns, Established by Freed Slaves After the Civil War, Are Dying Out," *The Washington Post*, March 27, 2015, www.washingtonpost.com/local/black-towns-established -by-freed-slaves-after-civil-war-are-dying-out/2015/03/26/25872e5c -c608-11e4-a199-6cb5e63819d2_story.html.

95 At Freetown, there . . . : Lam, "Edna Lewis and the Black Roots of American Cooking."

95 Lewis's grandmother, Mama . . . : Michael Twitty, "Edna Lewis," in *Icons of American Cooking*, ed. Elizabeth S. Demers and Victor William Geraci (Santa Barbara, CA: Greenwood, 2011), 158; Edna Lewis, *The Taste of Country Cooking* (New York: Alfred A. Knopf, 2006), 126.

96 Her recipe calls . . . : Lewis, *The Taste of Country Cooking*, 126.

96 "Line a deep . . .": George Washington Carver, "How the Farmer Can Save His Sweet Potatoes and Ways of Preparing Them for the Table,"(Revised and Reprinted) Fourth Edition (Alabama: Tuskegee Institute Press, 1937), aggie-horticulture.tamu.edu/vegetable /additional-resources/carver-sweetpotatoes.

CHAPTER FIVE

101 Napoleon was in . . . : Sarah Everts, "Processed: Food Science and the Modern Meal," Distillations, Science History Institute, January 4, 2014, www.sciencehistory.org/distillations/processed-food-science-and-the-modern-meal.

102 The nut is . . . : Ken Albala, *Nuts: A Global History* (London: Reaktion Books, 2014), 72.

102 Pecans were cultivated . . . : John Egerton, *Southern Food: At Home, on the Road, in History* (Chapel Hill: University of North Carolina Press, 1993), 334.

102 Despite this clear . . . : Albala, *Nuts*, 72.

103 Once this commercial . . . : Andrew F. Smith, *Food and Drink in American History*, 658.

103 References to pecan . . . : Dana Hatic, "A Brief History of Pecan Pie," Eater, Vox Media, November 23, 2016, www.eater.com/2016/11/23/13575790/pecan-pie-history-about.

103 There's some argument . . . : James McWilliams, *The Pecan: A History of America's Native Nut* (Austin: University of Texas Press, 2013), 121.

103 "Pecan pie is . . .": "Pecan Pie," *Harper's Bazaar*, February 6, 1886, 95.

104 "One cup of . . .": *Goshen Daily Democrat* (Indiana), November 26, 1898.

104 According to Ms. . . . : Lenny Wells, *Pecan: America's Native Nut Tree* (Tuscaloosa : University of Alabama Press, 2017), xx.

105 After canning kicked . . . : Anna Zeide, *Canned: The Rise and Fall of Consumer Confidence in the American Food Industry* (Berkeley: University of California Press, 2018), 13–14.

105 Naturally, the practice . . . : Everts, "Processed: Food Science and the Modern Meal."

106 Hardship begets hunger . . . : Zeide, *Canned*, 1.

106 Canned foods were . . . : Ibid., 16.

106 Before industrialization reshaped . . . : Ruth Schwartz Cowan, "The 'Industrial Revolution' in the Home: Household Technology and Social Change in the 20th Century," *Technology and Culture* 17, no. 1 (1976): 1–2.

106 Meanwhile, mechanization spread . . . : John Ikerd, "Corporatization of the American Food System," White Paper prepared for the Home Box Office Network, 2012, web.missouri.edu/~ikerdj/papers/HBOCorporatizationofAmericanFoodSystem.pdf.

107 Suddenly, food wasn't . . . : Ibid.

107 Unlike, say, an . . . : Ibid.

107 For instance, stores . . . : Linda Civitello, "Baking Powder," in *The Oxford Encyclopedia of Food and Drink in America*, 2nd ed., ed. Andrew Smith (Oxford, England: Oxford University Press, 2013), 109.

107 The 1890s also . . . : Douglas E. Bowers, "Cooking Trends Echo Changing Roles of Women," *A Century of Change in America's Eating Patterns*, 23, no. 11 (2000): 24.

107 Overall, food prices . . . : Katherine Leonard Turner, *How the Other Half Ate: A History of Working-Class Meals at the Turn of the Century* (Berkeley: University of California Press, 2014), 28.

108 Though it wasn't . . . : Paula Hook and Joe E. Heimlich, "A History of Packaging," Ohioline, Ohio State University Extension, May 11, 2017, ohioline.osu.edu/factsheet/cdfs-133.

108 Around the same . . . : Michael Krondl, "Advertising," in *The Oxford Encyclopedia of Food and Drink in America*, 2nd ed., ed. Andrew F. Smith (Oxford, England: Oxford University Press, 2013), 12–13.

108 Like the pressure . . . : Zeide, *Canned*, 22.

108 The transition away . . . : Bowers, "Cooking Trends Echo Changing Roles of Women," 24.

108 They were low-key . . . : Zeide, *Canned*, 28.

109 The unease was . . . : Quoted in ibid., 31–32.

109 Eventually, the disquiet . . . : Ibid.

109 The product was . . . : Jay Weinstein, "Karo Syrup," in *The Oxford Encyclopedia of Food and Drink in America*, 2nd ed., ed. Andrew F. Smith (Oxford, England: Oxford University Press, 2013), 410–11.

109 No one really . . . : Ibid., 411.

109 It wasn't the . . . : Hilde Lee, "Follow the Cornstarch and Corn Syrup History Path to a Scrumptious Pecan Pie," *Daily Progress*, August 27, 2014, dailyprogress.com/entertainment/hilde-lee-follow-the-cornstarch -and-corn-syrup-history-path-to-a-scrumptious-pecan-pie/article _2c2037ec-2953-11e4-9520-0017a43b2370.html.

110 Before the nationally . . . : Weinstein, "Karo Syrup," 410–11.

110 "a pure clear . . .": Advertisement for Karo Corn Syrup, *Success*, April 1904, 268.

110 Often, it was . . . : "Karo History," Karo, accessed February 27, 2021, www.karofoodservice.com/about.

110 In 1910, the . . . : Weinstein, "Karo Syrup," 411.

111 First of all . . . : Emma Churchman Hewitt, *Karo Cook Book: Being One Hundred and Twenty Practical Recipes for the Use of Karo Syrup* (New York: Corn Products Refining Co., 1920), 3.

111 "wholesome, sustaining, higher . . .": Ibid., 3.

111 "I find that . . .": Ibid., 4.

111 "thousands of people . . .": Ibid., 5.

111 "men at hard . . .": Ibid.

111 It also omitted . . . : Ibid., 15.

111 According to the . . . : Ibid., 5.

112 By 1920, the . . . : Lowell K. Dyson, "American Cuisine in the 20th Century," *A Century of Change in America's Eating Patterns* 23, no. 1 (2000): 4.

112 So somewhat unsurprisingly . . . : Ibid.

112 These developments were . . . : Cowan, "The 'Industrial Revolution' in the Home: Household Technology and Social Change in the 20th Century," 7.

112 Such changes dovetailed . . . : Dyson, "American Cuisine in the 20th Century," 4.

113 Because housewives *were* . . . : Cowan, "The 'Industrial Revolution' in the Home: Household Technology and Social Change in the 20th Century," 9–10.

113 The Karo pecan . . . : Weinstein, "Karo Syrup," 410–11.

114 "Was Hortense ever . . .": "Club Chatter," *Ward-Belmont Hyphen*, January 13, 1931.

114 Tucked amidst a . . . : Keystone Pecan Research Laboratory, *800 Proved Pecan Recipes: Their Place in the Menu* (Philadelphia: Macrae Smith Company, 1925), 270.

114 Other recipes abound . . . : "Favorite Recipe," *Democrat-American* (Sallisaw, OK), February 19, 1931; Sheila Hibben, *The National Cookbook* (New York: Harper & Brothers Publishers, 1932), 369.

115 "Surprise the Folks . . .": Advertisement for Karo Corn Syrup, *Big Spring Daily Herald*, April 17, 1941.

116 The marketing angle . . . : Volunteer Committee of Visiting Nurses Association of Milwaukee, *The New Milwaukee Cook Book* (Michigan State University Libraries Special Collections; Original Publisher: Visiting Nurse Association, 1938), 200.

116 Sometimes, the brand . . . : *The Delta's Best Cook Book* (Mississippi: The American Legion Auxiliary, unknown date), 74.

116 "fat men in . . .": Marjorie Kinnan Rawlings, *Cross Creek Cookery* (New York: Charles Scribner's Sons, 1942), 179–81.

116 By the 1950s . . . : Advertisement for Karo Corn Syrup, *Better Homes and Gardens*, December 1952, 89.

116 In her famous . . . : Marion Brown, *Marion Brown's Southern Cook Book* (Chapel Hill: University of North Carolina Press, 1980), 396.

116 Karo kept up . . . : *Happy Holidays: Recipes and "Goodies for Giving"* (New York: Corn Products Refining, undated, probably early 1960s) via "Pecan Pie," Pie & Pastry, The Food Timeline, accessed April 15, 2021, www.foodtimeline.org/foodpies.html.

117 As modern farming . . . : Weinstein, "Karo Syrup," 410–11.

117 It's even seeded . . . : Ibid.

DERBY PIE

120 A company called . . . : Danny Lewis, "Why Making 'Derby-Pie' Might Land You a Lawsuit," *Smithsonian Magazine*, Smithsonian Institution, May 5, 2016, www.smithsonianmag.com/smart-news/why-making -derby-pie-might-land-you-lawsuit-180959007.

120 "premium chocolate and . . .": "Our Story," Kern's Kitchen Derby Pie, accessed April 8, 2021, derbypie.com/pages/our-story.

120 And as for . . . : Ibid.

121 The pie proved . . . : "Tour the Timeline," Kern's Kitchen Derby-Pie, accessed April 8, 2021, derbypie.com/pages/tour-the-timeline.

121 Since then, its . . . : Lewis, "Why Making 'Derby-Pie' Might Land You a Lawsuit."; "Tour the Timeline."

121 Kern's Kitchen regularly . . . : Lewis, "Why Making 'Derby-Pie' Might Land You a Lawsuit."

121 One hostess working . . . : Ibid.

121 After Science Hill . . . : Nina Feldman, "What's Inside a 'Derby Pie'? Maybe a Lawsuit Waiting to Happen," The Salt, NPR.org, May 1, 2015, www.npr.org/sections/thesalt/2015/05/01/399842082/whats-inside -a-derby-pie-maybe-a-lawsuit-waiting-to-happen.

121 One Kentucky restaurateur . . . : Ibid.

122 In 1987, the . . . : Lewis, "Why Making 'Derby-Pie' Might Land You a Lawsuit."

121 Many bakers in . . . : Feldman, "What's Inside a 'Derby Pie'? Maybe a Lawsuit Waiting to Happen."

121 "Kern's Kitchen has . . .": "Tour the Timeline."

CHAPTER SIX

124 The '20s were a decade . . . : Luke Buckmaster, "The Greatest Decade in Cinema History?" BBC, June 1, 2020, www.bbc.com/culture /article/20200601-the-greatest-decade-in-cinema-history.

124 Monroe Boston Strause . . . : Monroe Boston Strause, *Pie Marches On* (United States: Ahrens Publishing Company, 1954), 7.

124 This sun-soaked childhood . . . : Ibid.

125 With the Southern . . . : "Inventing a City," Los Angeles, Britannica, accessed January 17, 2022, www.britannica.com/place/Los-Angeles -California/Inventing-a-city.

125 Between 1910 and . . . : Hilary Hallett, *Go West, Young Women! The Rise of Early Hollywood* (Berkeley: University of California Press, 2012), 5; Kevin Starr, *Material Dreams* (Oxford, England: Oxford University Press, 1991), 69.

125 And unlike the . . . : Starr, *Material Dreams*, 80.

125 Like most social . . . : Hallett, *Go West, Young Women!*, 4.

125 The whole thing . . . : Ibid., 5.

125 As cities on . . . : Ibid.

126 Charles Lummis . . . : Ibid.

126 "Many of these . . .": Ibid., 5–6.

126 Such opportunity applied . . . : Starr, *Material Dreams*, 86–88.

126 During the decade . . . : Douglas Gomery, *The Hollywood Studio System: A History* (London: Bloomsbury Publishing, 2019), "Introduction" and "Fox," Kindle.

126 Across the country . . . : Joel Waldo Finler, *The Hollywood Story* (London: Wallflower, 2003), 13; Hallett, *Go West, Young Women!*, 7.

127 "anything seems possible . . .": Quoted in Starr, *Material Dreams*, 70.

127 Strause's father was . . . : Mary Meade, "Pie 'Engineer' Is the Baking Industry's Friend: He's Also the Creator of Delectable Desserts," *Chicago Daily Tribune*, October 31, 1952.

127 That pivot came . . . : Charles Perry, "The Pie King," *Los Angeles Times*, January 9, 1997.

127 "tend to be . . .": "40 Kinds of Apple Pie, One Man Makes Them All," *Globe and Mail*, March 15, 1950.

127 "He has reduced . . .": Strause, *Pie Marches On*, 9.

128 "the tea cup . . .": Ibid.

128 Strause also obsessively . . . : Ken W. MacTaggart, "He Knows All Answers When It Comes to Pie," *Globe and Mail*, December 1, 1937.

128 "I'm afraid my . . .": Strause, *Pie Marches On*, 26.

129 He zeroed in . . . : Clementine Paddleford, "Its Inventor Tells How to Make a Chiffon Pie," *New York Herald Tribune*, May 15, 1939.

129 When she saw . . . : Clementine Paddleford, "Food for Conversation," *Los Angeles Times*, May 6, 1945.

129 Like Hollywood, Strause's . . . : Paddleford, "Its Inventor Tells How to Make a Chiffon Pie."

129 "a distinctive feature . . .": Strause, *Pie Marches On*, 263.

129 "a shell light . . .": Paddleford, "Food for Conversation."

129 One profile of . . . : Meade, "Pie 'Engineer' Is the Baking Industry's Friend"; Perry, "The Pie King."

129 "today chiffon pie . . .": Strause, *Pie Marches On*, 161.

130 Chiffon pie's launch . . . : Sherrie A. Inness, *Dinner Roles: American Women and Culinary Culture* (United States: University of Iowa Press, 2001), 55–58.

130 In the opening . . . : Strause, *Pie Marches On*, 8.

130 "Mary Pickford, America's . . .": Ibid.

130 One of the . . . : Finler, *The Hollywood Story*, 13.

130 With his mathematical . . . : "40 Kinds of Apple Pie, One Man Makes Them All."

131 "the most sensational . . .": Strause, *Pie Marches On*, 231.

131 "It came from . . .": Clementine Paddleford, "For Halloween . . . Black-Bottom Pie," *Los Angeles Times*, October 18, 1953.

131 "Add lemon juice . . .": Keystone Pecan Research Laboratory, *800 Proved Pecan Recipes: Their Place in the Menu* (Philadelphia: Macrae Smith Company, 1925), 263.

132 And Mrs. Breckenridge . . . : Myra Nye, "Doings Echoed Near and Far: Ripples of Clubdom Wash Strands of Women's World Here," *Los Angeles Times*, April 18, 1926.

132 The entire concept . . . : Rory Boothe, "Multiple Discovery," Indiana

Public Media, August 30, 2018, indianapublicmedia.org/amomentof
science/multiple-discovery.php.

133 "Fluffy unbaked pies . . .": Jean Anderson, *American Century Cookbook:
The Most Popular Recipes of the 20th Century* (New York: Clarkson Pot-
ter, 1997), 364, quoted in "Pie & Pastry," The Food Timeline, accessed
March 3, 2021, www.foodtimeline.org/foodpies.html#chiffon.

133 "One time a . . .": "GI's May Get Better Pies," *The Times Recorder* (Zanes-
ville, OH), January 16, 1951.

133 Eventually, Strause's pie . . . : Clementine Paddleford, "Food for Conversation," *Los Angeles Times*, May 6, 1945.

133 He traveled around . . . : MacTaggart, "He Knows All Answers When It
Comes to Pie."

133 By that year . . . : "Practical Recipes," *Los Angeles Times*, February 26, 1929.

134 And once the . . . : Advertisement for Ralph's Grocery, *Los Angeles Times*,
December 30, 1935.

134 Strause also followed . . . : Finler, *The Hollywood Story*, 13.

134 After selling his . . . : "He Bakes the Pies," *The Cincinnati Enquirer*, January 13, 1935.

134 He taught classes . . . : Paddleford, "Its Inventor Tells How to Make a
Chiffon Pie."; "Frozen Pie in Sky Flies to Market," *The Washington Post*,
February 26, 1947.

134 In Chicago, he . . . : MacTaggart, "He Knows All Answers When It Comes
to Pie."

135 He never stopped . . . : "Frozen Pie in Sky Flies to Market," *The Washington Post*, February 26, 1947.

135 "Monroe Boston Strause . . .": Strause, *Pie Marches On*, 9.

135 His success brought . . . : MacTaggart, "He Knows All Answers When It
Comes to Pie."

135 In the '90s . . . : Perry, "The Pie King."

KEY LIME PIE

138 As legend has . . . : Gwen Filosa, "We All Know Key Lime Pie Was
Invented in the Keys, Right? Seems Not Everyone Agrees," *The Miami
Herald*, August 6, 2018, www.miamiherald.com/living/food-drink
/article215758680.html.

138 Like the best . . . : Stella Parks, *BraveTart: Iconic American Desserts* (New
York: W. W. Norton, 2017), 171–72.

138 Parks identified a . . . : Ibid.

139 It's a very . . . : Filosa, "We All Know Key Lime Pie Was Invented in the Keys, Right? Seems Not Everyone Agrees."

139 According to the . . . : Ibid.

139 They'd soak the . . . : CJ Lotz, "A Slice of Key Lime Pie History," *Garden & Gun*, June 30, 2017, gardenandgun.com/articles/slice-key-lime-pie-history.

139 That geography is . . . : Ibid.

139 "Conch contribution to . . .": Quoted in Filosa, "We All Know Key Lime Pie Was Invented in the Keys, Right? Seems Not Everyone Agrees."

140 "makes a Key . . .": Nina Oliver Dean, "Candle Light," *The Orlando Sentinel,* October 17, 1937.

140 Sadly, Key limes . . . : Lotz, "A Slice of Key Lime Pie History."

CHAPTER SEVEN

142 "an excellent substitute . . .": "Quaker Minnie—Out-of doors & Indoors," *Brookville American* (IN), February 27, 1857, quoted in "Pies & Pastry," The Food Timeline, accessed January 15, 2022, www.foodtimeline.org/foodpies.html#mock.

142 "As apples are . . .": "Useful Receipts," *The Saturday Evening Post*, February 14, 1857, quoted in "Pies & Pastry," The Food Timeline, accessed January 15, 2022, www.foodtimeline.org/foodpies.html#mock.

142 "I have learned . . .": "Mock Apple Pie," *Crazy Pie Lady*, September 5, 2007, crazypieladys.blogspot.com/2007/09/mock-apple-pie.html.

143 "The deception was . . .": Ladies Social Circle, Simpson M.E. Church, *How We Cook in Los Angeles* (Los Angeles: Commercial Printing House, 1894), 240–41.

143 "wondered by what . . .": "Elizabeth Storrs—III," *The Emporia Gazette* (Emporia, Kansas), May 18, 1965.

143 "To one small . . ." : *Confederate Receipt Book: A Compilation of Over One Hundred Receipts Adapted to the Times* (Athens: University of Georgia Press, 1960), 16.

144 Written to help . . . : *Confederate Receipt Book*, 11, 16, 17.

144 "Perhaps I might . . .": Ellen McGowan Biddle, *Reminiscences of a Soldier's Wife* (Philadelphia: Press of J.B. Lippincott Company, 1907), 173.

144 "Soda crackers soaked . . .": Ibid.

145 *Housekeeping in Old* . . . : Marion Cabell Tyree, *Housekeeping in Old*

Virginia: Containing Contributions from Two Hundred and Fifty of Virginia's Noted Housewives, Distinguished for Their Skill in the Culinary Art and Other Branches of Domestic Economy (Louisville, KY: John P. Morton and Company, 1879), 413.

145   The pie also . . . : The Southern Ruralist, *Favorite Southern Recipes* (Atlanta: Southern Ruralist, 1912), 90.

145   And it also . . . : *The Kitchen Companion Cookbook* (Philadelphia: Richards, Warren & Flint Brothers, 1869), 22.

146   The worldwide GDP . . . : Robert A. Margo, "Employment and Unemployment in the 1930s," *Journal of Economic Perspectives* 7, no. 2 (1993): 43.

146   Herbert Hoover may . . . : Herbert Hoover, "Proclamation 1974—Thanksgiving Day, 1931," Online by Gerhard Peters and John T. Woolley, The American Presidency Project, accessed June 1, 2021, www.presidency.ucsb.edu/node/208700.

146   In 1933, one . . . : Michael Golay, *America 1933: The Great Depression, Lorena Hickok, Eleanor Roosevelt, and the Shaping of the New Deal* (New York: Simon & Schuster, 2016), 119.

146   "The myriad ways . . .": *Federal Aid for Unemployment Relief: Hearings, Seventy-second Congress, Second Session* (Washington, DC: U.S. Government Printing Office, 1933), 395.

146   Breadlines and soup . . . : James R. McGovern, *And a Time for Hope: Americans in the Great Depression* (Westport, CT: Praeger Publishers, 2000), 9.

146   Many struggling Americans . . . : Ibid., 10.

146   Hooverville residents scavenged . . . : Libby O'Connell, *The American Plate: A Culinary History in 100 Bites* (Naperville, IL: Sourcebooks, 2014), 214.

146   In Louisiana, Black . . . : McGovern, *And a Time for Hope*, 9.

146   One child recalled . . . : Milton Meltzer, *Brother, Can You Spare a Dime?: The Great Depression 1929–1933* (New York: Alfred A. Knopf, Inc., 1969), 42.

147   "Economy was chiefly . . .": Quoted in Janet Poppendieck, *Breadlines Knee-Deep in Wheat: Food Assistance in the Great Depression* (Berkeley: University of California Press, 2014), 20.

147   Among the changes . . . : Ibid.

147   "Millions of children . . .": Quoted in ibid., xvi.

147   "flour, lard, beans . . .": Quoted in Meltzer, *Brother, Can You Spare a Dime?*, 100.

147 They stretched resources . . . : Mary MacVean, "Food Lessons from the Great Depression," *Los Angeles Times*, December 10, 2008, www.latimes.com/style/la-fo-depression10-2008dec10-story.html.

148 "Every family knew . . .": Rita Van Amber, *Stories and Recipes of the Great Depression of the 1930's* (Neenah, WI: Van Amber Publishers, 2004), 8.

148 "Butternuts were for . . .": Ibid., 11.

148 "the mothers who . . .": Rita Van Amber, "The Way It Was," *Stories and Recipes of the Great Depression of the 1930's, Vol. 1* (United States: Van Amber Publishers, 2004), ii.

148 "as a result . . .": Ibid., iii.

148 A fictitious character . . . : Morleen G. Rouse, "Daytime Radio Programming for the Homemaker, 1926–1956," *Journal of Popular Culture* 12, no. 2 (1978): 317–18.

148 Her advice often . . . : Jane Ziegelman and Andrew Coe, "'Mock Duck' and Other Depression Thanksgiving Delights," *The New York Times*, November 24, 2016, www.nytimes.com/2016/11/24/opinion/mock-duck-and-other-depression-thanksgiving-delights.html.

149 Aunt Sammy's radio . . . : Edward Bottone, "The Radio Homemaker," The Smart Set, March 16, 2016, www.thesmartset.com/the-radio-homemaker.

149 Imitation foods were . . . : Natasha Frost, "How America Fell Into—and Out of—Love With Mock Turtle Soup," Gastro Obscura, Atlas Obscura, August 3, 2017, www.atlasobscura.com/articles/mock-turtle-soup-rise-and-fall-calf-head.

150 One Minnesota community . . . : Debbie Miller, "1930s Cookbooks," Collections, Minnesota Historical Society, accessed February 16, 2021, www.mnhs.org/collections/upclose/cookbooks.php.

150 Another cookbook, published . . . : The Garden Club of Cincinnati, *The Garden Club of Cincinnati Cook Book* (University of Michigan Janice Bluestein Longone Culinary Archive; Original Publisher: A.H. Pugh Print Co., 1937), 5.

150 That desire, in . . . : Kennan Ferguson, "Intensifying Taste, Intensifying Identity: Collectivity through Community Cookbooks," *Signs* 37, no. 3 (2012): 708.

150 "Beans, bacon, and . . .": "Beans, Bacon, and Gravy," Musixmatch, accessed February 21, 2021, www.musixmatch.com/lyrics/Pete-Seeger/Beans-Bacon-and-Gravy.

150   These include the . . . : Fruit and Flour Mission, *Choice Recipes* (Seattle: Lowman and Hanford Company, 1930), 254, 258.

150   Another frequent meaty . . . : Pat Willard, "Pies and Tarts," in *The Oxford Encyclopedia of Food and Drink in America, Volume 2*, ed. Andrew Smith (Oxford, England: Oxford University Press, 2004), 273.

151   One community cookbook . . . : Ladies of the Woman's Club of Benkleman, Nebraska, *The Benkleman Cook Book* (University of Michigan Janice Bluestein Longone Culinary Archive; Original Publisher: The Benkelman Post, 1937), 77–82.

151   "the cheap beans . . .": Kathleen Purvis, "'Tastes Like Apple Pie' Zucchini Pie," *Garden & Gun*, July 12, 2018, gardenandgun.com/recipe /tastes-like-apple-zucchini-pie.

151   "A genre of . . .": Emily Hilliard, "About," Nothing in the House: A Pie Blog, accessed February 16, 2021, www.nothinginthehouse.com/p /our-love-for-pies.html.

152   The popular product . . . : Lynne Olver, "Ritz Crackers," Cookies, The Food Timeline, accessed February 21, 2021, www.foodtimeline.org /foodcookies.html#ritz.

152   Other low-cost products . . . : Andrew F. Smith, *Food and Drink in American History*, 270.

152   These debuts also . . . : Ibid.

152   "see how they . . .": Advertisement for Ritz Crackers, *Good Housekeeping*, September 1936, 142.

152   One newspaper advertisement . . . : Advertisement for Ritz Crackers, *Chicago Tribune*, March 31, 1939.

152   Even the name . . . : *Encyclopedia of Consumer Brands, Volume 1: Consumable Products*, ed. Janice Jorgenson (Detroit: St. James Press, 1994), 494, quoted in The Food Timeline, www.foodtimeline.org/foodcookies. html#ritz; Jean Anderson, *American Century Cookbook*, 32, quoted in The Food Timeline, www.foodtimeline.org/foodcookies.html#ritz

153   Unlike plain Jane . . . : *Encyclopedia of Consumer Brands*, 494, quoted in The Food Timeline, www.foodtimeline.org/foodcookies.html#ritz

153   Most peg the . . . : Beth Kracklauer, "Putting on the Ritz," Saveur, February 28, 2008, www.saveur.com/article/Kitchen/Putting-on-the-Ritz; "Did Nabisco Invent Mock Apple Pie to Sell Ritz Crackers?," Culinary Lore, January 6, 2015, culinarylore.com/food-history:did-nabisco -invent-mock-apple-pie.

153 "Mock Apple Pie . . .": "Mock Apple Pie Recipe—Ritz Crackers," Recipe Curio, October 4, 2010, recipecurio.com/mock-apple-pie-recipe-crackers.

155 "3 egg whites . . .": Women's Society of World Service at South Bend Indiana, *Treasure of Personal Recipes* (Missouri: North American Press, 1947), 20.

156 "Ritz Cracker Mock . . .": "Ritz Cracker Mock Apple Pie Part of Forced Time Off Creations," NNY 360, April 28, 2020, www.nny360.com /news/ritz-cracker-mock-apple-pie-part-of-forced-time-off-creations /article_0e752b2d-40d1-5948-9e7b-62a1a52aaa7e.html.

156 "historic dishes born . . .": Sam O'Brien, "7 Historic Dishes Born From Tough Times That You Can Make at Home," Gastro Obscura, Atlas Obscura, March 30, 2020, www.atlasobscura.com/articles/unusual -dishes-to-make-with-pantry-staples.

157 "They're our ticket . . .": Luke Fater, "Even More Historic Dishes Born From Tough Times to Make at Home," Gastro Obscura, Atlas Obscura, April 27, 2020, www.atlasobscura.com/articles/easy-historical-recipes -to-make-at-home.

SUGAR PIE

160 Some people claim . . . : Katherine Coplen, "Vintage Vittles: Dreaming of Sugar Cream Pie," Historic Indianapolis, Aug. 17, 2013, historicin-dianapolis.com/vintage-vittles-dreaming-of-sugar-cream-pie; Dawn Mitchell, "Things You Didn't Know About Indiana Sugar Cream Pie (and a Cherished Recipe)," *IndyStar*, Jan. 17, 2019, www.indystar.com /story/news/history/retroindy/2018/01/23/things-you-didnt-know -sugar-cream-pie-and-cherished-recipe/1057180001.

160 Either way, it's . . . : *The Classic Hoosier Cookbook*, ed. Elaine Lumbra (United States: Indiana University Press, 2018), 236.

161 As with our . . . : Coplen, "Vintage Vittles: Dreaming of Sugar Cream Pie."

161 Wick's Pies in . . . : Mitchell, "Things You Didn't Know About Indiana Sugar Cream Pie (and a Cherished Recipe)."

161 In addition to . . . : Ibid.

161 Steeped in nostalgia . . . : "Hoosier Pie," Indiana Culinary Trails, Indi-ana Foodways Alliance, accessed January 15, 2022, www.indianafood ways.com/trail/31/Hoosier-Pie.

161 The dairy can . . . : Coplen, "Vintage Vittles: Dreaming of Sugar Cream Pie."

161 For what it's . . . : "Hoosier Pie."

161 And most controversially . . . : Kate Scott, "Desperate for Pie," Indiana Historical Society, accessed April 4, 2021, indianahistory.org/blog/desperate-for-pie/.

CHAPTER EIGHT

163 "AT LAST!" . . . : Advertisement for Jell-O, *Good Housekeeping*, 1951 (month unknown), via Etsy, www.etsy.com/listing/778889404/good-housekeeping-1951-magazine-ad-jello?show_sold_out_detail=1& ref=nla_listing_details.

165 "[Pie] symbolizes so . . .": Quoted in Inness, *Dinner Roles*, 146.

166 And some brands . . . : *Betty Crocker's Picture Cookbook* (Minneapolis: General Mills, 1950), 293.

166 "If I were . . .": Ibid.

167 In fact, 35 . . . : Douglas E. Bowers, "Cooking Trends Echo Changing Roles of Women," *A Century of Change in America's Eating Patterns* 23, no. 11 (2000): 26.

167 Those women who . . . : Stephanie Coontz, *The Way We Never Were: American Families and the Nostalgia Trap* (New York: Basic Books, 2000), 32.

167 Meanwhile, the housing . . . : Diane Boucher, *The 1950s American Home* (New York: Bloomsbury Publishing, 2013), 6–10.

167 "It is the . . .": "The Cover," *The Saturday Evening Post*, February 9, 1957, 3.

168 Stalking the American . . . : Coontz, *The Way We Never Were*, 24, 28.

168 As Stephanie Coontz . . . : Ibid., 28.

168 During the 1950s . . . : June Meyerowitz, *Not June Cleaver: Women and Gender in Postwar America, 1945–1960* (Philadelphia: Temple University Press, 1994), 4–6.

168 Meanwhile, poverty affected . . . : Coontz, *The Way We Never Were*, 31.

169 "Too much emphasis . . .": Eleanor Roosevelt, *It's Up to the Women* (New York: Frederick A. Stokes Company, 1933), 59.

168 With a rising . . . : Bowers, "Cooking Trends Echo Changing Roles of Women," 26.

169 Unsurprisingly, Home Economics . . . : Joan Jacobs Brumberg, "Defining the Profession and the Good Life: Home Economics on Film," in *Rethinking Home Economics: Women and the History of a Profession*, ed. Sarah Stage and Virginia B. Vincenti (Ithaca, NY: Cornell University Press, 2018), 195.

170 (In 1970, it . . .): Ediťh Kjaersgaard, "Home Economics and the Changing Roles of Men and Women," *International Review of Education / Internationale Zeitschrift Für Erziehungswissenschaft / Revue Internationale de
l'Education* 19, no. 1 (1973): 125.

170 Frozen Orange Juice . . . : Advertisement for Gold Medal Flour, *Ladies'
Home Journal,* July 1950, 19.

170 Fruit Basket Pie . . . : Advertisement for Crisco, *Family Circle
Magazine,* November 1950, via Pinterest, www.pinterest.com
/pin/558094578815679942.

170 Fruit Cocktail Eggnog . . . : "1956 Recipe for Fruit Cocktail Eggnog Pie,"
McCallum Vintage Recipe Divas, December 19, 2013, mccallumvintage
recipedivas.wordpress.com/2013/12/19/1956-recipe-for-fruit-cocktail
-eggnog-pie.

170 Even our good . . . : "Ko-Ko-Nut Pie: Vintage '50s Coconut Dessert
Recipe," Click Americana, accessed October 28, 2021, clickamericana
.com/recipes/dessert-recipes/ko-ko-nut-pie-recipe-1950.

170 "Karo supplies vital . . .": Ibid.

170 "a refreshing array . . .": "1956 Recipe for Fruit Cocktail Eggnog Pie,"
mccallumvintagerecipedivas.wordpress.com/2013/12/19/1956-recipe
-for-fruit-cocktail-eggnog-pie.

171 "the sure way . . .": Advertisement for Crisco, *Family Circle Magazine,*
November 1950, via Pinterest, www.pinterest.com/pin/558094578
815679942.

171 Carnation Evaporated Milk . . . : Advertisement for Betty Crocker Carnation Milk, 1953 (source unknown).

172 One ad boasted . . . : Advertisement for Jell-O, *Redbook,* November
1959, 161.

172 "Jell-O was all . . .": Laura Shapiro, *Something from the Oven: Reinventing
Dinner in 1950s America* (New York: Viking Penguin, 2004), 56.

172 The brand molded . . . : Laura Schenone, *A Thousand Years Over a Hot
Stove: A History of American Women Told through Food, Recipes, and
Remembrances* (New York: W. W. Norton, 2004), 320.

172 "Pliable in spirit . . .": Ibid.

172 "prepare 1 package . . .": Advertisement for Jell-O Puddings and Pie Fillings, *Ladies' Home Journal,* October 1951, 15.

173 That specific pie . . . : *Joys of Jell-O* (New York: General Foods Corporation, 1963), 31.

173 "The faster the . . .": Shapiro, *Something from the Oven*, 63.

173 According to Shapiro . . . : Ibid., 65.

174 "Stress should be . . .": Betty Friedan, *The Feminine Mystique (50th Anniversary Edition)* (New York: W. W. Norton, 2013), 305.

174 In *Something from* . . . : Shapiro, *Something from the Oven*, 6.

174 "The way my . . .": Friedan, *The Feminine Mystique*, 306.

175 "Rather than feel . . .": Ibid., 307.

175 "her personal participation . . .": Ibid., 308.

176 "The appeal should . . .": Ibid., 305.

176 "We help her . . .": Ibid., 324–25.

176 "Above all, creativity . . .": Shapiro, *Something from the Oven*, 64.

177 There was literally . . . : Mary Drake McFeely, *Can She Bake a Cherry Pie?: American Women and the Kitchen in the Twentieth Century* (Amherst, MA: University of Massachusetts Press, 2001), 1.

177 "This scrumptious pie . . .": *Knox On-Camera Recipes* (Johnstown, NY: Knox Gelatine, 1963), 32.

177 "Lady, you're *in* . . .": "Ko-Ko-Nut Pie: Vintage '50s Coconut Dessert Recipe."

177 This included claims . . . : Advertisement for Crisco, *McCall's*, January 1952, 61.

177 "homemakers voted this . . .": Advertisement for Betty Crocker Carnation Milk, 1953 (source unknown).

178 One 1950 ad . . . : Advertisement for Gold Medal Flour, *Ladies' Home Journal*, July 1950, 19.

178 "The flour you . . .": Ibid.

178 For beyond just . . . : *The Bisquick Cookbook: Recipes from Betty Crocker in Answer to Your Requests* (Minneapolis: General Mills, 1964), 58.

179 "There's warm and . . .": *Quicker Ways to Better Eating: The Wesson Oil Cook Book* (New Orleans: Wesson Oil & Snowdrift People, 1955), 53.

179 "nine out of . . .": Ibid.

179 "Soon you will . . .": Dorothy Hurst, *To the Bride* (Evanston, IL: Walter E. Botthof, 1956), 3.

179 "The talented gal . . .": Ibid., 84.

180 "Pie is a . . .": Ibid., 237.

181 "I understand that . . .": Peg Bracken, *The I Hate to Cook Book: More Than 180 Quick and Easy Recipes* (San Diego: Harcourt Brace Jovanovich, 1960), 103.

CHAPTER NINE

186 In 1930 in . . . : "Nation of Islam," Southern Poverty Law Center, accessed April 4, 2021, www.splcenter.org/fighting-hate/extremist -files/group/nation-islam.

187 Stories of evil . . . : *Modern Black Nationalism: From Marcus Garvey to Louis Farrakhan*, ed. William L. Van Deburg (New York: NYU Press, 1997), 97.

187 In a move . . . : Louis A. DeCaro, *On the Side of My People: A Religious Life of Malcolm X* (New York: NYU Press, 1996), 25.

187 Under Elijah Muhammad's . . . : "Nation of Islam."

187 Having converted and . . . : "Chronology," The Malcolm X Collection: Papers, 1948–1965, Manuscripts, Archives and Rare Books Division, Schomburg Center for Research in Black Culture, The New York Public Library, Astor, Lenox and Tilden Foundation, accessed January 15, 2022, archives.nypl.org/scm/21896.

187 His charisma, oratorical . . . : "Nation of Islam."

188 "Malcolm X preached . . .": John Henrik Clarke, *Malcolm X: The Man and His Times* (Trenton, NJ: Africa World Press, Inc., 1990), xviii–xix.

188 Eventually, under the . . . : "Nation of Islam."

188 Where Dr. King . . . : Edward E. Curtis, *Black Muslim Religion in the Nation of Islam, 1960–1975* (Chapel Hill: University of North Carolina Press, 2009), 3.

188 "The goal has . . .": Malcolm X., Ossie Davis, and Alex Haley, *The Autobiography of Malcolm X* (New York: Ballantine Books, 1992), 385.

188 Coupled with leaders' . . . : "Chronology."

189 And indeed, rhetoric . . . : Mattias Gardell, *In the Name of Elijah Muhammad: Louis Farrakhan and the Nation of Islam* (Durham, NC: Duke University Press, 1996), 80–81.

189 "a hate group . . .": "Nation of Islam."

189 As one of . . . : Simon Wendt, "Intellectual Predicaments: Black Nationalism in the Civil Rights and Post-Civil Rights Eras," in *Black Intellectual Thought in Modern America: A Historical Perspective*, ed. Brian D. Behnken, Gregory D. Smithers, and Wendt Simon (Jackson: University Press of Mississippi, 2017), 170–205.

189 "Cassius Clay is . . .": Stuart Cosgrove, *Cassius X: The Transformation of Muhammad Ali* (Chicago: Chicago Review Press, Incorporated, 2020), 217.

189 The movement away . . . : "The Foundations of Black Power," National Museum of African American History & Culture, Smithsonian, accessed April 13, 2021, nmaahc.si.edu/blog-post/foundations-black-power.

189 In the 1960s . . . : Harris, *High on the Hog*, 209.

190 As part of . . . : Ibid., 210.

190 In fact, leaders . . . : Opie, *Hog & Hominy*, 159.

190 "You know as . . .": Elijah Muhammad, *How to Eat to Live* (Phoenix, AZ: Secretarius MEMPS Ministries, 2008), 6.

190 ". . . sweet potatoes and . . .": Ibid., 5.

191 In their stead . . . : Harris, *High on the Hog*, 209.

191 "appeared on urban . . .": Ibid.

191 In the late . . . : Jennifer Jensen Wallach, "How to Eat to Live: Black Nationalism and the Post-1964 Culinary Turn," Study the South, July 2, 2014, southernstudies.olemiss.edu/study-the-south/how-to-eat-to-live.

192 *Ebony* even published . . . : Althea Smith, "A Farewell to Chitterlings: Vegetarianism is on the Rise Among Diet-Conscious Blacks," *Ebony Magazine*, September 1974, 104.

192 The NOI's training . . . : Opie, *Hog & Hominy*, 159.

192 Fasting became a . . . : Curtis, *Black Muslim Religion*, 133.

192 At one point . . . : Opie, *Hog & Hominy*, 164.

192 While meat wasn't . . . : Wallach, "How to Eat to Live: Black Nationalism and the Post-1964 Culinary Turn."

192 "They're blood-thirsty, they . . .": Malcolm X, "Afro-American History," *International Socialist Review* 28, no. 2 (1967): 28.

192 Beyond just dietary . . . : Wallach, "How to Eat to Live: Black Nationalism and the Post-1964 Culinary Turn."

193 Recognizing that food . . . : Ibid.

193 "teaches us the . . .": Josephine X, "Islam Has Started Life Anew for Me; Proud to Follow the Last Messenger," *Muhammad Speaks* 8, no. 17 (1969): 31.

194 "I stay off . . .": Allen 3X, "How Messenger Muhammad's Dietary Laws Saved My Life," *Muhammad Speaks* 10, no. 30 (1971): 28.

194 "Do not eat . . .": Muhammad, *How to Eat to Live*, 63.

194 "Allah (God) says . . .": Ibid., 170.

195 Lance Shabazz, an . . . : Mike Sula, "Bean Pie, My Brother?," *Chicago Reader*, November 18, 2013, www.chicagoreader.com/chicago/bean-pie-noi-sweet-potato-imani-muhammad/Content?oid=11544239.

195   Meanwhile, in one . . . : Mimi Sheraton, New York Times News Service, "Lana Shabazz's Culinary Wonders Keep Ali in Shape," *Shreveport Journal* (Shreveport, LA), September 29, 1976.

196   "Pastries and cakes . . .": Muhammad, *How to Eat to Live*, 10–11.

196   "You eat too . . .": Quoted in Curtis, *Black Muslim Religion*, 106.

197   "hawked by the . . .": Harris, *High on the Hog*, 211.

197   Muslim bakeries in . . . : Thérèse Nelson in discussion with the author, October 2018.

197   At the iconic . . . : Curtis, *Black Muslim Religion*, 103.

197   In Cleveland, Shabazz . . . : Advertisement for Shabazz Restaurant & Bakery, *Muhammad Speaks* 8, no. 45, July 25, 1969.

197   Later when the . . . : Lena Williams, "Bean Pies Have Grand New Home," *The New York Times*, March 1, 1995.

197   "It makes you . . .": Ibid.

198   As Shabazz wrote . . . : Lana Shabazz, *Cooking for the Champ* (New York: Jones-McMillon, 1979), 11.

198   A 1964 *New* . . . : Robert Lipsyte, "Day With Clay: TV, Song, Muslims; He Voices Pride in African Heritage to 'Ladies of Press,'" *The New York Times*, June 27, 1964.

198   *After Ali lost* . . . : Shabazz, *Cooking for the Champ*, 94.

199   Eventually, perhaps because . . . : Thérèse Nelson in discussion with the author, October 2018.

199   One theory behind . . . : "This Pie Tells One of the Most Essential Stories About Muslims in America. And It's Delicious," Slate, July 22, 2018, video, 7:56, www.youtube.com/watch?v=yWjDBWXzBLQ.

199   In his book . . . : Curtis, *Black Muslim Religion*, 107.

200   Bean pie, for . . . : Kwasi Konadu, *A View from the East: Black Cultural Nationalism and Education in New York City* (United States: Syracuse University Press, 2009), 77.

200   "Stomach ache, head . . .": Queen Latifah, vocalist, "Just Another Day . . .," by Apache and Dana Owens, recorded 1993, track 11 on *Black Reign*, Motown Records, compact disc.

200   When she performed . . . : Adler Hip Hop Archive, #8092, Division of Rare and Manuscript Collections, Cornell University Library.

200   "I might start . . .": Ice Cube, vocalist, "Steady Mobbin,'" recorded 1991, track 4 on *Death Certificate*, Lench Mob and Priority, compact disc.

200   Meanwhile, in one . . . : *In Living Color*, season 1, episode 2, "The

Wrath of Farrakhan," directed by Paul Miller, written by Keenen Ivory Wayans, Franklyn Ajaye, Jeanette Collins, Barry Douglas, Rob Edwards, Sandy Frank, Mimi Friedman, Jeff Joseph, Howard Kuperberg, Buddy Sheffield, Joe Toplyn, Damon Wayans, and Matt Wickline, featuring Damon Wayans and Jim Carrey, aired April 21, 1990, www.youtube.com/watch?v=slqtjqDHQqY.

201 When Martha Stewart . . . : "Navy Bean Pie," Martha Stewart, Meredith Corporation, accessed April 7, 2021, www.marthastewart.com /1162977/navy-bean-pie.

201 Abu's Bakery, curiously . . . : Idris Braithwaite in discussion with the author, September 2018.

201 "being creative, being . . .": Ibid.

201 "happens to be . . .": Ibid.

CHAPTER TEN

205 Feirstein went on . . . : "Bio," Bruce Feirstein, accessed January 16, 2022, brucefeirstein.com/bio.html.

206 In addition to . . . : Bruce Feirstein, *Real Men Don't Eat Quiche: A Guidebook to All That Is Truly Masculine* (New York: Pocket Books, 1982), 15.

206 According to Feirstein . . . : Bruce Feirstein, email to author, August 30, 2021.

206 And all the way . . . : Feirstein, *Real Men,* 35.

206 The book proved . . . : Beth Ann Krier, "A 'Real Man' Takes Aim at '80s Dating," *Los Angeles Times,* November 27, 1986.

207 "I don't believe . . .": Feirstein, email to author, August 30, 2021.

207 It was a . . . : Stacy J. Williams, "Subversive Cooking in Liberal Feminism, 1963–1985," in *Gender and Food: From Production to Consumption and After,* ed. Vasilikie Demos and Marcia Teller Segal (Bingley, UK: Emerald Group Publishing Limited, 2016), 265–86.

206 "The head of . . .": Feirstein, email to author, August 30, 2021.

207 The country was . . . : Robert W. Connell, "A Whole New World: Remaking Masculinity in the Context of the Environmental Movement," *Gender and Society* 4, no. 4 (1990): 452–78.

208 As one of . . . : Williams, "Subversive Cooking in Liberal Feminism, 1963–1985," 276.

208 "My biggest emotional . . .": Quoted in ibid.

208 With all these . . . : Emily J. H. Contois, *Diners, Dudes, and Diets: How Gender and Power Collide in Food Media and Culture* (Chapel Hill: University of North Carolina Press, 2020), Kindle.

208 "In the 1970s . . .": Barbara Ehrenreich, "A Feminists' View of the New Man," *The New York Times*, May 20, 1984.

208 This "new man" . . . : Contois, *Diners, Dudes, and Diets*, Kindle.

209 Suddenly confronted with . . . : Connell, "A Whole New World: Remaking Masculinity in the Context of the Environmental Movement," 452.

209 Ultimately, Feirstein's *Real* . . . : Contois, *Diners, Dudes, and Diets*, Kindle.

209 In the first . . . : Inness, *Dinner Roles*, 4.

210 Specifically, the press . . . : Ibid., 53–54.

210 As an example . . . : Ibid., 54–55.

210 Emerging from the . . . : Douglas E. Bowers, "Cooking Trends Echo Changing Roles of Women," *A Century of Change in America's Eating Patterns* 23, no. 1 (2000): 27.

211 It wasn't just . . . : Ibid., 28.

211 In addition to . . . : Ibid., 27.

211 "Back in the . . .": Candy Sagon, "It Was Up in the '70s and Down in the '80s. But, When Properly Prepared, Real Quiche is Most Certainly . . . : Stayin' Alive," *Los Angeles Times*, November 30, 1995.

212 "Americans had been . . .": Sylvia Lovegren, *Fashionable Food: Seven Decades of Food Fads* (New York: Simon & Schuster, 1995), 317.

212 "today's Real Man . . .": Feirstein, *Real Men Don't Eat Quiche*, 15.

212 Food was such . . . : Warren J. Belasco, *Appetite for Change: How the Counterculture Took on the Food Industry* (Ithaca, NY: Cornell University Press, 2007).

212 As he explains . . . : Ibid., 4.

212 "the implicit agenda . . .": Ibid., 28.

212 The countercultural youth . . . : Ibid., 7–8, 63.

213 Soon, quiche popped . . . : Ibid., 95.

213 "the symbol of . . .": Eric Sorenson, "A Question of Quiche," *The Burlington Free Press*, March 14, 1983.

214 Though counterculturists seized . . . : Belasco, *Appetite for Change*, 63.

214 "the assumption that . . .": Carol J. Adams, *The Sexual Politics of Meat— 25th Anniversary Edition: A Feminist-Vegetarian Critical Theory* (New York: Bloomsbury Publishing, 2015), xviii.

214 "Being a man . . .": Ibid., xvii.

215 "A month ago . . .": Quoted in ibid., 17.

215 In a less . . . : Ibid., xviii.

215 Accordingly to Polly . . . : Alan S. Rosenthal, "The Gender-Coded Stereotype: An American Perception of France and the French," *The French Review* 72, no. 5 (1999): 897–98.

215 Unlike French men . . . : Ibid., 898–99.

216 Such stereotypes sound . . . : Ibid., 903.

216 The renowned travel . . . : Ibid., 904.

216 "Most of us . . .": Quoted in ibid., 902.

216 "a satiric trope . . .": Feirstein, email message to author, August 30, 2021.

217 Examples include a . . . : Louis Diat, *Louis Diat's Home Cookbook: French Cooking for Americans* (Philadelphia: J.B. Lippincott, 1946), 76; Irma S. Rombauer, *Joy of Cooking*, facsimile 1931 edition (New York: Scribner, 1998), 60–61.

217 "It seems odd . . .": Craig Claiborne, *The New York Times Cookbook* (New York: Harper & Row, 1961), 26–27.

217 "a spineless and . . .": John Kelso, "Quiche Foes Join Forces," *Austin-American Statesman*, June 18, 1983.

217 "the epithet of . . .": Charlene Varkonyi, "Let 'em Eat Quiche," *Fort Lauderdale News*, May 18, 1983.

218 "I absolutely don't . . .": Ibid.

218 "Yes, I do . . .": Ibid.

218 "It's difficult to . . .": Diane White, "Quiche's True Significance," *The Vidette-Messenger* (Valparaiso, Indiana), June 30, 1982.

218 "Some of the . . .": Eric Sorenson, "A Question of Quiche."

218 According to one . . . : Kelso, "Quiche Foes Join Forces."

218 "We really have . . .": Ibid.

219 "The Hole in . . .": Ibid.

219 One article that . . . : Cheryl Cornacchia, "Real Men Do Eat Quiche," *Calgary Herald*, November 30, 1983.

219 "rugged, energetic, adventurous . . .": Kathleen Kelly, "Real Fathers Do Eat Quiche," *The Wichita Eagle*, June 15, 1983.

219 "You like eggs . . .": Mike Kelly, "All My Men Eat Quiche," *Austin-American Statesman*, November 5, 1982.

220 "Instead of calling . . .": Kelly, "Real Fathers Do Eat Quiche."

220 According to one . . . : Varkonyi, "Let 'em Eat Quiche."

221 "Never let it . . .": Pat Brockenborough, "Quiches for All Tastes, Made

with All Sorts of Ingredients," *The Paducah Sun* (Paducah, KY), September 7, 1983.

221 "I thought for . . .": Elaine Corn, "It's Said Quiche Isn't Manly, but it Sure Comes in Handy," *The Courier-Journal* (Louisville, KY), April 11, 1984.

221 As Schlafly plotted . . . : Louis Romano, "Political Pie," *The Philadelphia Inquirer*, January 27, 1983.

221 "Of course I'm . . .": Ibid.

221 "We're very upset . . .": Ibid.

221 "ERA: Real Men . . .": Quoted in ibid.

221 "I was writing . . .": Gabrielle Hamilton, "Real People Eat Quiche," *The New York Times*, November 21, 2018.

CHAPTER ELEVEN

225 One February day . . . : "Gates Won't Press Charges After Pie Attack in Belgium," *The Wall Street Journal*, February 5, 1998, www.wsj.com /articles/SB886697459798333000.

225 As the sun . . . : "Bill Gates Pie in Face," YouTube, January 1, 2010, video, 0:44, www.youtube.com/watch?v=iK6SS8CXYZo.

226 "revolutionary bakers and . . .": *Pie Any Means Necessary: The Biotic Baking Brigade Cookbook* (Oakland: AK Press, 2004), vi.

226 "the technocrats who . . .": Ibid., viii.

227 More than three thousand . . . : Thomas Vinciguerra, "Take Sugar, Eggs, Beliefs . . . And Aim," *The New York Times*, December 10, 2000.

227 "A vat of . . .": Monica Hesse and Manuel Roig-Franzia, "Murdoch is the Latest in a Long Line of Pie-Throwing Pranksters' Targets," *Washington Post*, July 19, 2011, www.washingtonpost.com/lifestyle /style/murdoch-is-the-latest-in-a-long-line-of-pie-throwing-pranksters -targets/2011/07/19/gIQASokmOI_story.html.

227 Some pie activists . . . : *Pie Any Means Necessary*, 16; Andrew Duffy, "Pied Snipers," *The Gazette* (Montreal, Canada), January 31, 1999.

227 Forçade was the . . . : Albert Goldman, "Thomas King Forcade: Living and Dying the Great Adventure," *Conjunctions*, no. 17 (1991): 371–79.

227 "counterculture guru and . . .": Ibid., 371.

227 In the spirit . . . : Ibid., 371–79.

228 One of Forçade's . . . : Ibid., 382.

228 Taking his stand . . . : Sean Howe, "Glass, Pie, Candle, Gun," *Longreads*, May 2019, longreads.com/2019/05/13/glass-pie-candle-gun.

228 His rant mostly . . . : Goldman, "Thomas King Forcade: Living and Dying the Great Adventure"; Howe, "Glass, Pie, Candle, Gun."

228 He capped things . . . : "Witness Presents Pornography Commissioner With a Pie (in the Face)," *The New York Times*, May 14, 1970.

228 He claimed it . . . : Fred P. Graham, "White House Bars a Radical Reporter," *The New York Times*, November 14, 1971.

228 "Cottage cheese dribbling . . .": "Witness Presents Pornography Commissioner With a Pie (in the Face)."

228 The event wasn't . . . : Howe, "Glass, Pie, Candle, Gun."

229 One such activist . . . : Charles Whited, "Pumpkin Tart Tough to Find—So an Apple Pie Has to Do," *The Miami Herald*, December 26, 1972.

229 Small was a . . . : Fred Barger, "Beach Turns Down Nondelegate Campsite," *The Miami Herald*, June 24, 1972.

229 His most prominent . . . : Whited, "Pumpkin Tart Tough to Find—So an Apple Pie Has to Do."

229 Small was subsequently . . . : Pamela Doran, "3 Hollywood Youths Participate and Now It's a Zippie Pie-In," *Fort Lauderdale News*, July 11, 1972.

229 It wasn't just . . . : Tom Hale, "The Yippie Pie Man, America's Unlikely Hero of the Radical Left," Huck, September 18, 2018, www.huckmag .com/perspectives/activism-2/the-yippie-pie-man-americas-unlikely -hero-of-the-radical-left.

229 "Goaded by the . . .": Rex Weiner, "Here's Pie in Your Eye," *The Paris Review*, April 1, 2014, www.theparisreview.org/blog/2014/04/01 /heres-pie-in-your-eye.

229 "Taking a businesslike . . .": Ibid.

230 Riding the pastry . . . : Ibid.

230 A pieing prodigy . . . : Hale, "The Yippie Pie Man, America's Unlikely Hero of the Radical Left."

230 Patti might have . . . : John Petkovic, "Patti Smith's legendary 1976 Cleveland Agora show: 'My Generation' and the year punk broke," *Cleveland.com*, January 11, 2019, www.cleveland.com/entertainment /2016/01/patti_smiths_legendary_1976_cl.html.

231 "It wasn't long . . .": Weiner, "Here's Pie in Your Eye."

231 With Nixon out . . . : Ibid.

231 Like many pie . . . : Hale, "The Yippie Pie Man, America's Unlikely Hero of the Radical Left."

231 "I was always . . .": Ibid.

231 "Get it? It . . .": Ibid.

231 As he broadened . . . : Ibid.

231 "he was out . . .": Hesse and Roig-Franzia, "Murdoch is the Latest in a Long Line of Pie-Throwing Pranksters' Targets."

231 "an apple crumb . . .": Hale, "The Yippie Pie Man, America's Unlikely Hero of the Radical Left."

231 "he got a . . .": Ibid.

232 "was a mushroom . . .": Ibid.

232 Kay's prolific pieing . . . : Ibid.

232 He founded the . . . : "Flanning: Rich and Famous Get Custard Pie Treatment," BBC News, February 3, 2000, news.bbc.co.uk/2/hi/uk _news/629352.stm.

232 "well-known in Belgium . . .": "Gates Won't Press Charges After Pie Attack in Belgium."

232 "He is the . . .": Quoted in *Pie Any Means Necessary*, 15.

233 Pie throwing also . . . : "Flanning: Rich and Famous Get Custard Pie Treatment."

233 Indeed, pie throwing . . . : *Pie Any Means Necessary*, x.

233 "We talk without . . .": Chumbawamba, "Just Desserts," recorded 2003, track 2 on *Un*, 2004, Mutt Records, compact disc.

233 Elsewhere, in Canada . . . : Andrew Duffy, "Pied Snipers."

234 "There are issues . . .": Chris Morris, "Cream and Punishment in P.E.I.," *The Windsor Star* (Windsor, Canada), May 17, 2001.

234 "This is a . . .": Ibid.

234 "The pie gives . . .": Andrew Duffy, "Pied Snipers."

234 This explanation makes . . . : Ibid.

235 "There is this . . .": Vinciguerra, "Take Sugar, Eggs, Beliefs . . . And Aim."

235 "This uprising has . . .": *Pie Any Means Necessary*, vi.

235 For instance, Frank . . . : Vinciguerra, "Take Sugar, Eggs, Beliefs . . . And Aim."

234n The one person . . . : Duffy, "Pied Snipers."

235 During the protest . . . : Gregory Scruggs, "What the 'Battle of Seattle' Means 20 Years Later," Bloomberg, November 29, 2019, www.bloomberg.com/news/articles/2019-11-29/what-seattle-s-wto -protests-mean-20-years-later.

236 The protestors in . . . : Ibid.

236 This willingness to . . . : Nick Davies, "The Bloody Battle of Genoa," *The Guardian*, July 16, 2008, www.theguardian.com/world/2008 /jul/17/italy.g8.

236 Once, a protestor . . . : Eric Asimov, "Gentlemen, Choose Your Sausage," *The New York Times*, February 15, 1998.

236 Another time, a . . . : Ibid.

237 "Pies defuse the . . .": Vinciguerra, "Take Sugar, Eggs, Beliefs . . . And Aim."

237 "Pie is goopy . . .": Ben Paynter, "How Pie Became a Powerful Punchline in Political Provocation," Fast Company, November 20, 2017, www.fastcompany.com/40467645/how-pie-became-a-powerful -punchline-in-political-provocation.

237 "ridicule is [hu]man's . . .": Quoted in *Pie Any Means Necessary*, 17.

237 One group that . . . : Ibid., 16".

238 Such victims, for . . . : Vinciguerra, "Take Sugar, Eggs, Beliefs . . . And Aim."

238 "As multinational corporations . . .": *Pie Any Means Necessary*, vi.

238 One of the . . . : Andrew Duffy, "Humble Pie on the Menu," *Edmonton Journal* (Edmonton, Canada), August 17, 2000.

238 "You can't punch . . .": Ibid.

238 Brown went on . . . : *Pie Any Means Necessary*, 16.

238 The arrests of . . . : Ibid., viii.

239 The Biotic Baking . . . : Ibid., vi.

239 The group had . . . : Ibid., ix.

239 For example, the . . . : Ibid., 9.

239 More seriously, they . . . : Ibid., 10.

240 "If we hold . . .": Ibid., 11.

240 As a result . . . : Ibid., 12.

240 "Opponents of the . . .": Ibid., 2–3.

240 "experienced activists involved . . .": Ibid., vii.

240 The BBB emphasized . . . : Ibid., 8, 16.

241 They weren't the . . . : J. D. Wallace, "Al Pieda Member Says the Arrest Was Worth the Stunt," KOLD, last updated February 19, 2009, www.kold.com/story/2485057/al-pieda-member-says-the-arrest-was -worth-the-stunt.

241 Made with ingredients . . . : *Pie Any Means Necessary*, 2.

241 "Using some variation . . .": Ibid., 108.

CHOCOLATE HAUPIA PIE

244 Haupia is a . . . : Sheldon Simeon, *Cook Real Hawai'i* (New York: Clarkson Potter, 2021), 240.

244 The sweet, gelatinous . . . : Kalei Talwar, "Recipe: How to Make Hawaii-Style Chocolate Haupia Pie," *Hawai'i Magazine*, August 5, 2009, www.hawaiimagazine.com/recipe-how-to-make-hawaii-chocolate-haupia-pie.

244 Particularly one that . . . : Tiffany Hill, "How Hawaii's Cacao is Making the World Sweeter," *Hawai'i Magazine*, June 17, 2019, www.hawaiimagazine.com/how-hawaiis-cacao-is-making-the-world-sweeter.

245 Easily the most . . . : "Our Story," Ted's Bakery, www.tedsbakery.com/story.

245 Ever ones . . . : Kathy Chan, "Special Menu at McDonald's Hawaii," Onolicious Hawai'i, June 19, 2019, onolicioushawaii.com/mcdonalds-hawaii-special-menu.

CHAPTER TWELVE

248 Such mentions included . . . "The Boss Watering Place 'Done' by 'Derrick Dodd,'" *Napa County Reporter*, July 1, 1881; "A Perilous Pie," *The Boston Globe*, May 15, 1881.

248 Meanwhile, as far . . . : "Grand Opening of Kaiser's Model American Restaurant," *The Sydney Morning Herald* (Sydney, Australia), June 15, 1885.

249 "The devotees of . . .": "A Good Apple Crop," *The Sentinel* (Carlisle, PA), October 12, 1887.

249 "All history shows . . .": Ibid.

249 "A rumor which . . .": "Corner in Dried Apples," *The Macon Telegraph* (Macon, GA), March 28, 1889.

249 That year, an . . . : "The National Emblem: What is the Matter With the American Apple Pie?," *Sacramento Daily Record-Union*, July 13, 1889.

250 "We should embody . . .": Ibid.

250 "Queen Victoria recently . . .": "Personals," *The Yonkers Statesman* (Yonkers, NY), March 12, 1890.

250 One of the . . . : "Pie," *The New York Times*, May 3, 1902, 8.

250 "Pie is the . . .": Ibid.

251 "Back from the . . .": "Salvation Army Worker Tells of Need for Pie at the Front," *New-York Tribune*, May 18, 1918.

251 "one of the biggest . . .": "Women Cheer Up Soldiers Abroad; Tribute to Work," *The Morning Union* (Grass Valley, CA), October 16, 1918.

251 "What better reminder . . .": "American Girl in France," *The Meriden Daily Journal* (Meriden, CT), March 14, 1919.

251 The *New York* . . . : James Young, "The Tourist Apple Pie Hunt Is Ended," *The New York Times*, October 3, 1926.

252 "Nothing in European . . .": M. E. W. Sherwood, "Ambrosial Dainties," *The Daily Independent* (Helena, MT), July 5, 1891.

252 "The French have . . .": "Apple Pie," *The Johnson City Staff* (Johnson City, TN), May 31, 1917.

252 "The color was . . .": Myrick H. Sublette, "French Cannot Bake Apple Pie," *The Republic* (Columbus, IN), December 1, 1917.

253 "Such a pastry . . .": "Not Lemon Meringue," *New-York Tribune*, December 25, 1918.

253 "German inventive genius . . .": "Not Real Apple Pie," *The Tucson Citizen* (Tucson, AZ), March 13, 1921.

253 "The American pie . . .": "America's National Dessert, Pie, Termed Most Wholesome of Foods," *The Journal and Tribune* (Knoxville, TN), September 23, 1923.

253 "We shouldn't therefore . . .": Anne Rittenhouse, "What Has Become of American Cookery?," *The News Journal* (Wilmington, DE), July 5, 1921.

253 "American pie breeds . . .": Quoted in "Britons Denounce Yankee Apple Pie," *The North Adams Transcript* (North Adams, MA), October 27, 1927.

254 "Why, they even . . .": "French Survey Finds Workers Proud in U.S.," *The Kokomo Tribune* (Kokomo, IN), August 21, 1929.

254 There are many . . . : "Ysaye and the American Apple Pie," *Evening Star* (Washington, DC), September 17, 1904; "Pilsudski Pleased by American Apple Pie," *The Morning News* (Wilmington, DE), May 25, 1921.

254 Even King Peter . . . : "Monarch Finds Time to 'Discover' Treat: King Peter Loses Heart to American Favorite, Apple Pie and Cheese," *The Cincinnati Enquirer*, June 25, 1942.

254 "I like American . . .": Frederic J. Haskin, "The Apple, King of Fruits," *The Butte Daily Post* (Butte, MT), July 5, 1907.

254 "This conversion is . . .": Ibid.

255 One early example . . . : Advertisement for Humphrey's The Blue Store, *The Burlington Free Press* (Burlington, VT), June 4, 1924.

255 Meanwhile, a 1928 . . . : Anne Rerendeen, "Mrs. Hoover, Too, Has Served the Nation," *The New York Times*, July 22, 1928.

255 By 1940, it . . . : "John Garfield and Ann Shirley Stars of Rialto's Drama," *Medford Mail Tribune* (Medford, OR), June 30, 1940.

255 Sometimes the phrase . . . : Henry P. Davis, "Dogs Save Game," *The Dispatch* (Moline, IL), December 23, 1938.

255 "As American as . . .": "Apple Pie Order," *The Daily News* (Mount Carmel, PA), August 9, 1901.

255 Other times, it . . . : "America Stands for 'Isolation' In Its Real Sense, Says Harper," *The Pantagraph* (Bloomington, IL), November 6, 1940.

255 "advertising is just . . .": Richard Harrison, "America Today," *Lincoln News Messenger* (Lincoln, CA), April 13, 1939.

255 Promotions for a . . . : "'The Patsy' Will Make You Laugh—It is So Guaranteed," *The Noblesville Ledger* (Noblesville, IN), March 25, 1930; "American Detail," *Daily News* (New York, NY), September 30, 1934; Advertisement for "Steamboat Round the Bend," *The Knoxville-News Sentinel*, September 6, 1935; Advertisement for Young Tom Edison, *The Twin Falls News* (Twin Falls, ID), May 5, 1940.

256 The saying was . . . : Advertisement for Walt Horan for Congress, *The Spokesman-Review* (Spokane, WA), October 25, 1942.

256 In 1935, Congress . . . : Catherine Mackenzie, "Apple Pie Raises an Issue," *The New York Times*, May 5, 1935, 18.

256 "The crust was . . .": Ibid.

256 "apple pie made . . .": Ibid.

256 "the foundation of . . .": "Connecticut's Pie Claims," *Democrat and Chronicle* (Rochester, NY), April 22, 1935.

256 "The Statue of . . .": "Back to America," *The Pantagraph* (Bloomington, IL), January 19, 1924.

256 "to banish pie . . .": Merrill Herald, "Political This or That," *Leader-Telegram* (Eau Claire, WI), May 24, 1934.

256 "an ancient and . . .": Henry W. Clune, "Not as Mother Made 'Em," *The Ithaca Journal* (Ithaca, NY), January 19, 1935.

256 "Let those in . . .": Ibid.

257 Someone also dramatically . . . : Lew Fitch, "Claims Good Old Apple Pie Libeled," *The Oklahoma News* (Oklahoma City, OK), August 30, 1934.

257   "It's a sad . . .": "For Shame, Don, For Shame," *The Kansas City Times*, August 24, 1934.

257   "Kidnapers, jail breakers . . .": Fitch, "Claims Good Old Apple Pie Libeled."

257   In 1951, Franklin . . . : Victoria Henrietta Kugler Nesbitt, *The Presidential Cookbook: Feeding the Roosevelts and Their Guests* (Garden City, NY: Doubleday, 1951), 161.

257   Calvin Coolidge and . . . : L. Clare Davis, "Passed by the Censor," *Stockton Daily Evening Record* (Stockton, CA), August 17, 1923; "Apple Pie," *The Ogden Standard* (Ogden, UT), October 23, 1911.

257   During World War . . . : "Apple Pie Still No. 1 in Army," *Rushville Republican* (Rushville, IN), January 12, 1942.

258   "How much pie . . .": "Fighting for Pie," *News-Journal* (Mansfield, Ohio), May 10, 1943.

258   "The smell of . . .": Advertisement for Globe Furniture Co., *Chillicothe Gazette* (Chillicothe, OH), September 29, 1943.

258   "the homely American . . .": Mary Sears, "Red Roses is Johnny Doughboy's Choice for Mom, Sweetheart or Wife on Easter," *Fort Worth Star-Telegram*, April 5, 1944.

258   When a solider . . . : Hazel Fowler Nelson, "Young Navy Vet Sure of Plans for Future," *The Miami Herald*, October 7, 1945.

258   "his manners are . . .": Ezra Goodman, "Huston the Ambassador," *The New York Times*, March 7, 1943.

258   "the apple is . . .": Frederic J. Haskin, "The Apple, King of Fruits."

259   "pie followed the . . .": "Mathilda, Thou Hast Done Well," *The Des Moines Register*, September 23, 1945.

259   "The meat pie . . .": H. H. Bushnell, "American Apple Pie," *Los Angeles Times*, January 29, 1932.

259   Another paper in . . . : "Mathilda, Thou Hast Done Well."

259   Sometimes apple pie . . . : *Plattsburg Leader* (Plattsburg, MO), October 9, 1925.

259   "Are we unworthy . . .": Bushnell, "American Apple Pie."

259   "Lynching is as . . .": Ernest L. Meyer, "Making Light of the Times," *The Capital Times* (Madison, WI), March 6, 1938.

260   "The Ku Klux . . .": James H. Madison, *The Ku Klux Klan in the Heartland* (Bloomington: Indiana University Press, 2020), 1.

260   The same goes . . . : Rickey Hill and Tazinski P. Lee, "The Killing of

Black People by the U.S. State is as American as Apple Pie: Groundwork toward a Critique," *Journal of Race & Policy* 11, no. 2 (2015): 5–22.

260   Audre Lorde, too . . . : Emma Parker, "'Apple Pie' Ideology and the Politics of Appetite in the Novels of Toni Morrison," *Contemporary Literature* 39, no. 4 (1998): 614–643.

260   "oppression is as . . .": Quoted in ibid.

260   After being confined . . . : "Japanese-American Youths Praised by Scout Executive," *The Havre Daily News* (Havre, MT), August 16, 1944.

260   "One of the . . .": "Re-Location of Japanese," *Freeport Journal-Standard* (Freeport, IL), October 2, 1942.

261   "Born and raised . . .": Jimmie Fidler, "Studios Restrict Sports of Big Actors," *The St. Louis Star and Times*, September 17, 1937.

261   This can be . . . : "Jimmy Stewart Statue Unveiled at Actor's 75th Birthday Party," *The Danville News* (Danville, PA), May 23, 1983.

261   "A glance into . . .": Jane Eddington, "The Most Glorious Yield of the Old Apple Tree is the Ever Refreshing Apple, but There is Apple Pie in the Offing," *Argus-Leader* (Sioux Falls, SD), October 1, 1927.

261   An American named . . . : Gabriella Petrick, "Why Americans Love Their Apple Pie," *Smithsonian Magazine*, September 2019, www.smithsonianmag.com/arts-culture/why-americans-love-their-apple-pie-180972852/.

261   "The Communist pie . . .": Quoted in ibid.

262   "When you say . . .": Quoted in "American Apple Pie," The Food Timeline, accessed October 29, 2021, www.foodtimeline.org/foodpies.html#applepie.

263   "The phrase 'as . . .'": Libby H. O'Connell, *The American Plate*, 71.

263   "the story of . . .": Ranya Tabari Idliby, *Burqas, Baseball, and Apple Pie: Being Muslim in America* (New York: Palgrave Macmillan, 2014), 3.

263   "its superpower ability . . .": Ibid., 225.

263   This dessert has . . . : Linda Bassett, *From Apple Pie to Pad Thai: Neighborhood Cooking North of Boston* (Beverly, MA: Commonwealth Editions, 2002).

263   "Speaking Spanish at . . .": America Ferrera, *American Like Me: Reflections on Life Between Cultures* (New York: Gallery Books, 2018), xv.

264   Such experiences can . . . : Edmund S. Wong, *Growing Up in San Francisco's Chinatown: Boomer Memories from Noodle Rolls to Apple Pie* (Charleston, SC, The History Press, 2018), 141; Valerie J. Matsumoto, "Apple

Pie and Makizushi: Japanese American Women Sustaining Family and Community," in *Eating Asian America: A Food Studies Reader*, ed. Robert Ji-Song Ku, Martin F. Manalansan, and Anita Mannur (New York: NYU Press, 2013), 259.

264 "apples are a . . .": Anne Dimock, *Humble Pie: Musings on What Lies Beneath the Crust* (Kansas City: Andrews McMeel Publishing, 2005), 56.

INDEX